BRUNO'S EARTH

GAMEBOOK

This tome is a compilation of information for role-play gaming, it is presented for your use, with the hope of improving your game.

Respectfully dedicate to my fellow advetureres

Keith Boyd, Jim McNair, John Daughrety, Craig Boyd, Kevin Boyd, Gale Mehler, Rick Slover, Karen Boyd, Randy Knapp, Dave Johnson, Pat Oaks, Bobby, Randy Inboden, Henry Traylor, Terry, Sam, Billy Booth, Timmy Booth, Jamie Booth, Tony Gozales, Kath Gonzales, John York, Ron Volz, Gene Schull, Nick Braker, Doug Lafayette, Ian Cloes, Lisa Guyer, Sherry Guyer, Lyle Guyer

BrunosEarth.com

JimGuyer@hotmail.com

Table of Contents

Player Characters

To play the game, a player must generate a character. The referee will assist the player in generating a list of abilities

.

Races

Human - Humans is the race on which all other races are based due to the familiarity to the players. Humans in the game are nearly identical to modern humans, aside from that humans in the game will be slightly less evolved intellectually, and slightly stronger physically.

ALBINO – Albinos are smaller than humans. Their bodies are proportionally similar aside from a slightly enlarged head. They have whitish skin. Albonis are either completely bald or have only then and wispy hair. Albinos are vulnerable to the sin can cannot stay out of doors without adequate protection. Albinos tend to be physically weaker then most of the other races, however, their mental abilities are greater.

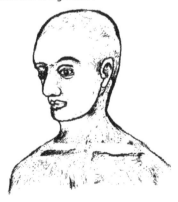

DWARF – Dwarves have short stocky bodies and tend to have thick bushy facial hair. Dwarves are strong, but not agile. They are healthy breed and have a strong constitution.

Elf – Elves have slender bodies with thin arms, legs, and neck. Elves have round chins and pointed ears. Elvish men have a boyish appearance, while elvish females have an almost ethereal beauty. Elves are very dexterous and make excellent craftsmen.

Giant – Giants are tall with broad shoulders and massive heads with shaggy hair. They have sharp protruding facial features. Giants are immensely strong, however, they are clumsy and walk in a teetering gait.

GNOME – Gnomes have short slender bodies with very round heads and pointed chins. Gnomes have pointed chins and very round heads. Their eyes are close set and beady. Gnomes noses are pointed and their mouths are a cluster of sharp pointed teeth.

ORC - Orcs are generally slightly shorter than then humans but tend to be stronger and heavier. Orcs have wide mouths with large teeth, jowl cheeks and snout-like noses. Orcs have excessive, burly body hair. Orcs usually cannot swim, never bathe and despise water in general. Orcs eat nearly anything organic and are not affected by spoiled foods or ingested poisons.

Hobbits – Hobbits are the shortest amongst the player-character races. They have round heavy bodies. Hobbits have a extremely high metabolism and can eat almost constantly they will consume 5 to 6 meals per day if possible, although they can subsist on much less. Hobbits have very thick leathery skin on their feet with thick fur on top. Hobbits generally dislike footwear and will favor going barefoot even when walking in snow or marching on rocky terrain.

Racial Ability Adjustments

Race	Cha	Int	Mem	Wis	Com	Con	Dex	Str
Albino	-4	+8	+4	+2	-2	-10	+6	-12
Dwarf	0	-2	-2	+4	-3	+15	-4	+8
Elf	+2	+2	+6	-2	+15	0	+12	-5
Giant	-8	-8	-8	-8	-6	+15	-10	+20
Gnome	+2	+4	0	-2	-4	-5	+6	-8
Hobbit	+2	0	+12	+8	-2	+5	+15	-8
Human	0	0	0	0	0	0	0	0
Orc	0	-15	-5	-5	-25	+8	+5	+12

Racial Physical Adjustments

Race	Initial Hit-points	Height	Weight
Albino	3D4	50-59"	70-100
Dwarf	3D10	44-54"	135-200
Elf	3D6	54-66"	90-120
Giant	3D20	72-96"	250-400
Gnome	3D6	39-45"	65-85
Hobbit	3D6	33-39"	175-250
Human	3D8	60-84"	150-250
Orc	3D12	62-70"	175-275

Character Classes - overview

Once the race of the character is chosen, the player must select a class for the character. The class represents the profession of the character, and most of the character's skills, abilities, restrictions and limitations.

Character classes are divided into two basic types, spell-casters and non-spell-casters. Generally, spell-caster characters are more difficult to play and require a higher level of involvement from the player. Beginning players are recommended to try a non-spell-caster first, then later on, move to a playing a spell-caster when they have become more seasoned. In advanced campaigns where the referee has elected to allow players to run more than one character at a time, it is recommended that only one of a player's characters be a spell-caster.

Within a class there may be sub-classes that are available to the player. A sub-class character uses the same tables and has basically the same abilities as the normal for the standard class, other than a few extra abilities and few extra restrictions.

Non-Spell-Caster Classes

FIGHTER - A fighter is one of the easiest characters to play and therefore, is often a good choice for new players. A fighter has foregone all other sorts of abilities to pursue excellence in fighting with weapons. A fighter is allowed the best armor and weapons and has the best chance of being able to strike an opponent in combat. **Prime requisites: Strength, Constitution.**

MARTIAL ARTIST - A martial artist is specially trained in the art of weaponless fighting, and also has use of some special exotic weapons not available to the other classes. A marital artist will either be a monk (and be part of a monastery) an assassin (and be part of a guild) or a rogue. **Prime requisite: Dexterity**

RANGER - The ranger class character is an outdoorsman, survivalist type of character. Rangers are skilled in hunting, foraging for food, path finding, and other various skills necessary in a wilderness setting. **Prime requisites: Strength, Dexterity**

THIEF - The thief class has the most developed and widest use of thieving abilities. These abilities involve stealth, sleight-of-hand, and general deception and distraction techniques. Also, thieves speak a special slang, known as "thieves cant" that sounds like a mix of non-sensical random words. **Prime requisite: Dexterity**

Spell-Caster Classes

CLERIC – The cleric is a spell caster that receives all spell abilities through divine asssistance. The spells available to a clerics are not as offensively powerful as those employed by other spell caster classes, however, the clerics is allowed better armor and weapons than other spell casters. Most clerical spells involve healing and curing the body. A cleric also has special abilities in regard to fighting undead and evil creatures. **Prime requisite: Wisdom. Memory**

DRUID - Druids are the worshipers and guardians of nature. Druidic spells generally involve the manipulation of plants and animals, weather, and the laws of nature. Druids have some healing and curing spells at their disposal and are able to employ some minor thieving abilities. **Prime requisite: Dexterity**

MAGE - The mage class encompasses the greatest array of magical abilities, but is the most limited in the use of combat weapons and armor. The spell abilities of a mage came vary greatly from one character to the next, due to the spells being divided into 7 different schools of magic. When a mage character is originated, the player will select three schools for the character to study. The mage will only be able to cast spells from their own school of study (unless using a scroll). A mage prepares for spell casting by studying spell text, and instructions of performing the somatic gestures involved. **Prime requisites: Intelligence, Charisma, Memory**

PSYCHIC - Psychics are not true spell casters since the use of psychic powers is not derived from magic, but from the power of the mind. A psychic performs "feats" that are often similar in nature to magical spells. Feats cannot be altered, dispelled, or influenced by most game factors that affect magic. Nonetheless, a psychic is considered to be a spell-caster class for most game purposes. **Prime requisite: Charisma**

Fighter

Fighter characters have forgone all other abilities in order to hone their skill with weapons. Therefore the fighter class has use of the best weapons and is the most formidable in physical combat.

Favored Weapons - When a fighter class character is created, the player should select a weapon type that will be the fighter's favored weapon. When using a favored weapon, the fighter gains special to-hit and damage bonuses on combat rolls.

As the fighter advances in experience, the bonuses increase in value. Eventually, the fighter is permitted to take on more weapons as favored weapons.

The fighter derives the class title from the first favored weapon. For example, Axe-Man. Bow-man, Swords-Man.

A favored weapon is a class of weapon. For example, a swordsman receives favored weapon bonuses for any sort of sword, 2-handed sword, long-sword, short-sword, etc.

Fighter Favored Weapon Bonus

Experience	#Favored Level Bonus	To-hit Weapons	Damage Bonus
0-4	1	+1	+2
5-9	1	+2	+3
10-14	1	+2	+4
15-19	1	+3	+5
20-24	1	+3	+6
25-29	2	+4	+7
30-34	2	+4	+8
35-39	2	+4	+9
40-44	2	+5	+10
45-49	2	+5	+11
50-54	3	+6	+12
55-59	3	+6	+13
60-64	3	+7	+14
65-69	3	+7	+15
70-74	3	+8	+16
75-79	4	+8	+17
80-84	4	+9	+18
85-89	4	+9	+19
90-94	4	+10	+20
95-	4	+10	+21

Martial Artist

The terms "Martial-artist" is a somewhat modern term that describes a class of character that is, in a made up of Monks, Rogues and Assassins. All of the subclasses use the same attack matrix and have similar abilities. Individual information, pertinent to each of the subclasses is listed later.

A martial artist is person trained in open-hand combat and use of exotic fighting weapons. A martial-artist is also trained in fighting, stealth, and killing.

Thieving Abilities - The martial-artist has the following thieving abilities: Disguise, move silently, lurk in shadows, climb walls, walk tightrope. A martial-artist is a character highly trained in fighting, stealth, and killing.

Open-hand - Anytime a martial-artist rolls a natural 19 or 20 when attacking a natural humanoid with a punch or kick, the creature must make a constitution saving throw or be stunned (normal damage for the 19 or double damage for the 20 occur regardless). A stunned humanoid will not be able to take action for 1 round (10 seconds) plus an additional round for each 20 level of experiences of the monk inflicting the stun.

Martial Artist Open-hand Stun Attack

Experience Level	Natural Roll-to-hit
1-19	19
20-39	18
40-59	17
60-79	16
80-	15

Special Abilities -
1. Initiative bonus - The martial-artist gains +1 to all initiative rolls, after each 20 levels of experience, and additional +1 to initiatives is gained.
2. Running - A martial artist is able to run 5 yards per round (1 mile per hour) faster then what is normal for their race. After 4 levels of experience, the martial-artists speed will increase another 5 yards per round untl the martial artist is reaches the maximum of double normal running speed.
3. Falling - A martial-artist is able to slow his/her fall if within 10 feet of a cliff face

Advanced Training – A martial-artist will is mostly able to maintain their training on their own. Eventually, a martial artist hit a platteu and will need to seek training from someone with greater skills. Every eight levels, a martial artist will must find training from a higher level martial-artist. Wihtout this new training, the character will stop advancing in level. During a period of no advancement, the character's If the character's experience points will continue to accrue and will later be redeemed into experience levels once the training is received.

Martial-Artist Thieving Abilities Percentages

	0-Level	Max
Move-silently	60%	99%
Lurk-in-shadows	60%	99%
Climb-walls	70%	99%
Walk-tightrope	70%	99%
Assume-disguise	20%	99%

Thieving Ability Adjustments per Level

Modified Dexterity	Adjustment
1-19	No adjustment
20-39	+1
40-59	+2
60-79	+3
80-	+4

Special Weapons

Throwing stars - Throwing stars can be thrown 3 at a time, and have a cycle rate of 3 seconds, allowing them to be thrown up to 9 stars in a single round. When martial-artist is throwing more than one star at a time, they must declare if they are throwing in a wide pattern or a narrow pattern.

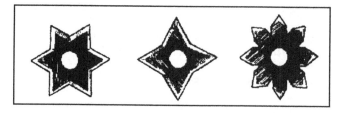

Narrow pattern - When a martial-artist throws stars in a narrow pattern, only 1 roll-to-hit will be made. All the stars will hit, or they will all miss. This is a good strategy when the martial-artist needs to deliver maximum damage and lesser damage would be ineffective. The drawback is that there is more potential of doing no damage at all.

Wide pattern - When a martial-artist throws stars in a wide pattern, a separate roll-to-hit is made for each star. If some stars miss others may hit. This is a good strategy when the martial-artist wants the best chance to deliver some damage, for example scrubbing the spell of a spell-caster. The drawback is that there is more of chance of some stars missing and less total damage is delivered.

Nunchaku - The use of this weapon allows the martial-artist an additional attack per round

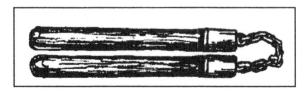

Sai - When a martial-artist uses this weapon, they are able to improve their armor class (attacks from a missiles and some buffet attacks are not affected). By using the side mounted hooks defensively, the martial-artist gains a +4 bonus to the armor class. Also, if an opponent using a hand weapon scores a natural 1 on a roll-to-hit, or the martial-artist scores a natural 20, it indicates that the martial artist was able to snag the weapon from the opponents grasp and toss it over their shoulder or to the side.

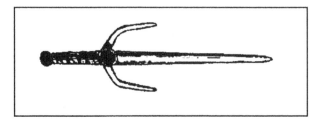

Baghnak - When a martial -artist uses this tool, the chance of successfully climbing a wall is increased to 99%. In hand combat, the Baghnak does 2D6 hitpoints of damage.

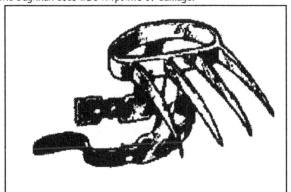

Throwing Net - To use this device, the martial-artist must be located above the intended target, If the target is unsuspecting; the martial-artist must a roll to hit armor class 0. If the target is aware, armor class adjustments for dexterity are allowed. If a target forgoes other action to attempt a dodge, a dexterity saving throw is allowed. The netting is fitted with barbs that do damage to if the barb thrashes about. To escape the net, a person trapped inside must make a strength saving throw. If the throw is successful, the character will suffer 10D6 damage from the nets barbs, but will be able to escape.

Rogue (Martial Artist Sub-class)
A rogue is a generic form of martial artist that is neither assassin nor monk, and does not have any of the abilities or restrictions that come with the other two subclasses.

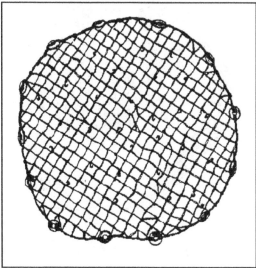

Affiliation - Nearly all rogues are former monks or assassins. Even a newly created rogue class character is assumed to have a history of a membership in either a monastery or a guild (or both, but left the monastery or guild early in their career. A rogue will usually seek their advance training from an assassins guild (who are usually happy to do so for money) or from another rogue. Monasterys will never train a non-monk.

Changing subclass - Changing from a rogue to an assissin is often quite easy since guilds generally always happy to have new paying members. The potential for switching to a monk subclass depends on the character's history. A former monk will have a difficult time making a reentry and joining a monastery, but under some conditions, is possible. No monastery will ever accept a former assassin into their ranks.

If a rogue does not join a local guild and become an assassin, the local guild will tolerate their presence so long as the character does not perform assassinations for hire, sell poisons, or interfere with the affairs of its members. If a rogue performs an assassination, the guild will be politely ask to receive 50% of the fee and request that the rogue join the guild or immediately leave town.

Guilds will often do business with rogues and sell them services and supplies, althought the prices will be greatly elevated from those available to members.

Monk (Martial Artist Sub-class)

A monk class character is a martial-artist subclass that is a member of a monastery.

Restrictions - A monk is required to maintain a lawful-good alignment and a humble demeanor at all times. Any overtly evil act will bring disfavor to the monk from the monastery's master.

A monk is never allowed to own real estate, money beyond what they need for personal needs, or any property that they cannot carry on their person, other then what they intend to save back to donate to the monastery when they return for their periodic training.

Training - At least once every 8 levels of experience, a monk must return to the monastery to receive new training. Without it, the monk will accrue experience, but will not realize the benefit of being a higher experience level.

Abilities - All of a monks special subclass abilities are granted through the monasteries deity. If the monk is ever ex-communicated from the monastery, the monk loses all abilities unique to the subclass and becomes either an assassin subclass (if they affiliate with a guild) or a rogue.

Monk Subclass Abilities - The monk subclass gains the following abilities at the following experience levels.

1st - **Self healing** - The monk may take a quiet moment of mediation that will heal bodily damage at the rate of 1 hit-point per minute at the cost 1 mana-point per.

3rd - **Speak to Animals** - The monk will gain the ability to talk to animals telepathically. The ability will not bring animals into friendly status with the monk, or enable the monk to read the thoughts that the creature is expressing towards the monk. Animals of low intelligence will be limited in their ability to carry on complex conversations.

5th - **Mind shield** - The monk becomes completely immune to all metal char affects, illusions, reading of the mind etc, from either magical or psychic sources. This protection requires no conscious effort on the part of the monk, and the monk will have no sensation of such an attack being attempted.

7th - **Immunity to sickness** - The monk gains immunity to all natural diseases and illnesses. Spells and affects that cause incapacitation due to nausea no longer affect the monk.

9th - **Immunity to paralyzation** - The monk becomes immune to all paralytic affects and magics.

11th - **Immunity to poisons** - The monk becomes immune to venoms and poisons.

13th - **Immunity to lycanthropy** - The monk becomes immune to all forms of lycanthropy.

15th - **Immunity to pertification** - The monk becomes immune to petrification. This protection applies only to the monk's person and not to clothing or any carried items.

17th - **Immunity to energy-drain** - The monk gains immunity to all magics and affects that drain mana and/or experience levels.

19th - **Quivering Palm** - The monk may touch any natural humanoid to gain complete control of their cardio-vascular system (charisma save negates) By use of this ability, the monk can speed up or slow down the victim's heart-rate or cause the breathing to be labored. The monk will be able cause the victim to feel nauseous, become comatose, or die.
Maintaining the link, when it is not actively being used, requires no concentration on the part of the monk, however using the link requires high concentration. Once established, distance is not a factor for the link. Every 24 hours, if the monk maintains the link, the subject is allowed a new charisma saving throw.

Affiliation - Although the character belongs to a monastery, they usually spend little time there. Player character monks travels about with the special permission of the monastery's master.

Changing subclass - Monks can easily change to a rogue or assassin subclass, but such a move should not be taken lightly. All monk type abilities will immediately start to fade and be totally gone over the course of the next eight levels. Regaining the subclass would require reentrt into the monastery which is extremely difficult for rouges and impossible for assassins.

Assassin (Martial Artist Sub-class)

An assassin generally comes from one of two origins. An assassin might be
1. A former monks who, for whatever reason, has become disassociated with the monastery
2. A rogue who has joined/rejoined a guild
3. An assassin that has maintained the same subclass since the first level or expereince.

All assassins must become part of the guild. Local guilds are always happy to receive new members since that is their source of income. A guild demands 10% of all treasure and moneys that an assassin acquires regardless if they acquire it by hired killings or other means. If an assassin is visiting a different town, they are obligated to pay the sister guild 10% plus the standard 10% to their own guild when they return home.

For an assassin, the guild is a vital source of weapons, poison ingredients, poison making knowledge, and general information (all for a fee). The sharing of information or skills, or even speaking openly of the guilds existence is strictly prohibited. Guild spies are everywhere and transgressions against the guild are usually detected.

Assassins are businessmen, and although they kill for a fee, are lawfully aligned. Assassins observe a strict code of completing an accepted contract and never double-crossing a client. Breaking this code will infuriate other members of the local guild and such infractions are dealt with swiftly and harshly. Assassins cannot sell their services if there is a general fear that they have a tendency to turn on their clients.

Assassins consider themselves professionals loathe killing when there is no pay. They will never kill wantonly or for personal vendettas. Such acts are considered the marks of an amateur would earn them immediate disrespect from fellow guild members.

At the 8th level of experience, the 16th level of experience, and ever 8 levels thereafter, an assassin must return to the guild for a week of rigorous training. Without such training, an assassin cannot acquire the next level of experience, regardless of the amount of experience they acquire. An assassin can continue to acquire experience points to later be redeemed in levels, but the abilities of the new level will not be awarded until the training is completed.

Usually, the assassin will offer a large sum of money or other valuable gift as a gratuity when returning for training.

Poison creation - Each time an assassin returns to their home guild for physical training they also receive training in the creation of poisons and the antidotes for them.

Assassin Ingested Poison Creation

Level		Onset Time	Duration	Damage
1-8	None	None		None
2-16	1 hour - 4 hours	Up to 5 min		1D20/Minute
17-24	45 min - 8 hours	Up to 6 min		1D20/ Round (10 sec)
25-32	35 min - 12 hours	Up to 7 min		2D20/ Round (10 sec)
33-32	30 min - 1 Day	Up to 8 min		3D20/ Round (10 sec)
41-40	25 min - 3 Days	Up to 9 min		4D20/ Round (10 sec)
49-48	20 min - 1 week	Up to 10 min		5D20/Round (10 sec)
57-56	15 min - 2 weeks	Up to 11 min		6D20/Round (10 sec)
65-64	10 min - 4 weeks	Up to 12 min		7D20/Round (10 sec)
73-72	5 min - 6 Weeks	Up to 13 min		8D20/Round (10 sec)
81-80	2 min - 8 weeks	Up to 14 min		9D20/Round (10 sec)
89	30 sec - 10 weeks	Up to 15 min		10D20/Round (10 sec)

Assassin Insinuated Poison Creation

Level		Onset Time	Duration	Damage
1-16	None	None		None
17-32	1 round	1 round		1D20/ Round (10 sec)
33-48	1 round - 2 rounds	Up to 2 rounds		2D20/ Round (10 sec)
25-64	1 round - 3 rounds	Up to 3 rounds		3D20/ Round (10 sec)
65-80	1 round - 4 rounds	Up to 4 rounds		4D20/ Round (10 sec)
81	1 round - 5 rounds	Up to 5 rounds		5D20/ Round (10 sec)

Assassin Contact Poison Creation

Level		Onset Time	Duration	Damage
1-32	None	None		None
33-64	1 round	1 round		1D20/ Round (10 sec)
65-48	1 round - 2 rounds	Up to 2 rounds		2D20/ Round (10 sec)

Ranger Character Class

Weapons - Long sword, short sword, dagger, staff, whip, club,
Armor - Leather, Bracers

General - A ranger class character is an outdoorsman, survivalist type of character. Their talents are best employed and most useful in a wilderness setting, but can be utilized anywhere. Ranger's interests are typically not at odds with that of druids. Most rangers do not kill for sport, but for sustenance, and in general, do not disrespect the wilderness

Whip - A rangers most useful weapon/tool is the whip. The whip can be used to fight, grab an overhead tree limb to swing from, or snag a small item.

Keeping an opponent at bay - The longer reach of the whip Bwil allow a ranger to repeatedly crack the whip to keep a regular size humanoid creature at bay for 3-6 rounds (1-4 rounds if the opponent is employing a shield). During this time, the ranger can deal damage with the whip without receiving damage in return. When an opponent breaks through the defense, the ranger will lose one round to change to a different weapon since a whip is ineffective in close quarters.

Snagging an ankle - If the player announces that they are trying to snag an opponent's ankle, a natural roll of 19 or 20 indicates that the ranger has managed to snag the opponent's ankle and pull them off their feet. The ranger will have 2 free attacks to deal damage with the whip as the opponent gets up. If the opponent tries to engage the ranger again, the ranger may start a fresh 3-6 rounds of keeping the opponent at bay.

Snagging a weapon - If the player announces that the ranger character is attempting to snag an item from an opponent's hand and rolls a natural 19 or 20 on a roll-to-hit, the snag is successful.

Smaller items that are being held by only one hand are snagged without a saving throw. With larger items that are held by two hands the holder is allowed to attempt a strength saving throw to be able to hang on. Sharp edged weapons cannot be snagged because the edge of the blade will cut the whip.

Non-snagging whip attack - If the ranger is not attempting a snag, the affect of rolling a natural 19 or 20 is normal in that a 19 always hits and a 20 always hits doing double damage.

Foraging - A ranger is always able to find and identify ample foods in a forest unless the area is extremely barren, Finding food adequate to feed a meal to a party of 12 or more typically takes only 15-20 minutes in the deep woods.

Set snares and traps - Rangers typically use this ability for catching small animals in the wilderness, but the same skills can be employed to make larger traps and mechanisms that will affect larger creatures

Ranger Abilities - Rangers gains the following abilities at the following experience levels.

1st - **Tracking** - The monk may take a quiet moment of mediation that will heal bodily damage at the rate of 1 hit-point per minute at the cost 1 mana-point per.

3rd - **Animal calming** - The ranger gains the ability to calm wild beasts. By speaking in low tones and approaching slowly, a ranger is able to calm a woodland creature into to tolerating its presence, and even other party members who keep their distance. If the animal is wounded or already riled, the process will be slower and more difficult. Any load noise or other distraction can upset the affect.

5th - **Find medicinal plants** - The range gains the ability to forage for and find medicinal plants. The referee will first secretly determine if there are medicinal plants in the area and how many are around. Then if there are, the referee will secretely make a intelligence saving throw to determine if they are found in 1 round (10 minutes) of searching. Only the success (or lack of) should be reported to the player. It should not be know if there are none in the are or if they simply haven't been found yet. Typically, the plants will have 1-4 small fruits that heal 1D8 hit-points apiece.

7th - **Bird Handling** - A ranger may capture and train (or purchase an already trained) bird of prey, typically either a falcon or eagle, but crows, sparrows, and other fowl can be used similarly. By the use of whistles and chirps, the ranger is able to give the bird primitive commands. The bird can to catch small creatures, find a path, or be sent ahead to find enemies. It will expose them by circling overhead and screeching loudly. A bird can be ordered to attack, (possibly to disrupting an opponent's concentration for the use of magics)

9th - **Find Poison antidotes** - The ranger is able to find antidotes for poisons in the wild. Usually, when a ranger is in the wild, they will casually look for poison slowing herbs that affect all poisons (players must announce intent). The ranger will use the poison slowing to delay the poison affects (consult slow poison spell) until the cure for the particular poison is found..

Thief Character Class

Thieves are masters of hiding, sneaking, and stealing. They are the most adept and have the widest use of thieving abilities.

Major/Minor Thieving Abilities - With each experience level, a thief's abilities will increase. Allowing for a more favorable success percentage. The amount of the increase depends on the thief's modified dexterity score (a dexterity score of < 10 allows no increase) when a thief is created, the player should select 3 thieving abilities to major in. These abilities are the skills the character will focus on and gain proficiency at the quickest. With every level of experience the percentile chance on the thief's major thieving abilities improve 1 percentile point for ever 10 points of dexterity has the potential to increase there A thief character improves the percentile when a thief character is create

THE THIEF ABILITIES ARE:
1. MOVE-SILENTLY
2. LURK-IN-SHADOWS
3. OPEN-LOCKS
4. CLIMB-WALLS
5. WALK-TIGHTROPE
6. Loosen Bounds
7. ASSUME DISGUISE
8. PICK-POCKETS
9. SLIEGHT-OF-HAND.
10. FIND-TRAPS
11. FIND-DOORS

Thieving abilities Min/Max Percentages		
	0-Level	Max
Move-silently	60%	99%
Lurk-in-shadows	60%	99%
Open-locks	10%	95%
Climb-walls	70%	99%
Walk-tightrope	70%	99%
Loosen Bounds	20%	95%
Assume-disguise	20%	99%
Pick-pockets	20%	79%
Sleight of hand.	10%	75%
Find/remove traps	20%	79%
Find secret doors	20%	90%

Dexteriy adjustments to Thieving Abilities per Level		
Modified Dexterity	Major	Minor
1-9	0	0
10-19	+1	0
20-29	+2	+1
30-39	+3	+1
40-49	+4	+2
50-59	+5	+2
60-69	+6	+3
70-79	+7	+3
80-89	+8	+4
90-	+9	+4

Cleric Character Class

Diety-selection - When a cleric is first created, the player will need to select a primary deity for the character. While deities are sometimes colloquially referred to as gods, they are not gods

in that they are not omni-powerful supreme beings. They are creatures from another plane of existence that have super-natural powers beyond the kin of normal mortals.

Bloodletting - The spilling of blood in battle is strictly prohibited to clerics, and therefore, they never employ edged weapons. Even an evil aligned cleric will only use edged weapons in a religious ritual and never frivolously spill blood on a battlefield. Such an act would be an aggregous offense to the character's patron deity and would surely cause a harsh punishment to be bestowed on the offending cleric.

Alignment-change - Alignment change and alignment drift is a serious matter for any class and particularly so for a cleric character class. A deity will normally not accept a cleric that is of a different alignment from themselves.

Cleric Undead Turning Matrix

Experience Level	Sk	Zo	Gl	Sh	Wi	Ga	Wr	Mu	Sp	Va	Gs	Li	Sp
0	11	14	17	18	19	20							
1	10	13	16	17	18	19	20	*	*	*	*	*	*
2	9	12	15	17	18	19	20	*	*	*	*	*	*
3	8	11	14	17	18	19	20	*	*	*	*	*	*
4	7	10	13	16	17	18	19	20	*	*	*	*	*
5	6	9	12	15	17	18	19	20	*	*	*	*	*
6	5	8	11	14	17	18	19	20	*	*	*	*	*
7	4	7	10	13	16	17	18	19	20	*	*	*	*
8	3	6	9	12	15	17	17	19	20	*	*	*	*
9	2	5	8	11	14	17	18	19	20	*	*	*	*
10-11	T	4	7	10	13	16	17	18	19	20	*	*	*
12-13	T	3	6	9	12	15	17	18	19	20	*	*	*
14-15	T	2	5	8	11	14	17	18	19	20	*	*	*
16-17	D	T	4	7	10	13	16	17	18	19	20	*	*
18-19	D	T	3	6	9	12	15	17	18	19	20	*	*
20-21	D	T	2	5	8	11	14	17	18	19	20	*	*
22-23	D	D	T	4	7	10	13	16	17	18	19	20	*
24-25	D	D	T	3	6	9	12	15	17	18	19	20	*
26-27	D	D	T	2	5	8	11	14	17	18	19	20	*
28-29	D	D	D	T	4	7	10	13	16	17	18	19	20
30-32	D	D	D	T	3	6	9	12	15	17	18	19	20
33-35	D	D	D	T	2	5	8	11	14	17	18	19	20
36-38	D	D	D	D	T	4	7	10	13	16	17	18	19
39-41	D	D	D	D	T	3	6	9	12	15	17	18	19
42-44	D	D	D	D	T	2	5	8	11	14	17	18	19
45-47	D	D	D	D	D	T	4	7	10	13	16	17	18
48-50	D	D	D	D	D	T	3	6	9	12	15	17	18
51-53	D	D	D	D	D	T	2	5	8	11	14	17	18
54-56	D	D	D	D	D	D	T	4	7	10	13	16	17
57-59	D	D	D	D	D	D	T	3	6	9	12	15	17
60-63	D	D	D	D	D	D	T	2	5	8	11	14	17
64-67	D	D	D	D	D	D	D	T	4	7	10	13	16
68-71	D	D	D	D	D	D	D	T	3	6	9	12	15
72-75	D	D	D	D	D	D	D	T	2	5	8	11	14
76-79	D	D	D	D	D	D	D	D	T	4	7	10	13
80-83	D	D	D	D	D	D	D	D	T	3	6	9	12
84-87	D	D	D	D	D	D	D	D	T	2	5	8	11
88-91	D	D	D	D	D	D	D	D	D	T	4	7	10
92-95	D	D	D	D	D	D	D	D	D	T	3	6	9
96-	D	D	D	D	D	D	D	D	D	T	2	5	8

Cleric Spell Capacity

Experience Level	1st	2nd	3rd	4th	5th	6th	7th
0	3	2					
1	3	2	1				
2	4	2	1				
3	4	3	1				
4-5	4	3	2				
6-7	4	3	2	1			
8-9	5	3	2	1			
10-12	5	4	2	1			
13-15	5	4	3	1			
16-18	5	4	3	2			
19-22	5	4	3	2	1		
23-26	6	4	3	2	1		
27-30	6	5	3	2	1		
31-35	6	5	4	2	1		
36-40	6	5	4	3	1		
41-45	6	5	4	3	2		
46-51	6	5	4	3	2	1	
52-57	7	5	4	3	2	1	
58-63	7	6	4	3	2	1	
64-70	7	6	5	3	2	1	
71-77	7	6	5	4	2	1	
78-85	7	6	5	4	3	1	
85-92	7	6	5	4	3	2	
93-	7	6	5	4	3	2	1

it, although nothing would prevent them from changing the nature of the place if the desire and wherewithal existed. In similar fashion, they avoid slaying wild animals or even domestic ones except as necessary for self-preservation and sustenance.

If druids observe any creature destroying their charges, the druids are unlikely to risk their lives to prevent the destruction. Rather, it is probable that the druids will seek retribution and revenge at a later date as opportunity presents itself.

Druids gain the following powers at the following levels:

1st Level - Thicket pass - All natural undergrowth will part easily to make way for a Druid to pass. A druid moave throught the heaviest of briars and thickets with no encumbrance.

3rd Level - Speak to animals - A cleric is able to speak to all woodland animals ba undersanting and mimmmicing their primitive forms of communication.

3rd Level - In connection with their nature worship, druids have certain innate powers which are gained at higher level. At 3rd level (Initiate of the Ist Circle), a druid gains the following abilities:

1. Identification of plant type
2. Identification of animal type
3. Identification of pure water
4. Power to pass through overgrown areas (undergrowth of tangled thorns, briar patches, etc.) without leaving a discernible trail and at normal movement rate (q.v.)

At7th level (Initiate of the 5th Circle), the following additional powers are

gained:

the 9th Circle. (Note: It is possible that other henchmen and hirelings, as well as worshippers, will be found with any particular druid. All servitors of upper- level druids are faithful protectors. They are not otherwise considered henchmen (q.v.) per se.)

At such time as a druid class player character attains experience points sufficient to advance him or her to Druid (12th level), the corresponding powers are gained only:

1. If there are currently fewer than nine other characters of Druid level, or
2. The player character bests one of the nine Druid level characters in spell or hand-to-hand combat. If the combat is not mortal, the losing combatant drops the exact number of experience points necessary to place him or her in the beginning of the next lower level. If the player character succeeds, he or she becomes a Druid, with full powers, and the former Druid (assuming case 2, above) becomes an initiate of the 9th Circle. If the player character loses, he or she remains at lower level and actually has fewer experience points in the bargain. This process is repeated with respect to a Druid becoming an Archdruid and for an Archdruid becoming the Great Druid. Multiple attempts to move up the heriarchy are possible as long as the character survives.

Druid Character Class

Armor - Leather
Weapons - Mace, flail, club, staff
Druids are the priest of nature and seek to preserve the natural order.

Druidic spells are a

Spells usable by druids are more attuned to nature and the outdoors than are the spells of other clerics or mages. Nonetheless, druids serve to strengthen, protect, and revitalize as the usual cleric does. The more powerful druidic spells, as well as their wider range of weaponry, make up for the fact that druids are unable to use any armor or shields other than leather armor and wooden shields (metallic armor spoils their magical powers). They must speak or read spells aloud.

They hold trees (particularly oak and ash), the sun, and the moon as deities. Mistletoe is the holy symbol of druids, and it gives power to their spells. They have an obligation to protect trees and wild plants, crops, and to a lesser extent, their human followers and animals. Thus, druids will never destroy woodlands or crops no matter what the circumstances. Even though a woods, for example, were evilly hostile, druids would not destroy

Mage Character Class

Armor - None
Weapons - Dagger, staff

General - Although weakest in hand combat, th mage class has the most powerful spells of all the classes. Mages must keep the the study text for their spells in a special tome. A mage cannot memorize or refresh spells without this spell book.

Schools - Mage spells are divided into 7 separate schools of study. They are;
1. Alteration
2. Conjuration
3. Divination
4. Enchantment
5. Evocation
6. Illusion
7. Necromancy

Alteration - Alteration spells deals with transforming objects and events.

Conjuration - This school specializes in magically creating or summoning objects or creatures.

Divination - Divination is a study of magics that are used to gather information, or find places or things.

Enchantment - Enchantment spells are used to imbue creatures and objects with a magical nature or to create magical affects.

Evocation - Evocation spells are used to trigger the release of massive amounts of elemental energy. Most of the heavy damage combative spells are evocation.

Illusion - This school includes all illusions and charm type spells that affect of influence the mind.

Necrmancy - Necromancy spells include those that deal with altering the body, as well as spells affecting the dead.

School selection - When a mage class character is created, the player must choose three schools of magic. One will be the character's primary study, with the other two being secondary schools of study.

Learning spells to primary school - To acquire a new spell and use it, a mage must either acquire a scroll of have another mage teach them the spell. If the spell is of a type belonging to the mage's primary the learning of the spell is automatically successful and the mage may enter the spell study text in the spell book to be relearned and used thence forth.

Learning spells to a secondary school - If a spell is of a type belonging to a secondaryschool, the referee will make a percentile roll to determine if the spell was successfully learned. A roll less than or equal to the mage's modified intelligence score indicates that the mage has able to learn the spell and it was committed to memory. Thereafter, the mage can cast the spell and/or make notes in their spell book to relearn or refresh the spell at a later time.

Learning spells from a scroll - The easiest way to learn a new spell is to acquire a scroll. A mage may read the scroll silently to commit it to memory. If the mage successfully learns the spell, they may then make notes in their spell book to be able to study the spell again at a later time.

Learning spells from a spell book - A mage who acquires a copy of another mage's spell book is *not* able to study the spell book and learn all the spells in it. Every mage has their own style of note-keep and short-hand of encrypted notes that help them learn or refresh the spell. For one mage to make sense of another mage's notes they must have the benefit of the teaching of the mage who inscribed them

Learning spells from a mage - To learn a spell from another mage requires a full day of study (8 hours) per level of the spell. Learning a new spell is mentally fatiguing. The additional time per day to shorten the number of days. At the end of 8 hours, the learning mage will be mentally exhausted and need the rest and relaxation of the remaining 16 hours of the day to recoup for the next day's study. At the end of the training, if the mage has successfully learns the spell, they may then make notes in their spell book to be able to study the spell again at a later time.

Psychic Character Class

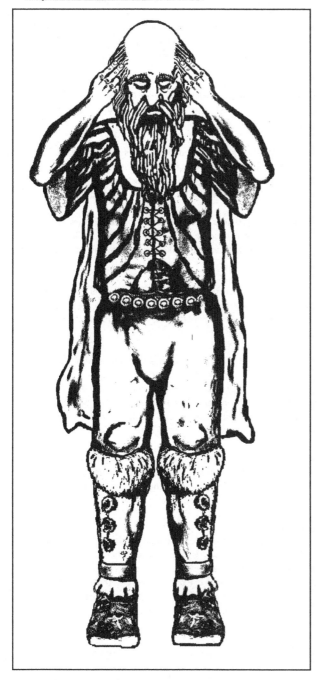

Runes - Runes are small gray flat circular ceramic pieces that are 1" to 2" in diamter and about ¼ inch thick. They are constructed of very pure clay.

Learning a rune - Just like spells and psychic feats, the use of a particular ttype of rune must be taught from another psychic.

Rune creation - The ability to create a rune is integral to the knowledge of the rune itself. Any psychic that has access to very pure gray clay nad a kiln can craft runes that they have the skills to use. Unlike magical items, runes are farilly easy to create and can usually be purchased in towns at a minimal cost. The use of some runes (such as exploding runes) destroys the rune. While others runes can be reused repeatedly.

Runes are small circular ceramic pieces 1 to 2 incehs in diameter and ¼ inch thick. They are inscribed with a symbol. Runes are precision made to be tuned to the be activated by the psionic waves created by a psychic's minds

A psychic is a character who has opted to develop the mind onto a formidable weapon. Psychics do not use magic, but the psionic feats they perform are similair in nature. Although no a trues spell caster, the spychic character class is considered to be a spell-caster class of character.

Psychics do not use scrolls AS disciplines cannot be inscribed with magical ink. They are, however able to use runes.

Character Statistics

Ability Score Generation

All ability scores run from 1 to 100. To originate a character, the player will generate 8 ability scores. Ability scores.

3D6 - Scores are generated by rolling three 6-sided dice for each score, totaling the amount, then multiplying by 5. This method utilizes the most common dice type, but creates scores that are rounded to increments of 5, and produces a base range of 15-90.

3D30 - Scores are generated by rolling three 30-sided dice for each score then totaling the amount. This method creates scores that are rounded to increments of 5, and produces a base range of 3-90.

4D24 - This is the preferred method. Scores are generated by rolling four 24-sided dice for each score then totaling the amount. This method can produce any score from 4-96. Although the range is larger, since 4 dice are rolled instead of 2, the bell curve is sharper and extremely high or low scores will be more uncommon.

Raw Scores - Once 8 ability scores are generated the player will assign the scores to each of the 8 abilities tailoring the character to fit the chosen class. Instead of die rolling, this can also be accomplished by computer score generation.

It should be noted that, none of the methods will produce a base score of 100. After the scores are generated, there are racial adjustments and other factors to be applied to the scores. Also, socres less than 100 allow the referee to introduce more ability enhancing magics without upsetting the balance of the game. Even with game factors to enhance abilities, a prudent referee will keep modified scores of 100 or higher extremely rare.

Random Assignment of Abilities - There are two different schools of thought for ability assignment. It is, or course, more realistic to force random assignment on the player and not allow them to choose which abilities are stronger. Doing random assignment, however, either forces a player to create a character that is not suited to their class (for example, if the character want to play a mage but is stuck with a low intelligence score) or forces the player to create a character of a class they are not interested in playing (for example, opting to play a fighter since the character has a low intelligence).

Selective Assignment of Abilities - While perhaps slightly less realistic, allowing the player to assign the ability scores prevents the player from having to play a class not suited to their abilities, or playing a character that he/she is not interested in. It is recommended that the referee remove this freedom only if it is the consensus of the group that the game is becoming unbalance due to too many players selecting the same class of character to play

Ability Explanations

A character's abilities scores represent the bulk of a character's power early in the game. Later, as the character is played, the importance of ability scores begins to diminish in place of power gained through experience levels.

Charisma - Charisma is the characters basic metal strength and power of will. A person with a high charisma is more able to influence other people and less susceptible to mental attacks.

Intelligence – Intelligence is the quickness of learning and the ability to comprehend. A character with a high intelligence is more likely to figure out a puzzle, decipher a code, learn a new language, etc.

Memory – Memory is the ability to store information rapidly and in large amounts. A character with high memory will retain information longer and with more accuracy.

Wisdom - Wisdom represents a character's judgmental abilities. A character with a high wisdom is better able to compare choices. A character with a high wisdom score has better ability to reason, and is less likely to be fooled or swindled.

Comeliness - Comeliness is the person favorability to the idea, or physical beauty. A character with a high comeliness will be better received by strangers and more likely to arouse the interest of the opposite sex,

Constitution – Constitution is a character's physical hardiness. A character with a high constitution can endure more physical abuse, is less likely to become ill, is not as venerable to poisons, and does not tire as easily.

Dexterity – Dexterity is a character's nimbleness of action and gracefulness of movement. A character with a high dexterity is less apt to get struck in battle by being better able to dodge and parry attacks. A character with a high dexterity is better marksman with distance weapons and is better able to perform a delicate task requiring nimbleness of hands.

Strength – Strength is the characters physical power for lifting, carrying, and moving objects in the game. When using a hand weapon, a character with a high strength is better able to hit an opponent and will deal extra damage.

Senses

After the abilities are created the player will generate scores for the character's senses. Unlike abilities, it is recommended that the referee require that scores be assigned in the order they are rolled. If players are allowed to selectively assign sensory scores, the group will quickly become compromised of characters with a high awareness and vision scores, and low taste and touch scores.

Awareness – The awareness score reflects how alert the character is. A character with a high awareness score is more likely to notice the things around them, and less likely to have some one sneak up on them.

Vision - The vision score reflects the quality of character eyesight. Characters with good eyesight are more likely to spot an enemy from afar.

Hearing – This score reflects how well a character can hear. This sense is relevant when a character is listening at a door, or trying to overhear a conversation. A character with an acute sense of hearing is more likely to hear an enemy slipping up on them.

Smell - A character with a high sense of smell is more likely to detect poisonous vapors, smell an approaching enemy, etc.

Taste – A character with a high sense of taste is more likely to notice poison or impurities in food and drink.

Touch – Touch reflect the sensitivity of a character's skin and the extent of what might be perceived by the use of feel. Although obviously a sense, this attribute seldom comes into play and the referee may elect to omit its use from the game.

Racial Score Adjustments

After the raw scores have been designated to the abilities, the scores will need to be adjusted for race. These adjustments reflect the general aptitudes of the particular races. Humans, due to inherent familiarity are used as the standard for adjusting all the other races. These adjustments allow for the fact that elves are generally more dextrous then humans, giants tend to be stonger, orcs are uglier, etc.

Racial Ability Adjustments

Race	Cha	Int	Mem	Wis	Com	Con	Dex	Str
Albino	-4	+8	+4	+2	-2	-10	+6	-12
Dwarf	0	-2	-2	+4	-3	+15	-4	+8
Elf	+2	+2	+6	-2	+15	0	+12	-5
Giant	-8	-8	-8	-8	-6	+15	-10	+20
Gnome	+2	+4	0	-2	-4	-5	+6	-8
Hobbit	+2	0	+12	+8	-2	+5	+15	-8
Human	0	0	0	0	0	0	0	0
Orc	0	-15	-5	-5	-25	+8	+5	+12

Hit-Points

Hit-Points are used to designate how much damage a character can sustain, and represent the character's current status in regard to bodily damage.

Initial-Hit-Points

A character's initial hit-points is the number of hit-points a charater has without regarding any experience levels. The amount of a character's initial-hit-points is generated by the roll of dice. The type and number of dice used is determined by the character's racial stock. Once the initial hit-points are determined, a character's initial hit-points will normally never change unless the character undergoes some sort of massive physical transformation. (In which case, all physical abilities would be regenerated also)

Initial Hit-Points by Race

Race	Initial Hit-points
Albino	3D4
Dwarf	3D10
Elf	3D6
Giant	3D20
Gnome	3D6
Hobbit	3D6
Human	3D8
Orc	3D12

Hit-Points-per-Level

When, first originated, a character begins the game with the Initial-Hit-Points plus whatever hit-points the character receives for being 1st level. Every time a character gains an additional level of experience, the character's overall hit-points will increase by the number of hit-points-per-level. The amount of hit-points-per-level the character will receive is based upon the character's **constitution** score. The amount can be taken from the table below or calculated algerbraically by hit-points-per-level = constitution/20

Hit-points per level

Constitution	Hit-Points/Level
0-19	0 Hit-points/level
20-39	1 Hit-points/level
40-59	2 Hit-points/level
60-69	3 Hit-points/level
80-99	4 Hit-points/level

Change in Constitution

If the character has a change in constitution score that puts them into a different hit-points-per-level bracket, the change is made retroactively for all already acquired experience levels. At any time, a character's full-hit-points can be calculated algebraically by: **Full-Hit-Points = Initial-hit-points + Hit-points/level * Experience-level.**

Hit-point-tally

A character's hit-points represents the number of points they will have when they are in their prime, completely healed, physical condition. It does not represent the current status of the character. A character who is recovering from physical wounds will not be at their maximum physical potential. A character's hit-point-tally designates the current status of a character's physical condition. When a character is wounded, the hit-point-tally will be reduced, as a character heals, hit-points will be regained. A referee will usually notify the player the number of hit-points that have been lost or recovered and let the player maintain the current hit-point tally. There may be occasions when the referee will deem it necessary to maintain the current hit-point-tally to keep it secret from the player, while only giving the player a general feedback of how the character is feeling.

Full-hit-points

When a character is completely healed and has no physical injuries, the current hit-point-tally will equal to the total hit-points allowed. Full-**Hit-Points = Initial-hit-points + Hit-points/level * Experience-level.**

Regaining Hit-Points

As a character rests, lost hit-points will heal at the rate of 1 hit-point per hour until the character is completely healed and restored to full-hit-points. There are also magics and other game factors that can help retore a character's hit-point-tally to to full-hit-points.

Losing hit-points

When a character becomes wounded or injured, the referee will inform the player how many hit-points of damage the character has suffered. (Unless the referee has a reason for keeping the hit-point-tally secret)

0 Hit-points

Reaching a hit-point tally of zero will cause a character to lose consciousness.

Negative Hit-Points

A character who reaches negative-hit-points will not only become unconscious, but may suffer hit-point-degradation.

Hit-Point Degradation – Sometimes, when a character is injured and left on the unattended on a battlefield, the character's condition will not improve, but will deteriorate. In the game, this is represented by damaged hit-point-degradation. If a character is suffering from hit-point-degradation the character will lose 1 hit-point per hour until the characters reaches -10 (and is dead) or receives aid (and begins to heal).

Determiming if hit-point-degradation occurs - The percentile chance of a character suffering hit-point-degradation is equal to the negative hit-point-tally * 10. If the roll is favorable, the character will recover without assistance. If the roll is unsuccessful, the character will deteriat at the rate of 1 hit-point per hour until the character reaches –10 and is dead.

Reversing Hit-point-degradation - At any time prior to death, hit-point-degradation will be reversed if the character receives physical aid, or healing affects. Once this aid is given, the character will begin to heal at the regular rate of 1 hit-point per hour of rest.

Additional damage - If a character in negative hit-points is healing, and receives further damage, a new percentile roll is made based off the new current hit-point-tally. If a character's hit-point-tally is already deteriorating and further damage is received, the new damage will be applied to the hit-point-tally and the hit-point-degradation will continue with no percentile roll being made for a recovery.

Example - A character reaches a hit-point-tally of -3. From the base chance of recovery (100%) the referee will deduct 30% (3 * 10%), giving the character a 70% chance of making an unaided recovery. If the percentile roll is 70 or less, the character will slip into hit-point-degradation.

-10 Hit-points Hit-points

A hit-point tally of -10 will result in death.

Mana-Points

Mana-Points are used to determine how the charater's mental stamina, and to designate what is the character's current state of mental fatigue.

Initial-Mana-Points

A character's initial-mana-points is the number of mana-points a charater has without regarding any experience levels. The amount of a character's initial-mana-points is determined by the character's racial stock.

Initial Mana-Points by Race	
Race	Initial Mana-points
Albino	4
Dwarf	2
Elf	3
Giant	2
Gnome	4
Hobbit	3
Human	3
Orc	2

Mana-Points per Level

When, first originated, a character begins the game with the the game with the Initial-Mana-Points plus whatever mana-

points-level the character receives for being 1st level. Every time a character gains an additional level of experience, the character's overall mana-points will increase by the number of mana-points-per-level. The amount of mana-points-per-level the character will receive is based upon the character's **charisma** score. The amount can be taken from the table below or calculated algerbraically by mana-points-per-level = charisma/20

Mana-points per level	
Charisma	Mana-Points/Level
0-19	0 Mana-points/level
20-39	1 Mana-points/level
40-59	2 Mana-points/level
60-79	3 Mana-points/level
80-99	4 Mana-points/level

Change in Charisma

If the character has a change in charisma score that puts them into a different mana-points-per-level bracket, the change is made retroactively for all already acquired experience levels. At any time, a character's full-hit-points can be calculated algebraically by: Full-Mana-**Points** = **Initial-hit-points** + **Hit-points/level** * **Experience-level**.

Mana-point-tally

A character's mana-points represents the number of points they will have when they are in their prime, completely rested, mental condition. It does not represent the current status of the character. A character who is recovering from mental fatigue will not be at their maximum potential. A character's mana-point-tally designates the current status of a character's mental condition. When a character is mentally exerted or mentally attacked, the mana-point-tally will be reduced, as a character rests and recovers, mana-points will be regained. The most common type of mental fatigue is from spell casting. In the case of mental attacks, the referee will usually notify the player the number of mana-points that have been lost or recovered and let the player maintain the current mana-point tally. There may be occasions when the referee will deem it necessary to maintain the current mana-point-tally to keep it secret from the player, while only giving the player a general feedback of how the charater is feeling.

Full-mana-points

When a character is completely rested and has no mental fatiguethe current mana-point-tally will equal to the total mana-points allowed. Full-Mana-**Points** = **Initial-hit-points** + **Mana-points/level** * **Experience-level**.

Mana-point Loss/Recovery

As a character cast spells or suffers mental attacks, they will lose mana-points, When a character rests they will regain mana-points at the rate of 1 mana-point per hour until the character is completely restored to Full-mana-points

0 & Negative Mana-points

Reaching a hit-point tally of zero or les will cause a character to lose consciousness. A character will not normally die from negative hit-points, but the tally is kept to resolve how long it will take for the character to recover. It is possible for a recovery to take many hours or even days before the character regains conciusness.

Armor Class

A character's armor class rating is a value designating how difficult a character or creature is to hit. All player-characters have a base armor class of zero (no armor). Dexterity bonuses, armor, and protective magics, and other game factors can raise the value of the character/creature's armor class making them more difficult to be struck.

Dexterity Adjustments

A character's dexterity allows for an adjustment to armor class since a more nimble character is harder to hit in combat. The adjustments in the chart represent the adjustment allowed while the character is in combat and attempting to strike an opponent. If the character is attempting to cast a spell, unaware of the attack, the dexterity adjustment is not included in the armor class score. If the character is not fighting, or taking other action, but expending all their energies to dodging a blow, the dexterity adjustment is doubled.

Dexterity Adjustment to Armor Class	
Dexterity	**Adjustment**
0-19	No adjustment
20-39	+1 to Armor Class
40-59	+2 to Armor Class
60-69	+3 to Armor Class
80-99	+4 to Armor Class

Armor Adjustments

The wearing of armor makes a chacter more difficult to hit. The heavier the armor, the greater the protection. Wearing armor impedes the dodging capabilities, those restriction are figure in to the armor-wearing adjustments. A character in full plate that has a high dexterity can still evade strikes better then a character with a low dexterity. Therefore, the dexterity adjustments to armor class are not lessened of discounted due to the wearing of armor

Armor Adjustment to Armor Class	
Armor	**Adjustment**
Buckler Shield	+1 to Armor Class
Shield	+2 to Armor Class
Leather Armor	+2 to Armor Class
Studded Leather	+3 to Armor Class
Chail Mail	+4 to Armor Class
Plate Mail	+5 to Armor Class

Armors made from dragon leather

Leathers made of dragon skin have a greater tensile strength and are more durable than normal leathers. The greater tensile strength of Dragon leather affords more protection than normal leathers and therefore, offers the wearer a better armor adjustment. Also, since dragon leathers are finer and more supple than normal leathers, they are able to retain continuous magical affects that enhance their protective ability.

Dragon Leather Armor Class Bonuses		
Dragon	**Tensile Adjustment**	**Potential Magical Adjustment**
Yellow	+1 to Armor Class	None
Orange	+1 to Armor Class	None
Violet	+1 to Armor Class	None

Armors made from extraordinary metals

Most normal metal armor is made or plain iron. There are metals available in the game that have a greater tensile strength that affod the wearer more dues to their greater tensile strength. Also, since extraordinary metals are are able to retain continuous magical affects that enhance their protective ability.

Extraordinary Metals Armor Class Bonuses		
Metal	**Tensile Adjustment**	**Potential Magical Adjustment**
Steel	+1 to Armor Class	None
Titanium	+2 to Armor Class	+1 to Armor Class
Mithril	+3 to Armor Class	+2 to Armor Class
Adamanite	+4 to Armor Class	+3 to Armor Class

To-Hit Rolls

The minimum roll required on the roll of a 20-sided dice to hit a creature with no armor. All player characters start out at 1st level, requiring a 10 to hit an armor class of zero. As a character rises in levels of experience, the score required to hit armor class of zero will become more favorable as the character's ability increases with experience.

Base-to-Hit

Base-to-hit is simply the attacker's THAC0 value added to the opponent's armor class rating to produce a base-to-hit. Once the base-to-hit for a particular armor class is established, the player may then add to-hit bonuses for strength and other adjustments.

Non-Spell Caster Attack Matrix				
<--------Character Class/Level--------->				Roll To
Fighter	Martial-Artist	Ranger	Thief	Hit AC-0
0	0	0	0	11
1	1	1	1	10
2	2	2-3	2-3	9
3	4-6	4-5	4-6	8
4-5	7-10	6-8	7-10	7
6-7	11-16	9-11	11-15	6
8-9	17-24	12-15	16-21	5
10-12	25-34	16-20	22-28	4
13-15	35-46	21-26	29-36	3
16-18	47-60	27-33	37-45	2
19-22	61-77	34-41	46-55	1
23-26	78-	42-50	56-67	0
27-31		51-60	68-81	-1
32-36		61-71	82 -	-2
37-42		72-83		-3
43-48		84-		-4
49-55				-5
56-62				-6
63-70				-7
71-79				-8
80-89				-9
90-				-10

Spell Caster Attack Matrix				
Roll to	<---------Character Class/Level--------->			
Hit AC-0	Cleric	Druid	Mage	Psychic
11	0	0	0	0
10	1-2	1-3	1-3	1-4
9	3-5	4-8	4-9	5-12
8	6-9	9-15	10-19	12-25
7	10-14	16-24	20-33	23-42
6	15-20	25-35	34-51	37-64
5	21-28	36-48	52-73	65-
4	29-38	49-63	74-	
3	39-50	64-80		
2	51-64	81-		
1	65-80			
0	81-			

To calculate a base-to-hit, consult the appropriate attack matrix for the character's class. Find the column that matches the class and go down the level listing to the the range that includes the character's experience level. Add the value in the leftmost column to the opponents armor class to arrive at the base-to-hit.

Example – A 14th level fighter is attacking an armor class of 7. Consult the Non-Spell-Caster attack matrix and go down the "Fighter" column until you find the "13-15" level range. Follow the row rightuntil you see the THAC0 (Roll-to-hit-Armor-Class-zero) of "3". The THAC0 of 3 is added to the armor class of 7 for a Base-to-hit of 10.

Score-to-hit

Once the Base-Score-to-hit is established, the character may have credit for other bonuses that enable a better chance for a successful strike. The final value needed to strike an opponent after all adjustments have been applied to the Base-to-hit.

Example: An attacker needs a 7 to hit armor class 0. The opponent has an armor class of 5, creating a base-to-hit of 12. The attacker bonuses for strength and other factors, is calculated to be +4, creating a minimum roll on a 20-sided die of 8.

Strength to-hit & damage adjustments on hand weapons

A high strength score enables a character to be more likely to hit with a hand weapon and to deliver more damage.

Strength Hand Weapon To-hit/Damage Bonuses	
Strength	Bonus
0-19	No adjustment
20-39	+1 On Rolls-To-Hit
40-59	+2 On Rolls-To-Hit
60-69	+3 On Rolls-To-Hit
80-99	+4 On Rolls-To-Hit

Dexterity to-hit adjustments on missle weapons

A high strength score enables a character to be more likely to hit with a missle weapon (damage is not adjusted for dexterity).

Dexterity Missle Weapon To-hit Bonuses	
Dexterity	Bonus
0-19	No adjustment
20-39	+1 On Rolls-To-Hit
40-59	+2 On Rolls-To-Hit
60-69	+3 On Rolls-To-Hit
80-99	+4 On Rolls-To-Hit

Favored Weapon to-hit & damage adjustments

A high strength score enables a character to be more likely to hit with a missle weapon (damage is not adjusted for dexterity).

Fighter Favored Weapon Bonuses	
Level	Bonus
1-3	+1 On Rolls-To-Hit
4-9	+2 On Rolls-To-Hit
10-19	+3 On Rolls-To-Hit
20-33	+4 On Rolls-To-Hit
34-51	+5 On Rolls-To-Hit
52-73	+6 On Rolls-To-Hit
74-	+7 On Rolls-To-Hit

Spell Capacities

A character' spell capacity is the amount of spell knowledge they can have memorized at any one time. A character's spell capacity is determined by their class, level, and memory score.

Level Spell Capacity

In time, a spell caster partices the craft and beomes more adept at memorizing spells. As the character increases in level and experience, the caster is able to memorize more spells, longer spells, and more complicated spells. Each class has it's own matix for determing the level number of spells useable by level.

Memory Spell Capacity

A spell-caster character gains spell usage from their memory score. The higher the score, the larger amount of spells the character is able to retain in memory. Non-spell casters cannot cast spells based on their memory scores

Memory Bonus to Spell/Feat Capacity

Memory	Spell/Feat Capacity Bonus		
	1st	2nd	3rd
0-19	0		
20-39	1		
40-59	2		
60-79	2	1	
80-	3	2	1

Cleric Spell Capacity

Experience Level	Spell Level						
	1st	2nd	3rd	4th	5th	6th	7th
0	3	2					
1	3	2	1				
2	4	2	1				
3	4	3	1				
4-5	4	3	2				
6-7	4	3	2	1			
8-9	5	3	2	1			
10-12	5	4	2	1			
13-15	5	4	3	1			
16-18	5	4	3	2			
19-22	5	4	3	2	1		
23-26	6	4	3	2	1		
27-30	6	5	3	2	1		
31-35	6	5	4	2	1		
36-40	6	5	4	3	1		
41-45	6	5	4	3	2		
46-51	6	5	4	3	2	1	
52-57	7	5	4	3	2	1	
58-63	7	6	4	3	2	1	
64-70	7	6	5	3	2	1	
71-77	7	6	5	4	2	1	
78-85	7	6	5	4	3	1	
85-92	7	6	5	4	3	2	
93-	7	6	5	4	3	2	1

Druid Spell Capacity

Experience Level	Spell Level							
	1st	2nd	3rd	4th	5th	6th	7th	8th
0	3	2						
1	3	2	1					
2-3	3	2	2					
4-5	3	2	2	1				
6-8	3	3	2	2				
9-11	3	3	2	2	1			
12-15	4	3	3	2	1			
16-20	4	3	3	2	2			
21-26	4	3	3	2	2	1		
27-33	4	4	3	3	2	1		
34-41	4	4	3	3	2	2		
42-50	4	3	3	2	2	1		
51-60	5	4	3	3	2	2	1	
61-71	5	4	4	3	2	2	1	
72-83	5	4	4	3	3	2	2	
84-	5	4	4	3	3	2	2	1

Psychic Feat Capacity

Experience Level	Spell Level							
	1st	2nd	3rd	4th	5th	6th	7th	8th
0	3	2						
1	3	2	1					
2	4	2	1					
3	4	3	1					
4	4	3	2					
5	4	3	2	1				
6	5	3	2	1				
7-8	5	4	2	1				
9-10	5	4	3	1				
11-12	5	4	3	2				
13-14	5	4	3	2	1			
15-16	6	4	3	2	1			
17-18	6	5	3	2	1			
19-21	6	5	4	2	1			
22-24	6	5	4	3	1			
25-27	6	5	4	3	2			
28-30	6	5	4	3	2	1		
31-33	7	5	4	3	2	1		
34-36	7	6	4	3	2	1		
37-40	7	6	5	3	2	1		
41-44	7	6	5	4	2	1		
45-48	7	6	5	4	3	1		
49-52	7	6	5	4	3	2		
53-56	6	5	4	3	2	1		
57-60	8	6	5	4	3	2	1	
61-64	8	6	5	4	3	2	1	
65-69	8	7	5	4	3	2	1	
70-74	8	7	6	4	3	2	1	
75-79	8	7	6	5	3	2	1	
80-84	8	7	6	5	4	2	1	
85-89	8	7	6	5	4	3	1	
90-94	8	7	6	5	4	3	2	
95-	8	7	6	5	4	3	2	1

Mage Spell Capacity

Experience Level	1st	2nd	3rd	4th	5th	6th	7th	8th	9th
0	3	2							
1	3	2	1						
2	4	2	1						
3	4	3	1						
4	4	3	2						
5	4	3	2	1					
6	5	3	2	1					
7	5	4	2	1					
8	5	4	3	1					
9	5	4	3	2					
10	5	4	3	2	1				
11-12	6	4	3	2	1				
13-14	6	5	3	2	1				
15-16	6	5	4	2	1				
17-18	6	5	4	3	1				
19-20	6	5	4	3	2				
21-22	6	5	4	3	2	1			
23-24	7	5	4	3	2	1			
25-26	7	6	4	3	2	1			
27-28	7	6	5	3	2	1			
29-30	7	6	5	4	2	1			
31-33	7	6	5	4	3	1			
34-36	7	6	5	4	3	2			
37-39	7	6	5	4	3	2	1		
40-42	8	6	5	4	3	2	1		
43-45	8	7	5	4	3	2	1		
46-48	8	7	6	4	3	2	1		
49-51	8	7	6	5	3	2	1		
52-54	8	7	6	5	4	2	1		
55-57	8	7	6	5	4	3	1		
58-60	8	7	6	5	4	3	2		
61-64	8	7	6	5	4	3	2	1	
65-68	9	7	6	5	4	3	2	1	
69-72	9	8	6	5	4	3	2	1	
73-76	9	8	7	5	4	3	2	1	
77-80	9	8	7	6	4	3	2	1	
81-84	9	8	7	6	5	3	2	1	
85-88	9	8	7	6	5	4	2	1	
89-92	9	8	7	6	5	4	3	1	
93-96	9	8	7	6	5	4	3	2	
97-	9	8	7	6	5	4	3	2	1

Memoryl Spell Capacity

A spell-caster character gains spell usage from their memory score. The higher the score, the larger amount of spells the character is able to retain in memory.

Example: Finding the spell capacity of a 5th level cleric with an adjusted memory of 75.

Consult the "Cleric Spell Capacity" Matrix and go down the left most column to find the experience level range of "4-5". The row shows capacities of a qty of 4 first level spells, 3 second level spells, and one 3rd level spell.

Next, consult the "Memory Bonus to Spell Capacity" and to find the "60-79" Memory range. The bonus is two 1st level spells, and one 2nd level spell. Last, add the two for a total of six 1st level spells, four 2nd level spells, and two 3rd level spells.

Spell Inventory – Every 1st level spell casters begins the game with a set of feats/spells at their disposal that is equal in number and spell level to their starting spell capacity. Early in the game, there is no daily spell selection, since the caster is able to retain all the spells they posses in memory. As a caster adds more spells to their repitoire, the caster will have make daily selections as to which spells they will hold in their memory and which spells are stored away for future use.

Saving Throws

A saving throw is used to determine if a character has resisted, partially escaped, or completely avoided various dangers or types of attack. The odds of a saving throw being successfule is determent by the level experience and the modified score of the relevant ability.

Rolling – Saving throws are attempted by making a roll with a 20-sided die. The roll must generate a score equal to or better than the amount required. It is recommended that a player keep track of the saving throw required for each of their players abilities.

Dodging (Dexterity saving throws) – The allowance of a dexterity saving throw is not automatice. In most situations, a referee will require that a player quickly call out that their character is dodging, diving away, etc as soon as the presence of the danger/attack first becomes known.

Mental Attacks (Charisma saving throws) - Mental attacks vary greatly situation by situation. Some charisma saving throws are automatically allowed with no penalty. With some mental attacks, the referee may inform the player they are feeling "light headed" or "a little antsy" or "nervous". If this is the prelude to a mental attack, the player should announce that there is mentally focusing on shutting out the attack. If the player fails to call for the save, the save may be forfeited, or rolled at a penalty (referee's disgression). Usually, this concentration effort to shut out a mental attack will preclude the character of taking any another action.

Calculation - Saving throws can be calculated algebraically, by using the formula: $Save = 20 - (Level/10 + Ability\ Score/10)$, or by using the table below

Saving Throw Matrix

Level	\<-- Modified Ability Score --\>									
	0-09	10-19	20-29	30-39	40-49	50-59	60-69	70-79	80-89	90-
0-9	20	19	18	17	16	15	14	13	12	11
10-19	19	18	17	16	15	14	13	12	11	10
20-29	18	17	16	15	14	13	12	11	10	9
30-39	17	16	15	14	13	12	11	10	9	8
40-49	16	15	14	13	12	11	10	9	8	7
50-59	15	14	13	12	11	10	9	8	7	6
60-69	14	13	12	11	10	9	8	7	6	5
70-79	13	12	11	10	9	8	7	6	5	4
80-89	12	11	10	9	8	7	6	5	4	3
90-	11	10	9	8	7	6	5	4	3	2

Experience Levels

Experience levels is what designates how the character is advancing in their fighting skills, and how they are developing the skill for their particular class.

Initial Experience

Every new character begins the game at first level with 1,000 experience points. As a character participates in adventuring, they will become more proficient in their skills and more powerful. This is represented by gaining experience and rising in experience levels.

Experience Distribution rate

Experience points are awarded based on the amount of real time (not game time) a player spends playing the character in the game. At the start of the campaign, the referee will announce the amount of experience points to be awarded per hour of play (usually from 50 to 100 experience points per hour) Once declared, a referee will seldom, if ever change the distribution rate of experience points.

Accruing experience

The character will stay first level until an additional 1,000 experience points have been accrued through game play. Once a character reaches 2,000 experience points, they will be awarded the status of 2nd level of experience. Thereafter, the character will be promoted to a new level with each additional 1,000 experience points

Usually, a referee will only award experience at the end of a session. If it is a crucial part of a campaign, and the distribution will make a difference in level, the referee may opt to award experience in mid session.

Experience drainage

There are conditions in the game under which a character may lose experience levels. It is possible, even, to lose experience past the starting level of 1,000 experience points and become a 0-level character.

Every time an experience level is lost, exactly 1,000 experience points will be deducted. The player should record the number of experience points prior to the loss in the case that a recovery of the experience becomes available at some later point in the campaign.

Recovery of Experience Levels

There are factors in the game that will enable a character to regain lost experience points, and thereby, lost levels. When a character's experience is restored, the character will be returned to the exact number of experience points they had prior to the drainage. Any experience points gained since the drainage and before the restoration are forfeited. To gain any benefit from experience restoration, it must take place prior to the points being regained my normal accruing of experience.

Example: An 8th level character with 8,500 experience points is drained for two levels. The tally of experience points is immediately lowered to 6,500, and the character becomes 6th level of ability. Through normal adventuring, the character acquires 700 experience points, for a total of 7,200 and becomes 7th level. At 7,200 experience points, the character undergoes a restoration and restored to 8,500 experience points. The 700 experience points that were accrued in between are lost and are not added to the tally.

Example: A 7th level character with 7,700 experience points is drained one level to 6,700 experience points. Over the course of play, the character again reaches 7,000 experience points by normal accruing of experience. Since the character has surpassed the former number of experience points, no benefit can be gained from restoration.

Alignment

The player should select an alignment for the character that denotes how they are basically going to play the game. Is the character going to be a "good guy" or a "bad guy"? Is the character going to be practical and methodical in approach, or wild and erratic? Will the character have a sense of honor and keep to their word, or be devoid of such values?

Alignment denotes a character's basic disposition and how a character might react to an influence. Alignment is a very general basis since a character might behave or react differently from day to day.

Alignment has two attributes, Good versus Evil and Law versus Chaos The alignment of a character designates where between the two extremes (for each attribute) a character's disposition tends to fall.

Alignment Selection - When a character is created, the player will select a position for each alignment attribute, Good, Neutral, or Evil for Lawful versus Evil, and Lawful, Neutral, Chaotic for Law versus Chaos.

In the case of a new player, the referee may allow the player to participate in a few sessions before the settling on a character alignment in order to get a feel for the concept. Mostly, experienced players will select an alignment when the character is first created.

Most characters will generally conceal their alignment other characters until they become well known, even if they are lawful good. There is nothing more insulting than bluntly asking a stranger their alignment.

Temporary Shifts - Mitigating circumstances might cause characters to temporarily behave outside of their alignment. This may include time when the character is in an emotional state. A good aligned character may commit evil acts against an enemy out of anger or revenge. An evil aligned character may behave as if good aligned for extended periods of time to function in a good aligned group of adventurers

Alignment Drift

When a referee deals that a character is being consistently played out of alignment to one being professed, the player and the referee should confer privately. The player will make a decision as whether the character's alignment should be changed, or if the behavior should be adjusted to come more align with the alignment being professed.

Alignment Change

Generally, a character can change alignment once or twice with no negative ramifications, especially if it is done in the early levels of experience. If a character's alignment changes to often, the referee may assign a percentile chance that the character is going, or has gone, insane.

Alignment Examples

Lawful-Good - Characters of lawful-good alignment believe that a structured society is necessary to make life better for the majority of people. Lawful-good character cling to an ordered method of accomplishing those things which will bring the most benefit to the greatest number of people and do the least amount of harm. They believe that when people work together to a common good, everyone benefits. **Examples:** A good and wise king, an honest working menial laborer.

Neutral-Good - Neutral-good characters believe in promoting of peace and harmony and are totally disinterested in rules and order. They tolerate lawful or chaotic pursuits for good because the methods are unimportant. **Examples:** A hermit who live by the side of the road and offers aid to passers by,

Chaotic-Good - Characters of chaotic-good alignment believe in the betterment of all people, but resent being told how to go about it. They consider rules and standards to be a hindrance to a good outcome. They believe in finding a path to goodness rather than a preperscribed method. Chaotic-goods feel that the end always justifies the means. **Examples:** A good and wise king, an honest and hard working menial laborer.

Lawful-Neutral - Lawful-neutrals believe in the need for order and structure to keep a society working and functioning. The root motive, be it good or evil, is not important, so long as order is established. **Examples** - A stern, but fair administrator of justice, a diligent soldier who never questions orders.

Neutral-Neutral - True Neutrals believe that a person should seek their own nature, whether it is good or evil, or, lawful or chaotic. They believe behaving in whatever way one feels inspired to act is the only way to be true to one's self. **Examples** - A creative artist, a wandering traveler.

Chaotic-Neutral - Chaotic neutral tend to act impulsively. They will follow whatever whim strikes them with little regard for whether or not their actions are good or evil.

Lawful-evil - Lawful-evils see a structured society as a means to suppress their lessers. They delight in power and dominion over others. Lawful-evil characters and creatures will seek to gain dominance over an enemy and bring them into service, rather than kill them outright. Lawful-evils, while self obsessed, recognize the need for order and will honor any promise or pact made. **Examples:** An iron fisted dictator, a devious greedy merchant who does not cheat customers.

Neutral-Evil - Neutral-evils seek power by conquering others. Their only interest is themselves and getting ahead by whatever means necessary. Neutral-evils have no loyalty and will betray anyone the moment it is in their best interest to do so. **Examples:** A double-crossing informant, someone who betrays comrades to save their own life.

Chaotic-Evil - Chaotic-evils delight in creating anarchy. They are an angry lot and despise order and goodness. They will seek to disrupt and cause misery in any way they can, and take pleasure in the suffering of others. Example: A person who deliberately accuses an innocent person and sees them punished, an arsonist, a random murderer.

Although certainly a legitimate alignment combination, a chaotic-evil does not function well with a group and is difficult to play in a group setting with other player-characters and still be true to the chosen alignment. For this reason, a referee may restrict the use of this alignment and possibly other evil alignments.

Combat

Combat is conducted in a series of melee rounds. A Melee is 10 seconds long. During a melee, watch character may attempt to take action. Melee actions may include striking an opponent, dodging, running, readying a weapon, or any other action the character wishes to attempt

Melees

Combat is conducted in a series of melee rounds. A Melee is 10 seconds long. During a melee, watch character may attempt to take action. Melee actions may include striking an opponent, dodging, running, readying a weapon, or any other action the character wishes to attempt.

Surprise

Surprise is usually only a factor in the first round of a battle. The referee will apply a surprise round when a creature or party is caught unawares and not prepared to do battle. In some cases, when both side meet unexpectedly, the referee may rule that there is mutual surprise and no purpose advantage is awarded to either side.

Ending Melee

When one part opts to break off the attack and flee, the opposing party is allowed one final attack as the opponent turns to run. Thereafter, the opponent may attempt a pursuit.

Initiative Actions

At the start of every round, the referee will call for an initiative roll. During a 10 second round of battle, several exchanges of strikes and blocks will take place. An initiative roll is used to determine what when in the round a successful attack will occur. Early in the campaign the referee will set a standard for the use of either a 10-sided die or 6-sided dies to be used to determine an initiative. In a complex battle, the referee determine that is determine that a separate initiative roll be made for every creature or character participating. In simpler confrontations, the referee may call for each player to make a single roll for all their character's. In the most basic of confrontations, the referee may call for only two rolls to be made, with one initiative roll being made by the referee to stand for all non-player-characters, and one by the calling player for all player-characters.

Roll-To-Hit

On the second of the round designated by the initiative roll, a creature will may attempt a to-hit by rolling a 20-sided die. The roll required is based on the modified to-hit-armor-class-0 of the attacker and the opponents armor class rating.

Example: An attacker needs a 7 to hit armor class 0. The opponent has an armor class of 5, creating a base-to-hit of 12. The attacker bonuses for strength and other factors, is calculated to be +4, creating a minimum roll on a 20-sided die of 8.

Default Hit

Even if an attacker has score-to-hit of less than 1 against an opponent, the attacker still has a chance to make a successful hit. Anytime a natural 20 or 19 is rolled on a 20-sided die, the hit is automatic regardless of armor class or other adjustments. Anytime a natural 20 is rolled, the hit is automatic and all damage is doubled.

Default Miss

Even if the attacker has a score-to-hit of 1 or less, the attacker might miss the opponent. A natural roll of 2 or 1 indicates that the strike attempt was a miss. Anytime a natural 1 is rolled, the miss is automatic and the referee will rule that a mishap has occurred. Mishaps might include striking a comrade, on the back swing, the attacker stumbling and being vulnerable for one round, the attacker dropping the weapon, etc, with the referee determining which, if any, are appropriate.

Advantage Attacks

If there is a situation where one combatant has a large advantage over the other, the referee may award an advantage attack. An advantage attack may include a +4 bonus on rolls-to-hit for the attacker, a –4 penalty for rolls-to-hit for the opponent, or both.

Flank Attacks – Flank Attacks are attacks that are itiated against characters or creatures that are already engaged in hand combat with a different opponent, or otherwise preoccupied and cannot defend themasleves as normal. An attacker making a flank attack receives a + 4 bonus on rolls to hit and any dexterity adjustments to armor class are not contented.

Blinded Attacker/Invisible Opponent - A blinded attack is a situation where the attacker cannot see the opponent, but the opponent can see the attacker. In such a case, the combatant that cannot see their opponent will suffer a –4 adjustment to all to-hit rolls.

Dazed Opponent – A dazed opponent is any creature or character that is stunned, slowed magically or hypnotically, etc and only partially able to defend themselves. An attacker striking at a dazed opponent receives a free attack a + 4 bonus on rolls to hit and any dexterity adjustments to armor class are not contented. Usually, the referee will rule that the pain from a wound is sufficient to shock the character back to full conciousness. When a dazed character returns to full conciousness, the attacker will usually get a second free attack (no to hit bonus on the second attack) as the opponent snacks back awake and turns to flee, readies a weapon for combat, or takes other action.

Specially Targeted Weapon Attacks

Sometimes, a character will want to attack a specific target on an opponent. In this situation, the referee will make an arbitrary call for a roll-to-hit penalty based on the smallness and the added difficulty of hitting a specific target. If the roll is successful, the target area is struck.

Example - A fighter is trying to hit the magical necklace of a mage. The fighter has a modified THAC0 of 4. The mage has an Armor 3. To hit the mage in a non-specific area would normally require the roll of a 7 or better. To hit the necklace, the referee imposes a penalty of 4, making the required roll an 11. The roll-to-hit is a 10 (which would normally hit). Since the attack was targeted, however, anything less than an 11 misses completely. On the subsequent round, the roll-to-hit is a 14 and the necklace is successfully hit.

Multiple Attacks

Multiple Hand Weapon Attacks – Some characters and creatures can have more than 1 attack per round in hand combat. The roll on the initiative die determines when the first attack takes place. Thereafter, a creature with multiple attacks can make additional rolls at the rate of one per second. The string is broken when any of the following occurs; an roll-to-hit is missed, the attacker has reached their maximum number of attacks per round, or there is no more time left in the 10-second melee.

Martial-Artist Hand Weapon Multiple Attacks	
Level	**Bonus**
1-3	1 Attack per round
4-9	2 Attacks per round
10-19	3 Attacks per round
20-33	4 Attacks per round
34-51	5 Attacks per round
52-73	6 Attacks per round
74-	7 Attacks per round

Non Initiative Action

Non-Initiative actions are those actions which do not require an initiative roll. Non-initiative actions include unobstructed actions and reactionary actions.

Surprise Attacks

Occasionally, a combatant will find themselves caught unawares by a sneak attack or happening on an enemy unexpectedaly. This is represented in the game by surprise. Depending on the situation, an attacker who surprises an opponent may receive 1 or 2 melees where they can attack without being counter-attacked.

2 Surprise Melees – If the surpised character/party first learns of of an attacker via the swing of the attack, and does not have a weapon ready, the refree will generally award two free melees. During the first melee, the recipient will have no action. During the second melee, the recipient will ready a weapon or turn to flee.

1 Surprise Melees – If the recipient already has a weapon at the ready, or the attacker must close on the recipient to initiate the attack, the referee will generally award only one melee as the opponent either resies a wepon or turns to flee

Mutual Surprise – Occasionally, both parties to a battle will be caught unready for battle. In this event, the refree will declare mutual surpise and no surprise melees are awarded.

Unobstructed actions

Unobstructed actions are those actions are not affected or hindered by other characters or creatures. Unobstructed actions are assumed to have been started on the first second of a melee round unless it is specifically announced otherwise. The most common types of unobstructed action are missile firing and spell casting.

Missile Attacks

No initiative roll is required for firing a missile weapon. The loading and firing speed of weapon determine the initiative for the attack. The base-to-hit for a particular armor class is for weapons fired at medium range. The referee may allow to-hit bonuses for firing a missile weapon at close range, or impose a penalty for firing at long range. Other adjustments might for such factors such as partial cover, poor visibility, an unstable firing position, etc.

Multiple Missile Attacks

If a missle weapon can be cycled (loaded, aimed, and fired) in less than 5 seconds, the attacker may attempt multiple attacks. If the player rolls a natural 1 on a roll-to-hit for a missile weapon attack, the attack will miss, no other attacks may be attempted for the rest of the round, and some mishap will occur.

Missle Weapon Multiple Attacks	
Cycling Time	**Number of attacks**
Greater than 5 seconds	1 Attack per round
5 – 4 Seconds	2 attacks per round
3 Seconds	3 attacks per round
2 Seconds	5 attacks per round
1 Second	10 attacks per round

Reactive Action

A reactionary action is any action which depends upon a host action to take place before being executed. For initiative purposes, the reactive action is considered to take place at same moment as the host action.

Dodging – The most common type of reactive action is a dodge. Most area affect damage spells allow for a dexterity saving throw to allow the character to attempt make a dodge. **A dodge attempt is <u>never</u> automatic, and should not be prompted by the referee.** Also, in combat be there may be times when a character may wish to forgo the option of attacking in order to devote all their energies to avoid being struck by a weapon. A character attempting to dodge or parry is not allowed to make a roll-to-hit, but is allowed to make a dexterity saving throw to avoid being struck.

Calling for a dodge in combat - A player must be quick to announce that their character is going to dodge. Usually, in the case of a area affect damage spell, the referee will pause the game for only 1 or 2 seconds to give the players an opportunity, then continue.

Calling for a dodge against a spell - To be allowed a dodge in combat, the player must call for the dodge prior to their rolling the initiative die. Once the player makes the initiative roll the window of opportunity has closed. A player is not allowed to "wait and see" who will strike first, or if the attacker's roll-to-hit is successful before deciding to dodge. For this reason, the referee most referees will roll initiative last. If the referee makes a mistake and rolls intiative first, and the player sees the results, the player may still call for a dodge as long as they have not rolled their own iniative die.

Rolling for a dodge – After the dodge is called for, the character making the dodge will make the dexterity saving throw as per the saving throw matrix. A saving roll equal to or greater than the required amount indicates the dodge was successful and the attacker is not allowed a roll-to-hit.

Dodge Adjustments - Depending on the circumstances, a referee may impose penalties or allow bonuses to the saving throw. Penalties may be levied for such things as the dodging character not having adequate room or good footing, being encumbered, etc. Bonuses might be awarded for the attacker being impaired, poor visibility, etc.

Spells

The casting of spells does not require an initiative roll. The spell caster will announce that they are casting a spell at the start of a melee. The casting time for the spell will designate when, in the round, the spell will be completed and the affects will occur. Spell casting takes a huge amount of concentration to perform and cannot be done while walking or on horseback (Once the spell is cast, the concetration required to maintain duration spells varies)

Spell Casting While Under Hand Weapon Attack – Casting a spell with a cast time of more than one second is impossible while under attack by a hand weapon. If a spell caster does not stop the spell to defend themselves, the attacker is allowed a non-defensible attack (no roll-to-hit require), and all damage will be doubled (as if a natural 20 were rolled), the spell will be scrubbed and the mana-points required to initiate the spell will be lost.

Spell Casting While Under Missile Attack – If an opponent is able to fire a missile at a spell-caster, who is casting a spell requiring more than one second of cast time, the caster must either stop and attempt to dodge the missile, or submit to an attack with no dexterity adjustment to armor class. If the caster opts to hope for a miss and continue the spell, the attack will be made with the spell-casters dexterity bonus to armor class disregarded. If the hit is successful the spell will be scrubbed and the required mana-points will be used. If the hit misses, the caster may continue the spell .

Instantaneous spells - If a character is casting a spell with a one second cast time of less, the spell is quick enough to be cast between the opponents swings and cannot be scrubbed by interference.

Scroll Reading

Scroll reading occurs more quickly then spell casting, and the normal casting time for the spell is irrelevant. Opening the tube and reading it takes 3 seconds. If the scroll is in hand at the start of the melee, the affect from the spell will have an intiative of 3. Scroll reading require minimal concentration and can be completed while walking or riding horesback. As long as the reader is not injured, the spell can usually be complete without disruption. If the scroll is not in hand, but tucked away, it will usually require the action of a melee to retreive

Potion Drinking

Opening a potion vial and drinking its contents takes 3 seconds. If the potion vial is in hand at the start of the melee, the affect from the potion will begin to occur at the 3rd initiative. Once the potion begins to take affect, the potions onset time will determine when the affects are fully realized. If the potionl is not in hand, but tucked away, it will usually require the action of a melee to retrieve

Magical Item Use

Employing a magical item require the same high level of concentration as casting as spell, and normally will have a lesser affect. The initiative is determined by the activation time of the item. Normally, the activation time for an items affect is the same as the spell which produces the same affect.

Non-Defensible-Attack

Occasionally, an attacker may be in a situation where there is no conceivable way the attack can miss. Missile weapon attacks are rarely Non-defensible-attacks. In a Non-defensible it is assumed that not only has the attacker made a successful hit, but has also achieved exceptional damage (as if a natural 20 was rolled). No roll is required and all damage is doubled.

Rear Attacks – The most common type of non-defensible-attack is an attack from the rear. If an attacker is able to slip up on an opponent unawares. The attacker is allowed two free attacks. The first attack is at double damage (as if a natural 20 were rolled). The second attack takes places as the opponent turns to fight or begins to flee.

Sleeping Opponent – When an attacker is sticking a sleeping opponent, the hit is automatic and all damage is tripled. If the opponent is not slain, he/she may cry out for help, and begon to take action. As the opponent gathers themselves, the attacker will usually get a second free attack (no to hit bonus on the second attack) as the opponent snacks back awake and turns to flee, readies a weapon for combat, or takes other action.

Multiple Non-Defensible-Attack

There are conditions in the game when an attacker will have unrestricted Non-Defensible-Attacks at their disposal. When this occurs, the opponent is at the mercy of the attacker. If the attacker does not break off the attack, and there is no outside intervention, the opponent is pronounced dead.

Restrained Opponent - A character who is completely restrained and cannot cry out for help will generally be pronounced dead by the referee.

Paralyzed Opponent – Depending on the cuase of the paralysis, the referee may rule that the pain from being wounded will create enough shock to end the paralysis. Depending on the situation, a charisma saving throw mya be in order. If the paralysis is not broken, is pronounced dead.

Equipment

Weapons

Hand Weapons

Below is a listing of the statistics to the basic weapons that are employed by the different classes. There are specialized weapons for particular classes that are included only in the character class information.

Hand Weapons		
Weapon	Damage	Size/Weight
Punch or Kick	1D4	Not applicable
Punch (Martial-Artist)	1D6	Not applicable
Kick (Martial-Artist)	1D8	Not applicable
Dagger	1D6	1'/4 pounds
Club	1D6	3"/6 pounds
Staff	1D6	6'/10 pounds
2' Sword	1D8	8 pounds
3' Sword	1D10	12 pounds
4' Sword	1D12	16 pounds
5' Sword	2D8	20 pounds
6' Sword	1D20	24 pounds
7' Sword	2D12	30 pounds

Swords

The damage a sword cause is relative to it's size. There is no such thing as "two hand sword" A hobbit's two-hand sword would be about 4 foot long, and require two-hands for a hobbit to use. A giant could use the same sword in one hand and use a shield, or a dagger in the other hand.

Secondary arm Sword-Shield usage – The smaller the sword (proportional to the weilder's body) the greater the ability to use the second arm.

Extraordinary Metals To-hit/Damage Bonuses		
Metal	Tensile Adjustment	Potential Magical Adjustment
Steel	+1 on rolls-to-hit	None
Titanium	+2 on rolls-to-hit	+1 on rolls-to-hit
Mithril	+3 on rolls-to-hit	+2 on rolls-to-hit
Adamanite	+4 on rolls-to-hit	+3 on rolls-to-hit

Hand weapons made from extraordinary metals

Most normal metal weapons are made or plain iron, and have no to-hit or damage bonuses. Upgrading to a steel weapon will give the weilder a +1 bonus on to-hit and damage rolls dues to the fact that it will hold a better edge. Also, some extraordinary metals are are able to retain continuous magical affects that enhance their to-hit and damage affects. All wepons with bonuses have the same bonus amounts for rolls-to-hit and damage.

Supplies

The handling of supplies varies from campaign to campaign. For some. The book work of remembering to purchase rations, material components for spells, supplies, etc in preparation for an adventure adds realism and mirrors the necessity of a character

Secondary Arm Shield/Sword Usablility							
	------------ Sword Size -------------						
Race	7	6	5	4	3	2	DG
Albino	*	*	2H	BS	FS	DG	2F
Dwarf	*	*	2H	BS	FS	DG	2F
Elf	*	*	2H	BS	FS	DG	2F
Giant	2H	BS	FS	DG	2F	3F	4F
Gnome	*	*	*	2H	BS	FS	DG
Hobbit	*	*	*	2H	BS	FS	DG
Human	*	2H	BS	FS	DG	2F	3F
Orc	*	2H	BS	FS	DG	2F	3F

2H = Heavy 2-Handed use, no shield
BS = Light 2-Handed use, strap on buckler
FS = 1-Handed Use, full shield
DG = 1 Handed use, secondary dagger
2F = 1 Handed use, secondary 2 foot sword

readying for the task. For others, it is just a hinderance to getting the game going and into the action.

Standard dungeoning equipment

If the referee decides to abbreviate the preparation time, the rule of "standard dungeon equipment" may be instituted. Basically, it is assumed that the characters are going to come equipped with the basics. Torches, string, rope, oil, sacks, chalk, pry-bars, door-wedges, etc are all assumed to be brought along for the journey. During the game, as the need arises, the player may ask the referee if particular items were brought along. So long as the items are fairly common and reasonably considered to bee "tools of the trade" the referee should assent to the assumption they had been brought along. Items such as potions, weapons, armor, etc are not included and must be specifed and inventoried before the character leaves to go on the adventure. If an item is borderline as far as commonality and if it may have been brought, the referee will make a judgement call, or declare a percentage chance and roll percentile dice to determine an outcome.

Game Standards Non-Magical

Ability Rolls

An ability roll is an attempt by a character to complete a particular task. The referee will consider the task, and what is being attempted and will determine what ability is relevant. The base chance for successful completion of the task is equal to the character's relevant score. Once the odds are determined, a roll is made on percentile dice to determine if it was successful.

Difficulty Adjustments

A referee will utilize difficulty adjustments to set the ease with which various tasks in the game can be performed. A difficulty adjustment can be penalty (a negative adjustment for more difficult tasks) or a bonus (a positive adjustment for easier tasks). After the referee has determined what ability is relevant, the referee will set the adjustment, then make the percetile roll (or, at the referee's disgression, if secrecy is not required, may allow the player to make the roll).

Example - A character is trying to open a jammed door. The referee determines the character's strength is the relevant ability that comes into play. Further, ther referee has determined that a person of average strength would have a difficult time opening the door and has assigned a difficulty adjustment of -20% to the task. The character making the attempt has a strength ability of 60. The odds of the door coming open are 40% (60 - 20). A percentil roll of 41 of higher will indicate failure, while a roll of 40 or loss will indicate success. The referee makes a roll of 35 and the door is opened.

Multiple Tries - A referee may assign a timeframe to a difficulty adjustment and have a secondary difficulty adjustments for subsequent tries. Normally, secondary difficulty adjustments are less favorable and/or have a longer time frame since their use indicates that the character has already made at least one unsuccessful attempt.

Example - A character is trying to decipher an encoded note. The referee determines that the character's intelligence is the relevant ability needed to be successful. Futher the refree has determined that the code is not very complex and has a initial difficulty adjustment of +25% with a timeframe of one hour. The character has a intelligence score of 40 allowing for a 65% chance be successful. The referee rolls 55 on the percenitle dice indicating failure. The player informs the refree that the character is going to spend more time in hopes of breaking the code. The refree determines that the timeframe for subsequent attempts is 4 hours and the difficulty adjustment is -25% (to reflect the greater difficulty of being successful after a first attempt has failed) Utilizing the intelligence score of 40 and applyiung the -35% penalty, the character has a 15% chance of success on the next attempt. The refree makes a roll of 20 on the percentile dice indicating the second attempt has also failed. The player opts to make a third attempt, expending an additional 4 hours. The refree makes a new roll, generating a 9 on the percentile dice, indicating success on the third attempt.

Lower limit - A referee may assign a limit to a difficulty roll to prevent a particular task from being impossible and/or an automatic success.

Example - A character is trying to pick up a wand with a loop of string. The refree has determined that it is a fairly difficult task and it has a dexterity difficulty adjustment of -40% Further the refree has determined that even a very clumsy character would some chance of success and assigns a 10% lower limit. A fighter with a dexterity score of 33 makes the attempt. Absent of tlower limit, the fighter would have no chance of success since the adjustment (-40%) is greater than the dexterity score (33) With the lower limit in play, the fighter still has a 10% chance regardless of the poor dexterity. A roll of 15 comes up on the percentile dice and the attempt has failed. A mage then makes an attempt. The mage has a dexterity of 44. Applying the difficulty adjustment of -40% would give the mage only a 4% chance of success. With the 10% lower limit in play, however, he has a 10% chance regardless of his dexterity ability. The percentil roll is 5, and the is success.

Upper limit - A referee may assign a limit to a difficulty roll to prevent a particular task from being impossible and/or an automatic success.

Time-Distance-Movement

Time in Play - Play time is simply real time as experienced by the players and reflects the amount of time the player is participating in the game. To maintain a conitent basis, experience points are awarded based on play time. Most other game factors are determined by game time.

Time in Game - Game time is the passage of time as experience by the characters. While a game session might last a few hours. During that play time

Time Table			
1 Segment =	1/10 Second		
1 Second =	10 Segments		
1 Round =	10 Seconds	100 Segments	
1 Minute =	6 Rounds	60 Seconds	600 Segments
1 Turn =	10 Minutes	60 Rounds	600 Rounds
1 Hour =	6 Turn=	60 Minutes	360 Turns
1 Watch =	4 Hour	24 Turns	240 Minutes
1 Day =	6 Watches	24 Hours	144 Turns
1 Week =	7 DAYS	42 Watches	168 Hours
1 Month =	4 Weeks	28 Days	168 Watches
1 Year =	12 Months	52 Weeks	365 Days
1 Decade =	10 Years	120 Months	520 Weeks
1 Century =	10 Decades	100 years	1200 Months
1 Millenium =	10 Centuries	100 Decades	1000 Years

Distance/Movement Table		
Distance		
1 Foot =	12 Inches	
1 Yard =	3 Feet	36 Inches
1 Mile =	1760 Yards	5280 Feet
Movement		
1.5 Feet per Second = 5 Yards per Round		
5 Yards per Round = 1 Mile per hour (actually 1.045 MPH)		

Pursuit

Pursuit takes place anytime one party is in pursuit and another party is attempting to flee. The success of a pursuit hinges on various factors that are adjudicated by the referee to produce a result.

Starting Distance – The first thing a referee must determine is how far about the two parties are when the chase begins. For easy calculation, it is recommended that the refeee will extablish the starting distance in yards.

Closing rate – This is simple calculation of difference in movement rate of the two parties. The referee may include adjustments to allows for conditions of the settings which may be to the benefit or detriment of either party's speed. It is generally assumed that the pursuer is the faster of the two. If the pursued is moving faster, the pursuer will often give up the chase when they see they are being outdistanced. For easy calculation, it is recommended that the refeee will establish the closing rate in yards per round (miles per hour * 5).

Length of Pursuit – Once the yardage for the starting distance and yards pre round of the closing rate are determined, it is simple enough to divide the distance by the yareds per round to come up with the total rounds the chase can last.

Endurance – After the length of pursuit is established, the referee must determine how many of the participants can last the entire pursuit. If the fleeing party can hold out, but pursuer cannot keep up the chase long enough to close the gap, the pursuit will usually end in faiure.

Finding Cover – If there is adequate cover, the fleeing party may opt to lose the pursuer rather than outrunning them.

Chance of Success - A percentile chance of the pursuer successfully catching the quarry. This is an arbitrary call made by the referee based on such factors as movement rates, endurance, seperation distance, available cover, level of motivation, etc.

Example: A large beast is pursuin a hobbit. The hobit runs at 35 yards per round (7 MPH) The beast moves at 50 yards per round (10 MPH) The chace begins with a starting distance of 150 yards.

The referee may determine : The pursuer is closing at a rate of 15 yards per round (50 YPR - 35 YPR). Since the starting distance is 150 yards, the length of pursuit is 10 rounds (150 yars/15 yards per round). However, the referee determines that the pursing beast is heavy and cannot endure a 10 round chase. After 6 rounds, the beast will tire and the hobbit will escape.

Attacking during a pursuit – Sometimes, a participant is able to fire missle weapons at an opponent during a pursuit. The referee will determine which of the participants can attack based on the ability to weild a weaponm and use it effectively while the chase is going on.

Example: A character in horseback is pursuing a horse drawn wagon. The chase takes place on an open round and begins with the participants 200 yards apart. The wagon has a speed of 60 yards per round (12 MPH) while the rider's horse travels at 150 yeards per round (30 MPH).

The referee may determine: The closing rate is 90 yards per round, and at 200 yards, the chase will last just over two rounds, causing the distance to be closed early in the 3rd round. During the chase, the rider cannot attack. During the chase, two characters riding in the back of the wagon may fire arrows from long bows at rider following on horseback. The characters firing the long bows will suffer a –2 to-hit penalty due to the jostling of the wagon. The long bow cycle rate allows for two attacks per round. Since it will take just over 2 rounds to close, each of the character in the back of the wagon are allowed 5 long bow attacks, for a total of 10 arrows fired at the rider on horseback

Holy Water

Holy water is uausally very attainable in any town at a church or abbey.

Holy water will cause 3-6 (3D6) hit-points of damage to any undead creature it is splashed on. To splash an undead creature, the person making the tosser must make a roll-to-hit an armor class of 0. Holy water is the material component for may spells, as well as having other assorted uses.

Poison

Poison is one of the deadliest aspects of the game. There are three basic types of poison in the game.

Ingested - These are typically the most potent types of poison but are also the most difficult to deliver. Ingested poisons are most often used on food and drink and then duping the victim into eating it. Ingested poisons usually have the longest on-set times and durations.

Insinuated - Insinuated poisons are used to coat the spikes and edges of weapons so as to introduce the poison into a victim's blood stream. Weapons that have been tainted with insinuated poison usually have a brown or bluish tint.

Contact - Contact poisons are the easiest to deliver but have the smallest affect. They operate by coating an object or surface with the poison then waiting for a victom to make physical contact. Contact poisons are the most difficult to find or produce. Also, to be effective, larger amounts are usually needed.

Venoms - For all intents and purposes, venoms are considered to be insinuated poisons, and all game factor are handled under this asumption. For example, if an affect such as poison neutralization (the basic purpose of which is to relieve a victim's body of poison) were used on a venomous snake, all poisons in the snakes body would be rendered inert, making it non-poison until its body had adequate time to create new venom.

When adjudicating the damage from a poisons affect, there are three basic factors to consider; onset-time, damage-rate, and duration.

Onset-time - Onset time time is the time that will elapse between when the poison is first initiated into/onto the subject and when the first affects of the poison will be felt.

Damage-rate - Poison damage is always handled with 20-sided dice. A constitution saving throw to ½ damage is almost always allowed. The damage-rate for a poison will determine how quickly the poison will afflict damage on the victim's body and in what amounts. Usually damage-rates are handled in 1 round (10 second) intervals.

Single roll versus multiple rolls - The referee may elect to roll the dice for the damage only once, at the first interval, then repeat the same damage for each interval; or re-roll the damage at individually for each interval.

Fair play insists that the referee announce which damage rolling method will be used (or allow the palyer the option) <u>before</u> the first intervals damage is rolled. If the damage for the first interval is rolled without the referee establishing the method (either by deliberation or ommision), the player is allowed to select the method. If the referee has already announced the results of the roll, this gives the player an advantage since a low roll could be replicated (by selecting the single roll method), or a high roll could be discarded for a fresh roll at every new interval (by selecting the multiple roll method). Once the rolling method is established, it must stay the same throughout the poisons duration.

Duration - A poisons duration is simply how long a victim will suffer the affects of the poison. During a potions duration, the victim will be overcome by nausea and convulsions and will not be able to take action.

Example - The referee has determined that the bite of a venomous snake has the following specifications;

When the character is bitten, the referee rolls a 4-sided dice to determine the amount of time before the affects of the poison will be felt. The roll is a '4' giving the player 3 rounds of action before being incapacitated by the poisons affects. When that time has elapsed, the affects begin, and the victim can no longer take action until the poisons duration is over.

The character makes a successful constitution saving throw, indicating that all poison affects will be suffered at ½ damage. (A successful save does not allow the victim to take action during the poisons duration).

The referee elects to make one a single roll for damage and repeat the same damage at every interval (in this case the intervals are in rounds). The roll of 3D20 generates a per round damage of 25. Since the constitution save was successful, the damage is halved (rounded down) to 12 points per round.

The referee then rolls a 6-sided die to detemine how many rounds the victim will suffer poison damage (since the duration is 1-6 rounds) The roll generates a '4', which means that the damage will be suffered for 4 rounds

Result - The victim will suffer 12 hit-points of poison damage per round, for a 4 round duration, causing a total of 48 hit-points of poison damage.

Fall Damage

Fall Damage	
Distance	Damage
1-9ft	None
10-19ft	1D4
20-29ft	2D6
30-39ft	3D8
40-49ft	4D10
50-59ft	5D12
60-69ft	6D12
70-79ft	7D12
80-89ft	8D12
30-39ft	9D12
40-49ft	10D12
50-59ft	15D6

Item Saving Throws

All saving throw requirements are based on 1-3 dice of the damage type. Adjust the required amount up by 1 for each additional 3 dice of damage. **Example** - Glass requires a roll of 8 to save against 1D6 to 3D6 of fire damage, 4D6 to 6D6 would require a roll of 9, 7D6 to 9D6 would require a roll of 10.

Item Saving Throws - Elemental					
Type	Energy	Fire	Cold	Lightning	Pelter
Bone	1	1	3	3	3
Book	1	4	3	8	12
Ceramic	1	3	12	12	18
Cloth	1	16	2	6	12
Crystal	1	5	16	16	19
Glass	1	8	17	17	20
Leather, Normal	1	12	5	9	12
Leather, 2nd dary Dragon	1	11	4	8	12
Leather, Primary Dragon	1	10	3	7	12
Leather, Black Dragon	1	9	2	6	12
Metal, Precious	1	12	4	19	11
Metal, Iron	1	9	5	16	7
Metal, Steel	1	8	4	15	6
Metal, Titanium	1	7	3	14	5
Metal, Mithril	1	6	2	13	4
Metal, Admanite	1	5	1	12	3
Paper	1	20	1	8	8
Potion vial	1	14	20	20	20
Rope	1	16	3	3	3
Staff	1	12	2	10	8
Stone, Plain	1	5	5	6	9
Stone, Precious	1	4	4	5	8
Wand	1	6	6	7	10

Game Standards Magical

Magic is treated as a science that was used and developed thousands of years ago, but the gradually faded into non-existence long before the modern age. Magic gains it's power from the balance of postive and negative energies. Certain verbal recitations, somatic gestures, and materials are capable of creating a conduit between the two energy poles and releasing their energy.

Magical Durations

Magic is appears in the game in various ways but all magical affects are always divided into three basic types. Instaneous, Enchantment and Continual magic.

Instantaneous Magical Affects

Instaneous magic has no duration. The magic is only in affect for a split-second. It is used to obtain a result which is non-magical in nature.

Enchantments

Many spells can generate a mild dweomer that will have a lingering affect that is not permanent and is the residual magical affects of a magical spell. All enchantment magics have a duration and will expire with time. Enchantments might be used on an object, but it does not create a magical item. An enchantment might be used to move temporarily animate an object but cannot be used to create a magical creature or magical item.

Enchantments are often controllable by the caster through command words

Continual magics

Continual magics is the most powerful form of magica always have a permanent duration is the creation if a magical item or a magical creature that is magical in and of itself. It is important to make the distinction between the two, for many spells and affects of the game will influence one, but no the other.

Any spell which has a duration of "permanent" is considered a continual magic. Continual magics are magics that are then enchantments, and hanve no continued association with the spell caster. If the magic is controllable through command words, anyone who knows the words and understand how to the use the magic may control it. Spells and affects that can dispel enchantments have no affect, or only limited temporary affect on continual magics.

Spells

Spell casting is the most common form of magic in the game. Spells can be used to create instantaneous magics, enchantments, or continual magics.

Spell Casting

The casting of spells can involve any combination of up to three types of components, which are, verbal (spoken allowed), somatic (hand gestures), and matrial (a physical item or substance to orientate the spell). Triggering the spell requires the use of some of the character to expend some of their personal psychic energy (Mana).

Spell casting in secret – At the beginning of every round, any character intending to cast a spell must announce their intent. A player is not required to reveal what spell has been chosen until casting is complete. To keep it secret, the player should place the spell card on the table face down (if spell cards are not used, the write the name of the spell on a piece of paper). When the casting time is complete, the player will turn the card over to reveal the spell.

Scrubbed Spells

Casting any spell requires a high level of concentration (after being cast, some spells require a lesser amounts of concentration to maintain). If a character who is casting a spell has their concentration interrupted, the spell will be scrubbed, and the mana-points required to cast the spell will be used.

Target Spells - If a spell has a range and the affected area is a single vreature of object it is considered to be a 'targeted" spell. To target a spell the caster must have a clear line of sight to the intended target. IF the caster begins the spell, but the target disappears from view before the casting is complete, the caster must quicky select a new target or the spell will be scrubbed and the mana will be sued.

Spell Memorization

If a character is already at full spell capacity and wishes to begin using a spell they do not currently have commited to memory, they must stop all other activities and spend the time necessary to commit the spell to memory. As the the new spell is memorized, the player must select a spell of the same level to be lost from memory as the new spell being studied takes its place. The type of study required to renew spells varies from class to class. A player should consult his/her class information to determine what method of spell study is appropriate for their class.

Spell Study – To study a spell, the caster must have rested at least 1 turn (10 minutes) for each spell level to be studied. The caster must be in normal mental status and have at least 50% of their hit-points.

Spell Refresh - Each morning, a player must which spells, from those available to them, they are going to use for the day.

Scroll Spell Memorization - If a character is wanting to commit a spell to memory and is in possession of a scroll of that same spell, the memorization process can be abbreviated by the spell caster silently reading the scroll.
If the spell caster is already at maximum spell capacity, they must select a spell of the same level to be overwritten as the new spell is read into memory.

Spell Memorization/Refresh Times	
Refresh	1 Minute (60 Seconds) per spell level
Memorize	10 Minutes (1 Turn) per spell level

Innate Magical Abilities

Some creatures in the game can cast spells, while others can cause magical affects without the use of spells. Innat magical abilities do not require spell study (although daily use may still be limitied) Innate magical abilites do not require the same high level of concentration that is necessarryu for spell casting.

Scrolls
Scrolls are fine

Scroll Paper - Scrolls are are magical command words inscribed on sheets of fine paper in magical ink by a spell caster. Scrolls are typically stored in tube of glass, metal, or other materials allowing for an air tight seal.

Writing Scrolls –A spell can be inscribed to a scrolls can be inscribed by any caster who has the spell committed to memory and has the required mana, and has aquired the necessary scroll paper and ink. Inscribing a scroll requires double the normal amount of mana and 4 x the normal casting time (1 turn/10 minutes for instantaneous spells) Psychic feats are not inscribable to scrolls.

Magic Scroll Ink - Magical ink is very flammable. If a scroll is opened near an open flame, it will burst into flames consuming the parchment and daling 1d6 fire damage to the reader. Dry scroll ink fades rapidly when exposed to air. A scroll must be sealed in an airtight tube immediately ofter it is written. If a scroll tube loses it's airtight seal, the writing inside will fade leaving only blank paper inside.

Reading a scroll - The moment a scroll tube is opened, the writing will start to fade. The opener must begin to read the scroll immediately or the writing will fade before the scroll can be used. The scroll will either need to be read aloud (to cast the spell) or silently (to commit the spell to memory) A scroll can only ge read by a character of the same class as the scroll author. As each word is read it immediately vanishes.

Scroll Marking – Often, a spell caster will mark the spell tube to label it with the spell inside since, if the caster forgets what spell is inside, opening the scroll to check will destroy the scroll.

Casting spells from scrolls - Casting a spell from a scroll requires no somatic or material components. The reader will not siffer any mana loss from casting the spell. The cast time is exactly the same as if the spell were being cast normally.

Scroll Casting Time - Casting spells from reading a scroll takes exactly the same amount of time as if the spell were being cast normally. The scroll itself is the material component for the spell and the reading is the somatic gestures. Should the reader pause or be interrupted, the writing will fade before the scroll can be completely read and the spell will be lost.

Gaining New Spells from Scrolls – If a spell caster finds a scroll that is not currently part of their repitoire of spells, the reade may use the scroll increase their spell inventory. The spell caster must first read the spell silenty to commit it to memory. Once the new spell is in memory, the spell caster must sit quietly for 1 turn (10 minutes) per spell level to study on the spell (in the case os a mage, make notes in the spell book) Once the spell study is finished, the new spell becomes part of the caster's spell inventory and can be used normally thus forward.

Example: A statue that has had a lightning glyph cast on it, is enchanted, but is not a magical item. A wand that can produce lightning bolts, is a magical item.

Enchantment dispelling: When enchantment are dispelled in area affect, usually neutralizes all enchantments in the affected area, and has not affect on magical creatures or magical items. When placed singularly on a magical item or creature, it may (depending on the item/creature) temporarily neutralize it.

Enchanted Potions
Potions are enchanted liquids that have a magical affect when consumed or poured on a subject. Potions are generally sored in stored generally sealed vials and have a liquid volume of ¼ cup (2 fluid ounces). Like spells, some potions have instantaneous affects while others have a duration of enchantment.
Duration
Most potions will last 60-90 minutes (5 + 1d4 Turns) Dome potions have magical affects

Shelf life
After their creation, most potions have a shelf life of 6-9 weeks.

Magical Items
Magiced items are objects that have very powerful continual magics placed upon them. Magical items are objects that are permanently magiced and can be used to cause or create magical affects. They are finely crafted from precious materials such as rare metals, fine gems, and inlaid rare woods and ivories. Once created physically, they are magically endowed by powerful magical forces.

Magic Item Use
Magiced items do not have any continued association with the spell caster. If the magic item is controllable through command words, anyone who knows the words and understand how to the use the magic may control it.

Magic Item Creation
Creating magical items is usually a daunting task for player-characters. First, the player-character must acquire the spell, then they must acquire the precious materials to create the item, then they must hire the item to be created before receiving the magic (fine jewelry crafting is normally not a part of player-character skills).

Often, to be able to receive the magic, an object must be of a certain configuration (wand, ring, staff) and material (gold, platinum, ivory, etc) set with precious stones (diaimonds, rubies, emeralds, etc)

To create the item successfully, requires two successful percentile rolls. If either roll fails, a mistake was made. The item will explode, peltering anyone in a 15' will suffer 3D12 pelter damage.

Intelligence roll - The caster must make a roll equal to or less then their modified intelligence score on percentile dice.
Experience roll - The caster must make a roll equal to or less then their experience on percentile dice.

Spells for Magical Item Creation on scrolls - Finding a spell to create a magic item inscribed on a scroll is extremely rare. Mage's do not usually inscribe magic creation spells to scrolls since the cast times tend to be extremely long (hours and sometimes days), and therefore a one use scroll would require massive amounts of scroll paper and ink. Also, scrolls are primarily used to have extra spells for combat, if a mage is home in their shop, they Mage's do not commonly inscribe rmanent magic to

Magical Creatures

Magiced creature are those non-living creature that are brought to life by continual magics. Unilike magical items, magical creatures will recognize orders and command words only from their creator. The size nature and type of creature varies with the spell.

Command words Some enchantments and most continual magics controlled by the verbal enuciation of command words. Often, these command words are required to be spoken while holding or manipulating the item in specific way. Learning the use of a magical item requires that a character be given meticulous training by someone already skilled in it's use. Merely overhearing the command words being spoken once or twice is not adequate to learn the proper tone and accent of syllables of the command words, or proper handling of the item.

If a magic item user is uable to speak, inebriated and unable to speak clearly, dizzy, dazed, or confused, he/she will not be able to summon the concentration necessary to properly acticate the item.

Magical creatures are any creatures who's life force is generated by the forces of magic, and not by natural body processes. They cannot be destroyed by enchantment dispelling, although one, might be immobilized for a time.

Magical ink, that is used to inscribe scrolls and for other magical writings is magical in nature, and cannot be permanently affected by enchantment dispelling.

Artifacts & Relics

Artifacts and Relics are extremely powerful magical item. They are normally one of a kind magical items that were created by a fluke, or extremely powerful creatures. The creations (and often use) of these is normally beyond the scope of mortals. Artifacts and relics can not be created, altered, duplicated, scryed, affected by wishes, into existence, located magically moved about magicallynormally not be , the creation

Artifacts cannot be teleported or moved magically in any way. The location of an artifact cannot be revealed by magical means, or by any sort of magical probing, An artifact cannot be made invisible (unless it is a function of the artifact) or influenced by any sort of outside enchantments such as glyphs, levitating, etc. An artifact can only be taken into other planes and dimensions if it is physically carried. Artifacts can only be destroyed by specific means, and in specific places (usually the place of its creation).

Elemental Damage

Shroud-type Magics
There are magics in the game which can cause a creature or character to be invisible. There are two basic types of invisibility, bodily invisibility and shroud invisibility
Invisibility
There are magics in the game which can cause a creature or character to be invisible. There are two basic types of invisibility, bodily invisibility and shroud invisibility.

Bodily Invisibility - The most common way to achieve bodily invisibility is to ingest an invisibility potion. Bodily invisibility turns the recipeint's entire body invisible, but all clothing and carried items remain visible. For bodily invisibility to be usefule, the recipient must be nude and carrying no items. Bodily invisibility is dispelled if the recipient casts a spell, uses a magical item, or is influenced by magic employed by others. Physical contact with creatures, objects, or surfaces will not dispel bodily invisibility.

Shroud Invisibility - With an invisible shroud, the magic will cause the subject and all carried items to become invisible, from their head to the soles of their feet. Walking or running will not dissapate the magic so long as the subject does not brush up against anything.

Casting a touch range spell on oneself will not dissapate the magic or dirnking a magical potion will not dissapate the magic.

The enchantment will be disappaited it any of the following happen; the character or anything carried by the character brushes up agains anyone or anything, any object or liquid falls on the character or anything the character is carrying, the character picks up anything, the creature is hit by any sort of missle, the character fires any sort of missle, the character is struck by a hand weapon, the character strikes anyone or anything with a weapon or other object, the character is influenced or damaged by an external spell or breath weapon, the character releases a touch spell onto anyone but themselves.

Teleporting
To teleport to anywhere using any sort of means, the character must either be able to see the new location, or have been there previously, or cans see the the target location with their own line of sight.

Elemental Maximum Damages						
Source	Energy	Fire	Cold	Lightning	Pelter	Poison
Ring	3D4	3D6	3D8	3D10	3D12	3D20
Wand	4D4	4D6	4D8	4D10	4D12	4D20
Staff	5D4	5D6	5D8	5D10	5D12	5D20
Innate Ability	6D4	6D6	6D8	6D10	6D12	6D20
Area spell	7D4	7D6	7D8	7D10	7D12	7D20
Targetspell	8D4	8D6	8D8	8D10	8D12	8D20
Touch spell	10D4	10D6	10D8	10D10	10D12	10D20

Scrying

The percentil chance for success of scrying a person or place depends on the scryers familiarity with the intded subject. To perform a successful scry, the scryer must at least be in physical contact with someone who is very familiar to the intended subject. The amount of time the scry lasts, and whether or not it includes audio or is only visual depends upon the means used.

Odds of Successfule Scrying

%Chance	Familiarity
90%	Very well known. Seen several times
80%	Touched only once
70%	In possession of tissue or soil sample
60%	Seen only once in a close quarters
50%	Seen only once from a distance
40%	Physical contact with creature who has had contact

Gaseous Form

Gaseous form is magical alteranation of creatures, objects or other solids into a cloud of colored gas. Artifacts and relics cannot be transformed into gaseous clouds

Gaseous Objects

If this spell is used on an object, the cloud will hang in one spot (if there is no draft), or willow about in the breeze until the magic is no longer in affect.

Gaseous Creatures

While in gaseous form, a subject is able to float in any direction horizontally or vertically at a rate of 25 yards per round (5 niles per hour) relative to the surrounding air. The subject will be able to control their form so as to leak through small cracks or openings.

Senses - While is gaseos from, a creature will have multi-directional "vision" due to being able to sense the light that is passing through their gaseous body. The subject will able to "hear" by sensing the vibrations of in the air. The subject can speak, but only in a hollow, whipery voice.

Spell casting - A subject will not be able to cast spells while in gaseous from since the voice will be distorted and not effective for verbal components. There are not limbs to complete somatic components. Any material components are either turned to gas with the spell caster or unable to be grasped by the spell caster.

Psychic feats and Innate Abilities - These can be employed while in gaseous form so long as they do not require any verbal, somatic, or material components.

Magical Flying

Various spells and other magis in the game might give the character the ability to fly. Learning to fly is difficult and novices will spend most of their time crashing into trees, buildings, and anything else in their path. A novice will always crash and roll when landing. When a novice lands, they will make a dexterity saving throw, failure of which indicates that the flyer has incurred 1D6 landing damage.

The time required to become proficient at fighting is an arbitrary call made by the referee based on the characters dexterity ability score. After the character masters the basics, they can move on to the more complex maneuvers such as hovering, wielding a weapon in flight, etc.

To credit for all time spent flying, a player should keep a log of the character's early flights and length of flight, until a prefeceincy is gained.

Wishes

Wishes are the most powerful form of magic in the game, and expend massive amounts of magical energy. It is not all powerful, however.

In the most basic terms, a magical wish interprets the spoken words of the person making the wish, then manufactures the magics necessary to comply.

The path of least resistance - The nature of wishes is like that of electricity in that it will always choose path of least resistance in which to function. A wish will always complete itself using the least amount of magics, and thereby, causing the least affect possible or no affect at all. It falls to the referee to find the interpretation of the spoken wish that renders the least affect to the game, or if possible, no affect at all.

Wording descrapancies - As with any situation of one person speaking and another person listening, there will be times of human error when the recollection of the player is that they worded the wish one way, while the recollection of the referee is that it was worded some other way. For this reason, it is recommended that the player write the wording of the wish on a sheet of paper. While this is slightly less realistic, it goes along way to removing the element of human error.

Writing it down - The player will write the wording down, read the wish of the sheet, then give the referee the page to review. If this method is used, so long as the player does not stumble during the reading, the wording on the paper is the accepted as being the exact wording used.

Just saying it - If the player declines to write the wish wording down, the wish will function as the referee *thinks* it was heard. Any disconnect between the referee's perception and the players's intent is assumed to be a misspeak on the part of the player regardless of who was actually in error or where the where the real fault lies.

Pitfalls - The wording of every wish must begin with "I wish...." Thereafter, the referee will exploit every legitimate mistake to render the wish useless or less effective. Some of the typical pitfalls are listed below.

Unintended wishes - Unitended wishes can occur anytime the character has wishes at the ready. This can occur in situation such as when the character is wearing a ring of wishes, is in the company of a dijinn or efreet that owes them wishes, or if the character has read a wish scroll but not yet made the wish.

If the player happens to speak the words "I wish" in passing, such as *"I wish we had brought more horses on the adventure"*, the wish will be used. Unless the referee is a real stickler, comments that are obviously intended to be out of game, due to modern connotations, will not be counted. Saying *"I wish we'd bought more cola at the pizza parlor"* in reference to the food on the gaming table, will probably not use up a wish. However, if the same comment is made with more ambiguity such as "I wish we had more drink", it could be either the player speaking or the character speaking.

All ambiguities should be decided in the disfavor of the player, accepting that the game itself is based on the spoken word and anytime the player is participating in the game the words *"I wish"* have the potential of triggering a wish.

False starts - The player begins speaking the words to a wish for a wand "I wish I had a wand of..." then realized that the number of charges was not specified. The player pauses, clears their throat, and starts again, *"I wish I had a fully charged wand of..."*

If the player only has one wish at the ready, the wish is scrubed with the first start, and the second start is just spoken words that have no wish power.

If the player has multiple wishes at the ready, the first wish is scrubbed but the second one may be effective if no other mistakes are made. More false starts will use more wishes until the supply is depleted.

Getting multiple wishes out of a single wish - For obvious reasons, a wish such as "I wish for three more wishes" cannot work. Likewise, there are other wordings which, in affect attempt the same thing, and therefore always end with the same result, which is, the wish is used but no affect takes place. Note, this is not the same as a false start, because each false start is a separate wish attempt and uses up a wish. Trying to get multiple wished will ounly scrub one wish as long as the words "I wish" are only used once

Wishing for a quantity - A wish cannot be used to acquire more than one of anything, because, in affect, it is combining multiple wishes. A wish of "I wish I had two vorpal swords" will use the wish and no affect will occur. The person will not receive two, or even one. The quantity stipulation kicks in even if the request seems rather small. A wish of "I wish I had a dozen normal arrows" -or- "I wish I had a dozen copper pieces" will not work because it is combining 12 wishes into one. The wisher will not receive the 12, or even a single one.

Wishing with conjuctions - Wishes will not function with most of the connotations of words like "and", "with", "plus", etc. A wish such as "I wish for a new steed <u>with</u> a fancy saddle" is combining two wishes into one. The wish will produce neither the horse nor the saddle. Likewise "I wish for a mithril suit of armor <u>and</u> shield" will produce neither the armor nor the shield.

Altering reality - A wish cannot be used to rewrite history. Wishes will will affect the events of the game going forward, but will not rewind and roll forward again creating new and different events.

Unique items and creatures - Artifacts, relics, and some unique creatures cannot be affected by wishes. If a wish such as "I wish the greater diety Zeus to come immediately into my prescence"

would work, Zeus will be blipping in and out every time a similair wish was made.

Missing descriptions - When a wish is made, the player will need to be specific as to how the wish will be executed. If information is missing the referee will choose the path of least resistance, if the avenues are similair in resistance, the referee will use random determination.

What do you want it to do? - Proper wishing requires the preface of "I wish" followed by at least a noun and a verb. If a character states "I wish for a horse" there is not verb designating what the horse should do. Fall dead? Enlarge? Obviously, the character was hoping to acquire a horse, but without a verb, there is no viable wish instruction and no affect will be produced. Since the "I wish" preface was utilized, the wish is scrubed.

When will it happen? - A player forgets to include a descriptive word of "now" or "immediately" to designate when the wish affect should occur. This is one error that does not automatically prejudice itself against the player, Using the "path of least resistance" theory, a wish requires the same magical forces to execute the wish after 2 seconds of elapsed time as it does after 2 centuries. Given that the magic is without instruction as to when the affect of the wish should occur, the referee will randomly determine how long it will take for the affects of the wish to be realized.

Example - The character states "I wish for a horse ot come into my possesion" but fails to state when he wants it. The referee rolls a 12-sided die that produces a result of "9", which indicates that the affect is months away from occurring. The range of months is 1-12. The referee rolls a second 12-sided die to determine how many months will pass. The roll generates a 6 indicating that the wish will occur 6 months in the future. If more precision is needed, the referee will also make descending rolls. For example, avter determining that the occurrence will be in 6 months, the referee then rolls for number of weeks, days,

Random Time Determination Table		
Roll on 12-sided die	Increment	Qty
1	Segment	1-10
2	Second	1-10
3	Round	1-6
4	Minute	1-10
5	Turn	1-6
6	Hour	1-20
7	Day	1-8
8	Week	1-4
9	Month	1-12
10	Year	1-10
11	Decade	1-10
12	Century	1-10

hours, minutes, seconds.

What is the condition? - "I wish for a horse ot come immediately into my possesion" could produce a young healthy horse or a worn out old nag. Using the path of least resistance, one outcome is as likely as the other the referee should use random determination the age and condition.

No charges - If a wish is stated as "I wish for an unowned, wand of fireballs to come immediately into my possession", assuming there are no other errors, a the wand with no charges would be created (random determination not to be used) since it takes more magics to create a fully charges wand.

Is there a previous owner? - "I wish for a young healthy adult horse to come immediately into my possesion" could cause the wisher to suddenly be holding the reins of such a horse, that was teleport from a few miles down the road, with horse's owner still atop it.

Add-ons (Getting carried away) - Sometimes a referee can be too overzealous in perverting wishes "I wish for a young, healthy, unowned adult horse to come immediately into my possesion" could be met with "He materializes 100 foot in the air, falls to the gorund, and splatters on the road before you. Or, "I wish my comrade Izengard to be immediately restored to life" can be met with referee responding "Sure, he's alive but he is turned into a grasshopper" -or- "Ok, but he is moved to the bottom the ocean, so he drowns again"

If wishes are going to exist in the game, there has to be the attainable capacity to use them effectively when they are properly employed. Certainly, a player must be precise in the wording of a wish, but a referee should not add "extras" just to foul the wish. Also, this violates the path of least resistance rule. For example, it takes more magics to restore a dead character to life **and** morph him into a grasshopper then just the life restoration alone.

Possibility and consistency - A referee may decide to not use some of the rules here, or may impose some of their own. In the end, it doesn't matter so long as;
1. Wishes can be completed successfully
2. The narture of wishes is handled consistently

Spell Listings

Spell Mechanics

Spell Components – Every spell has some components. These may include any combination of material, verbal, and/or somatic components.

Verbal Components – Verbal components are the most common type of components. Spells whcich do not employ verbal components are very rare. The verbal components are the magical command words which activate the spell.

Somatic components – Some spells require precise gestures and hand movements known as somatic components. A bound or otherwise physically restricted character cannot perform somatic components unless they have unrestricted free use of the hands. Somatic gestures may include such motions as appointing, a sweeping motion of the hand, a snap of the fingers, etc.

Material Components – Some spells require certain materials or substances to orient the magic. The spell might require the spell caster to merely hold the material components, tap it agains an object, crumble it beneath the finger, wave it in the air, etc.

Spell Capacity – A spell caster's spell capacity is the maximum number of spells that a character can have memorized at any one time. The number and level of the spells is determined by the character's level on the appropriate class' spell capacity chart and the memory spell capacity bonus chart below.

Spell concentration – Casting of any spell requires a high level of concentration. If the spell is a sort that has a duration other than instantaneous, the spell might require a level of concentration to keep the spell going.

High Concentration – To maintain the spell, the caster must remain motionless and concentrate diligently on the spell. Any loss of focus instantly ends the spell.

Standard Concentration – The caster is able to walk slowly and talk briefly while maintiaining the spell. The spell is broken if the caster attempts a new spell, employs a magic item, is wounded, or is suddenly startled.

Low Concentration – The spell requires only mimal concntration to maintiain. The spell can be kept in force as long as the caster is not wounded, does not fall asleep, and does not attempt to cast another spell.

None – The spell continues for its entire duration, regardless of the actions of status of the caster, so long as the it is not affected by enchantment dispelling and the caster does not call for the spel to end.

Continual Magic – The spell has a permanent duration and cannot be called to end by the spell caster. It will only be affected by magic (continual) dispelling.

Range – Range designates how far away the caster can center the spell.

Touch Range Spells – If a caster is trying to release a spell with a range of "touch" into an inwilling subject, the inteneded subject is allowed to forgo other action in attempt to dodge the casters touch. A successful roll indicates that the spell caster's touch has been avoided for one round and the spell caster's touch remains magiced.

Duration – Duration indicates how long the affects of the spell will last.

Affect Duration/Magical Duration - Some spells have a lingering affect that is non-magical.

Duration of "Up to" – Anytime a spell has a duration listing that is suffixed with the words "up to", it means that the caster can call for the spell to end at any time by uttering a command word. The command word must be aloud and near enough to the enchantment that is within range of the casters voice.

Affected Area –

"Shroud" Affected Area - If a spell has a "shroud" Affected Area, the subject and all carried items will be incased in the magical shroud.

Command words to End – Spells that have a range suffixed by up to can be ended early by use of the command words

Command Words to suspend – Some spells can have the affect turned off and on with out ending the magic.

Duration of "Up to" – Anytime a spell has a duration listing that is suffixed with the words "up to", it means that the caster can call for the spell to end at any time by uttering a command word. The command word must be aloud and near enough to the enchantment that is within range of the casters voice.

Command words to End – Spells that have a range suffixed by up to can be ended early by use of the command words

Command Words to suspend -

Clerical Spells

1st Level	2nd Level	3rd Level	4th Level
Cause Light Wounds	Augury	Cause Critical Wounds	Animate Dead
Cleanse	Cause Serious Wounds	Continual Light	Create Healing Potion
Create Water	Feign Death	Create Food and Drink	Detect Lie
Detect Evil Item	Find Doors	Create Holy Water	Flame Strike
Heal Light Wounds	Find Traps	Destroy Parasite	Gaseous Form
Holy Touch	Heal Seriuos Wounds	Dispel Magic	Know ALignment
Enchanted Light Spell	Holy Touch	Electric Touch	Pennance
Protection from evil	Resist Termperatures	Glyph	Rejuvenation
Purify food and drink	Sancutary	Heal Critical Wounds	Silence Area
Slow poison	Silence	Holy Bolt	Stone to Flesh
	Holy Touch	Sanctify	

Druid Spells

1st Level	2nd Level	3rd Level	4th Level
Entangle	Polymorph animal	Volcanic eruption	Lightining bolt
Water tap		Continual Light	
Find direction			
Part brush			
Heal Light Wounds		Destroy Parasite	
Holy Touch	Heal Seriuos Wounds		
Enchanted Light Spell			
Protection from evil	Resist Termperatures		
Purify food and drink			
Slow poison	Silence		

Druid Spells

5th Level	6th Level	7th Level	8th Level
Cause Light Wounds	Wall of thorns	Venom Strike	Earthquake

Mage Spell Schools – All mage spells are divided into 7 schools. When a Mage character is created, the player will select 3 of these schools to pursue.

Aleration – Spells of the alteration school deal with magic that transform objects

Conjuration (Summon) – Conjuration spells call or create objects, creatres, or magics

Divination – Divination spells detect and gather information .

Mage Spell Schools – All mage spells are divided into various schools

Aleration – Spells of the alteration school deal with magic that transform objects

Conjuration (Summon) – Conjuration spells call or create objects, creatres, or magics

Divination – Divination spells detect and gather information .

Enchantment – Enchantment spells are used to endow existing creatures are objects with magics

Evocation (Elemental) - Evocation spells summon and release massive amounts of elemental energy that can be employed as weapon

Illusion (Charm) – Illusion spells deal with alter or influence the mind.

Necromancy - Necromancy deals with spells that alter or influence the body

Mage Spells

Illusion (Charm) – Illusion spells deal with alter or influence the mind.

Necromancy - Necromancy deals with spells that alter or influence the body

1st Level	2nd Level	3rd Level	4th Level
A-Affect Fires	A-Air restoration	A-Water to oil	A-Adhesive Surface
A-Amplify	A-Change mass	C-Stinking cloud	A-Gaseous form
A-Mend	A-Crystalize Metal	C-Web	C-Poison cloud
A-Enlarge/Shrink Object	A-Glaze surface	D-Babble	C-Wall of iron
A-Purify food and drink	A-Heat metal	D-Tonuges	C-Wall of stone
A-Silence	C-Hold protal	D-Scan item	D-Locate
C-Create water	C-Encanted flame	E-Magic Ink	D-Probe Item
C-Enchanted Light	C-Pyrotechnics	E-Scry	E-Magic bottle
C-Floating platform	C-Reflective shield	E-Wizard lock	E-Wall of force
C-Smoke Cloud	C-Continual Light	N-Nuetralize poison	N-Regenerate
D-Comprehend	D-Find doors	N-Wizard eye	N-Xray vision
D-Detect creature	D-Find traps	V-Electric touch	V-Cone of Cold
D-Detect magic	E-Dimensional chamber	V-Fireball	V-Lightning Bolt
D-Identify	E-Dimension walk	V-Icy blast	V-Power fist
E-Enchanted Mouth	E-Dispel Magic		
E-Enchanted Lock	E-Invisibility		
E-Magic stone	E-Enchanted rope		
E-Enchanted lock	E-Enchanted shelter		
I-Babble	E-Knock		
I-Cause blindness	I-Charm		
I-Guise	I-Mesmeric touch		
I-Mesmeric Touch	I-Feign death		
I-Sleep	N-Dragon skin		
I-Ventriloquism	N-Fly		
N-Enlarge/Shrink Creature	N-Passwall		
N-Infravision	V-Freeze		
N-Jump	V-Energy bomb		
N-Resist temperatures	V-Flame Blast		
N-Water breathing	V-Icy touch		
N-Water walking			
V1-Combustion			
V1-Energy touch			
V1-Flame arrow			
V1-Flash			
V1-Nudge			
V1-Shatter			

Mage Spells

Illusion (Charm) – Illusion spells deal with alter or influence mind.

Necromancy - Necromancy deals with spells that alter or influence the body

3rd Level	5h Level	4th Level
A-Water to oil	A-Soften shape	A-Adhesive Surface
C-Stinking cloud	A-Gravity field	A-Gaseous form
C-Web	C-Poison cloud	C-Poison cloud
D-Babble	C-Wall of iron	C-Wall of iron
D-Tonuges	C-Wall of stone	C-Wall of stone
D-Scan item	D-Locate	D-Locate
E-Magic Ink	D-Probe Item	D-Probe Item
E-Scry	E-Magic bottle	E-Magic bottle
E-Wizard lock	E-Wall of force	E-Wall of force
N-Nuetralize poison	N-Regenerate	N-Regenerate
N-Wizard eye	N-Temporal Stasis	N-Xray vision
V-Electric touch	N-Xray vision	V-Cone of Cold
V-Fireball	V-Chain lightning	V-Lightning Bolt
V-Icy blast	V-Meteor blast	V-Power fist
	V-Telekenetics	

Cleric Spells

Cleric/1 - Bless

Level: 1	Components: V, S, M
Casting Time: 1 round (10 sec)	Duration: 6 rounds (1 min)
Range: 15' + 10'/level	Area of Effect: 15' Radius
Mana: 1	Damage: N/A
Save: None	Saving Throw: N/A
Components: V, S	Concentration: N/A
Somatic component:Pointing of caster's finger	
Material Component: Holy water	

Execution - Upon uttering this spell allcreatures in the affected area gain +1 on to-hit rolls.

Limitations - A blessing, will affect only those not already engaged in melee combat without also including the opponents, due to the movement of the participants during casting.

Cleric/1 - Cause Light Wounds

Class: Cleric	Level: 1
Cast Time: 1 Second	Duration: N/A
Range: Touch	Affected Area: 1 Creature
Mana: 1	Damage: 1D8 Death
Save: Dexterity	Save Affect: Avoids for 1 Round
Components: V, S	Concentration: N/A
Somatic component:Touch of the spell caster	
Material Component: None	

Execution - After this spell is complete the caster may make a roll-to-hit to touch a creature and cause 1-8 hit-points of damage.

Affect - The spell will cause opening of minor wounds and minor bleeding.

Limiations - This spell has no affect on undead creatures.

Cleric/1 - Cleanse

Class: Cleric	Level: 1
Cast Time: 1 Round	Duration: None
Range: 15' + 10'/level	Affected Area: 10,000 cubic'/level
Mana: 1	Damage: N/A
Save: N/A	Save Affect: N/A
Components: V, S	Concentration: N/A
Material Component: Bit of soap	
Somatic component:Swirling motion in the air with bit of soap	

Execution - By use of this spell, the caster is able to remove all dirt, dust, ash, and other wastes from an affected area. The spell might be used to remove stains from clothing, dirt from food, graffiti from wals, etc.

Aftermath - Once the spell is cast, the affected area retains no enchantment and is subject to normal adversarious conditions.

Cleric/1 - Command

Class: Cleric	Level: 1
Cast Time: 1 Round	Duration: 1 round
Range: 15' + 10'/level	Affected Area: 1 Creature
Mana: 1	Damage: N/A
Save: Intelligence	Save Affect: Negates
Components: V	Concentration: None
Material Component: None	
Somatic component:None	

Execution - This spell enables the cleric to issue a command of a single word. The command must be uttered in a language which the spell recipient is able to understand. The individual will obey to the best of his/her/its ability only so long as the command is absolutely clear and unequivocal, i.e. "Suicide!" could be a noun, so the creature would ignore the command. A command to "Die!" would cause the recipient to fall in a faint or cataleptic state for 1 round, but thereafter the creature would be alive and well. Typical command words are: back, halt, flee, run, stop, fall, fly, go, leave, surrender, sleep, rest, etc. Undead are not affected by a command. Creatures with intelligence of 13 or more, and creatures with 6 or more hit dice (or experience levels) are entitled to a saving throw versus magic. (Creatures with 13 or higher intelligence and 6 hit dice/tevels do not get 2 saving throws!)

Cleric/1 - Comprehend

Class: Mage	Level 1
Cast Time: 1 Second	Duration: 1 turn/level
Range: 15' + 10'/level	Affected Area: 1 Creature
Mana: 1	Damage: N/A
Save: None	Save Affect: N/A
Components: S	Concentration: None
Material Comp: None	
Somatic Comp: Placing a had to an ear as if to hear better	

Affect - This spell enables the caster to understand the speech or utterance of a pariticular creatuer.

Limitations - If there are several of the same sort creatures together speaking in the same unknown language, the caster will only be able to understand the one who is the subject of the magic. The magic will not enable the caster to speak, read, or write any particular language. The spell does not assist the caster in hearing the subject. If the subject is outside normal hearing range, the caster will not be able to hear the subjects speech regardless of the spell.

Cleric/1 - Create Water

Class: Cleric	Level: 1
Cast Time: 1 Second	Duration: N/A
Range: 15'	Affected Area: 4 Gallons/Level
Mana: 1	Damage: N/A
Save: N/A	Save Affect: N/A
Components: V, S	Concentration: N/A
Material Comp: None	
Somatic Comp: Squeezing of the fist as if wring water from a cloth	

Execution - Casting this spell creates water that is pure and drinkable. The water can be created inside a single open container, or create in the air to raind down on an object or creature.

Limitations - The spell cannot be used to create water inside a living creature or inside any sealed container or space.

Aftermath - Once created, the water retains no magical nature and is subject to normal adversaious conditions such as freezon, spillage, evaporation, freezing, etc.

Cleric/1 - Detect Curse

Class: Cleric	Level: 1
Cast Time: 1 Second	Duration: N/A
Range: 15' + 10'/level	Affected Area: 15' Radius
Mana: 1	Damage: None
Save: None	Save Affect: N/A
Components: V, S	Concentration: N/A
Material Comp: None	
Somatic Comp: Waving of the fore-finger back and forth	

Affect - When this spell is used, all cursed items in the Affected Area will begin to visibly glow.

Limitations - The spell will not reveal any detailed information such as what sort of curse is present

Errata - The spell will give the caster an impression of the relative strength of the cursed nature by the brightness of the glow.

Cleric/1 - Detect Magic

Level: 1	Components: V, S, M
Range: 3"	Casting Time: I round
Duration: 1 turn	Saving Throw: None
Area of Effect: 1" path, 3" long	

Affect - When this spell is used, all magical items in the Affected Area will begin to visibly glow.

Limitations - The spell will not reveal any detailed information such as what sort of magic/enchantment is present

Errata - The spell will give the caster an impression of the relative strength of the magic by the brightness of the glow.

Cleric/1 - Heal Light Wounds

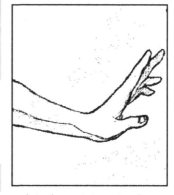

Class: Cleric

Level: 1

Cast Time: 1 Second

Duration: N/A

Range: Touch

Affected Area: 1 Creature

Mana: 1

Damage: 1D8 to undead

Save: Dexterity

Save Affect: Avoids

Components: V, S

Concentration: N/A

Somatic component: Touch

Material Component: None

Execution - After the spell is complete the caster may touch a creature and heal 1D8 hit-points of damage. The spell will cause closure of small wounds and cessation of light bleeding.

Affect - The spell will not affect creatures with a current hit-point tally of 0 or less. It the spell is relased onto a subject with less than 1 hit-point, no healing will take place and the caster's mana will be used.

Limitaitions - If this spell is used on an undead creature, it will cause rather then heal damage.

Cleric/1 - Enchanted Light

Class: Cleric	Level: 1
Cast Time: 1 Second	Duration: N/A
Range: 15' + 10'/level	Affected Area: 15' Radius
Mana: 1	Damage: None
Save: None	Save Affect: N/A
Components: V, S	Concentration: N/A

Material component: None

Somatic component: Snap of fingers

Execution - The spell can be cast into the air (where it will remain motionless) or on an object (in order to be moved about).

Affect - When this spell is cast, it creates a small, brilliantly glowing 2" sphere that will effectively light a surrounding 15' radius. Although different in appearance, a light sphere gives off roughly the same amount of light as a bright torch.

Adjustments - So long as the spell is in range, the caster may control the intensity of the light. By speaking command words, the caster can call upon the light to go black, brighten to full intensity, or any shade in between.

Limitations - A light spell cannot be cast onto living tissue of magical objects or creatures. The spell might, however, be cast onto the clothing or something carried by a living or magical creature. Lkiewise, the spell may be cast on a container for a magical item, or an a non-magical object attached to the magical item.

Aftermath - After the spell exhsts its duration, the light will begin to dim. Over the course of one round (10 seconds) the light will continue to darken until it is completely extinguished. If the spell is cast on an object and the object is cracked or broken, the light will be immediately extinguished. Likewise, if the enchantment is dispelled, the light will immediately go dark.

Errata - A light sphere give off no heat and consumes no oxygen. It cannot be blown out, doused, or extinguished by normal means. A light sphere has no physical mass of its own. It cannot be touched.

Cleric/1 - Protection From Evil

Class: Cleric	Level: 1
Cast Time: 1 Second	Duration: N/A
Range: Touch	Affected Area: 1 Creature
Mana: 1	Damage: None
Save: None	Save Affect: N/A
Components: V, S	Concentration: N/A

Material component: Holy water

Somatic component: Sprinkling of holy water on subject.

Executiion - The casting of this spell will cover 1 Creature in a magical shroud (see Game-standards-Magical/Spells/Shroud Area Affects) that will prevent the subject from being touched or bodily attacked by undead or extra-planar creatures.

Limitations - The spell will not affect natural or super-natural creatures. The spell will not prevent an undead from striking with a wepon, using a mental attacks, or hurling an object at the subject.

Cleric/1 - Purify Food and Drink

Class: Cleric	Level: 1
Cast Time: 1 Second	Duration: N/A
Range: Touch	Affected Area: 1 pound/level
Mana: 1	Damage: N/A
Save: N/A	Save Affect: N/A
Components: V, S	Concentration: N/A

Material component: None

Somatic component: Clasping of hands.

Exexution - By invoking this spell, the caster it able purify one pound (10 gold piece weight) of food and rink per level of experience of the caster. Any poison, spoilage, staleness, disease, parasites, impurities, or other contaminates will be completely neutralized.

Limitations - Casting the spell will reveal to the caster whether or not the food was contamintated prior to the magic. The spell will not alter the type, natural taste, or quality of preperation of the food. The spell will not warm or coll the food to any desired eating temperature.

Cleric/1 - Remove Fear

Class: Cleric	Level: 1
Cast Time: 1 Second	Duration: 1 Round/level (non-magical)
Range: Touch	Affected Area: 1 Creature
Mana: 1	Damage: None
Save: Dexterity	Save Affect: Avoids for 1 Round
Components: V, S	Concentration: N/A

Material component: None

Somatic component: Touch of spell caster

Affect - There are creatures, items, and other game factors which can cause such uncontrollable fear that a will a creature who fails a saving throiw will automatically creature turn and flee. This spell will cause a character to overcome such fear.

Limitations - The spell will no automatically force a character to stay and fight. A character may opt to flee the battle without doing so from uncontrollable fear.
as if the saving throw were successful.

Erratta - If the spell is used prior to the subject being subjected to the fear, and the subject is willing, the delivery of this spell is automatic and no charisma saving throw against fear will be required. If the subject has already failed the saving throw and has succumbed to the fear, the character will flee and avoid all contact with others. The spell caster must catch and/or corner the subject to administer the spell. If the intended subject is able to dodge, they will be compelled to do so and will make a dexterity saving throw to avoid the spell caster's touch. Once the spell has been administered, the subject will be free of the fear (as if the original charisma save against fear had been successful) and will be immune to further fear affects as long as the duration of the spell lasts

Aftermath - After the spell is administered, the affect is psychological and non-magical in nature. It cannot be ended prematurely by command words or magical dispelling. The protection will continue until the affect has exhausted its duration.

Cleric/1 - Sanctuary

Class: Cleric	Level: 1
Cast Time: 1 Second	Duration: N/A
Range: o	Affected Area: Caster's body
Mana: 1	Damage: 1D8 Death Magic
Save: Charisma	Save Affect: No affect
Components: V, S, M	Concentration: Medium

Material component: Holy Symbol
Somatic component: Clasp opf hands

Execution - When the cleric costs a sanctuary spell, any opponent must make a charisma saving throw in order to strike or otherwise attack him or her. If the saving throw is not made, the creature will attack another and totally ignore the cleric protected by the spell. If the saving throw is made, the cleric is subject to normal attack process including dicing for weapons to hit, saving throws, damage.

Limitations - The spell does not prevent the operation of area attacks (fireball, ice storm, etc.). To maintain the affect requires medium concentration to maintain. If the caster attacks or cast a new spell, this one will be negated.

Cleric/2 - Augury

Class: Cleric	Level: 2
Cast Time: 2 minutes	Duration: N/A
Range: Touch	Affected Area: 1 question
Mana: 2	Damage: N/A
Save: N/A	Save Affect: N/A
Components: V, S, M	Concentration: N/A

Material Component - Holy symbol
Somatic Component - Clasping of holy symbol in hands

Execution - After casting this spell, the carter may ask their patron diety questions as to wheter or not a particular action will be to the net benefit of the spell caster or the spell caster/s party. The percentile chance of divining the correct answer is equal to the spell caster's modified wisdom score. The referee

will roll the dice secretly to determine the outcome. A missed roll can either indicate no answer or an incorrect answer. If the spell caster should cast the spell a second time to ask the same question, the answer wil lbe the same and no roll is made. The answer will usually be short and non-explaining, often, in the form of a simple, "yes", "no", "maybe", or unknown"

Limitations - Mostly, a patron diety will give a correct answer (if the roll is successful) on rare occasions, the diety may not answer, may answer incorrectly, or not wish to divulge the information, even if the roll is successful.

Cleric/2 - Authenticate

Class: Cleric	Level: 2
Cast Time: 2 minutes	Duration: N/A
Range: Touch	Affected Area: 1 mark/message
Mana: 2	Damage: N/A
Save: N/A	Save Affect: N/A
Components: S, M	Concentration: N/A

Material Component - Holy symbol
Somatic Component – Running of fingers across mark

Execution – By means of this spell the caster is able to determine if a written note, signature, or identifying mark is genuine. It is used to validate any sort of identifying written text as being inscribed by the author identified in the writing.

Limitations – The spell may only be used on writings. It has no affect on an anonymously received note, nor will it help determine if a message is truthful. It will not reveal the identity or any other information about the author. The spell only serves to validate if It will not reveal the identity of the author or, in the case of a fake, the forger, or any other additional information other than whether or not the mark or message wes inscribed by the person it

Cleric/2 - Chant

Level: 2		Components: V, S
Class: Cleric	Level: 2	
Cast Time: 2 seconds	Duration: 1 Round/level	
Range: 15' + 10'/level	Affected Area: 15' radius	
Mana: 2	Damage: +2 to-hit	
Save: None	Save Affect: N/A	
Components: V, S	Concentration: High	

Material component: Holy smbol
Somatic component: Clutching of holy symbol and chanting

Execution - When this spell is cast all creatures inside a 30' diameter affected area receive +1 on rolls to-hit, +1 to weapons damage, and +1 to their armor class.

Limitations - The spell requires high concentration on part of the spell caster to maintain the spells duration. Any sort of interruptions will end the affect. After the spell is cast, the recipients can leave the 15' radius to attack, but they must remain within range of the caster (15' + 10'/level of caster). Anyone who moves out of range will lose the benefit of the affect and returning into range will not restore it.

Cleric/2 - Cause Serious Wounds

Class: Cleric	Level: 2
Cast Time: 2 Seconds	Duration: N/A
Range: Touch	Affected Area: 1 Creature
Mana: 1	Damage: 1D8 Death Magic
Save: Dexterity	Save Affect: Avoids for 1 Round
Components: V, S	Concentration: N/A

Material component: None

Somatic component: Touching of subject.

Execution - After the spell is complete the caster may make a roll-to-hit to touch a creature and cause 2-16 hit-points of damage.

Affect - The spell will cause opening of wounds and bleeding.

Limitations - This spell has no affect on undead creatures.

Cleric/2 - Detect Mind Control

Class: Cleric	Level: 2
Cast Time: 2 Seconds	Duration: N/A
Range: 15' + 10'/level	Affected Area: 1 Creature
Mana: 1	Damage: None
Save: None	Save Affect: N/A
Components: V, S	Concentration: N/A

Material component: None

Somatic component: Moving of the finger as if beckoning to come

Execution - This spell will be ablet o dectect if a person or creature is acting out of their own volition or under the influence of any magical or non-magical mind cotrolling or influencing affect.

Limitations - The spell will not reveal who or what is controlling or influencing the subject, nor will it reveal what sort of method is being used.

Cleric/2 - Find Doors

Class: Cleric	Level: 2
Cast Time: 1 Second	Duration: N/A
Range: 15' + 10'/level	Affected Area: 15' radius
Mana: 2	Damage: N/A
Save: N/A	Save Affect: N/A
Components: V, S	Concentration: N/A

Material component: None

Somatic component: Horizontal sweeping motion with the hand

Execute - When this spells is cast, all antrances and exits to any enclosure will be outline with brilliantly glowin luminescent lines.

Affect - Doors, doorways. Portals, secret doors, concealed doors, corks in bottles, plugs on scroll tubes, all portals will have a glowing line around the edges.

The spell will not reveal and hidden latching mechanisms or traps on the doors

Aftermath - The glowing lines will remain until the spell exhaust its duration, it is magically dispelled, or the caster speaks the command words calling for the spell to end.

Cleric/2 - Find Traps

Class: Cleric	Level: 2
Cast Time: 1 Second	Duration: N/A
Range: 15' + 10'/level	Affected Area: 15' radius
Mana: 2	Damage: N/A
Save: N/A	Save Affect: N/A
Components: V, S	Concentration: N/A

Material component: None

Somatic component: Touching of subject.

Execution - When this spell is cast, all mechanical type traps within the affected area will begin to glow brightly and illuminate light.

Affect - Traps illuminated by the spell are easy to see and avoid, but not always easy to disarm. Some can be as easy as closing a safety or throwing a lever. Others may require thieving abilities to neutralize.

Aftermath - Affected traps will glow until the enchantment is dispelled, the spell exhausts its duration, or the spell caster speaks the command word calling for the spell to end.

Cleric/2 - Heal Serious Wounds

Class: Cleric	
Level: 1	
Cast Time: 1 Second	
Duration: N/A	
Range: Touch	
Affected Area: 1 Creature	
Mana: 1	
Damage: 1D8 to undead	
Save: Dexterity	
Save Affect: Avoids	
Components: V, S	
Concentration: N/A	
Somatic component: Touch	
Material Component: None	

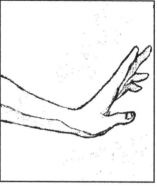

Execution - After the spell is complete the caster may touch a creature and heal 2D8 hit-points of damage.

Affect The spell will cause closure of wounds and cessation of bleeding.

Limitations - The spell will not affect creatures with a current hit-point tally of 0 or less. It the spell is relased onto a subject with less than 1 hit-point, no healing will take place and the caster's mana will be used.

Errata - If this spell is used on an undead creature, it will cause rather then heal damage.

Cleric/2 - Hold Person

Class: Cleric	Level: 2
Cast Time: 2 Secondss	Duration: 1 hour/level
Range: 15' + 10'/level	Affected Area: Up to three creatures
Mana: 2 per creature	Damage: None
Save: Charisma	Save Affect: Negates
Components: V, S, M	Concentration: Low

Material components: Small straight piece of iron

Somatic components: Rubbing oil drop onto skin

Explanation/Description: This spell holds immobile, and freezes in places, from 1-3 humans or humanoid creatures (see below) for 5 or more melee rounds. The level of the cleric casting the hold person spell dictates the length of time the effect will last. The basic duration is 5 melee rounds at 1st level, 6 rounds at 2nd level, 7 rounds at 3rd level, etc. If the spell is cast at three persons, each gets a saving throw at the normal score; if only two persons are being enspelled, each makes their saving throw at -1 on their die; if the spell is cast at but one person, the saving throw die is at -2. Persons making their saving throws are totally unaffected by the spell. Creatures affected by a hold person spell are: brownies, dryads, dwarves, elves, gnolls, gnomes, goblins, half-elves, halflings, half-orcs, hobgoblins, humans, kobolds, lizard men, nixies, orcs, pixies, sprites, and troglodytes. The spell caster needs a small, straight piece of iron as the material component of this spell.

Cleric/2 – Immunitity to Temperatures

Class: Cleric	Level: 2
Cast Time: 2 Rounds	Duration: 1 minute/level
Range: Touch	Affected Area: 1 Creature
Mana: 2	Damage: N/A
Save: N/A	Save Affect: N/A
Components: V, S, M	Concentration: None

Material components: Drop of oil

Somatic components: Rubbing oil drop onto skin

Execution - After casting this spell, the caster may touch a subject to envelope them with an enchantment that affords tolerance to non-magical heat and cold.

Affect - The subject will be able to stand in a blazing fire or artic storm with the same comfort as if they were basking in normal room temperature. The spell will also protect clothing, carried items or other items that may have intolerance to adverse temperatures. This spell will protect against magical elemental attacks or breath weapons that employ fire, cold, etc. The enchantment is affixed to the creature and moves about with them.

Limitations - The spell will only protect against the heat or cold of a single magical attack, then be dispelled by the introduction of new magics. If creature enchanted by this spell casts a spell, initiates the use of a magic item, or other wise influenced my magics, the enchantment will be dispelled. This spell will only function on natural creatures and has no affect on undead creatures, magical creatures, or inanimate objects.

Cleric/2 - Know Alignment

Class: Cleric	Level: 2
Cast Time: 2 Seconds	Duration: None
Range: 15' + 10'/level	Affected Area: Self
Mana: 2	Damage: N/A
Save: None	Save Affect: N/A
Components: V, S	Concentration: N/A
Material Component: None	
Somatic Component: Pointing at subject	

Exectuion - This spell enables the caster read the aura of a person and know their alignment of the person.

Limitations - Up to 10 persons can be examined with this spell. The reverse totally obscures alignment, even from this spell, of a single person for 1 turn, two persons for 5 rounds, etc. Certain magical devices will negate the ability to know alignment.

Cleric/2 - Sanctuary

Class: Cleric	Level: 2
Cast Time: 1 Segment	Duration: 1 Round/level
Range: 0	Affected Area: Self
Mana: 2	Damage: N/A
Save: Charisma	Save Affect: Negates
Components: V	Concentration: N/A
Material Component: None	
Somatic Component: None	

Invocation - When this spell is cast, any creatures who do not make a charisma saving throw become instantly unaware of the character's prescence.

Affect - The invisible magical shroud has will affect all creatures that fail a charisma saving throw, even if the spell caster is unaware of them.

Limitations - The spell caster will not be protected from incendental damages caused by attacks aimed at other members of the spell caster's party. Touching, striking, firing a missle at, or casting a spell upon on a creature will negate the affect with regard to the recipient only. It is feasible to cast supportive spells, advise, or hand weapons to fellow party members while still being protected from enemies.

Cleric/2 - Silence Creature

Class: Cleric	Level: 2
Cast Time: 2 Seconds	Duration: 1 Round/level
Range: Touch	Affected Area: 1 Creature or object
Mana: 2	Damage: None
Save: Dexterity	Save Affect: Avoids
Components: S	Concentration: N/A
Material Component: None	
Somatic Component: Placing a finger upright against the lips, then touching the intended subject	

Affect - This spell will immediately silence all emanations of sound from a creature or object.

Uses - The spell might be used to silence an alarm, cause a missle to strike without noise, stop a spell-caster from using spells with somatic components.

Cleric/2 - Slow Poison

Class: Cleric	Level: 2
Cast Time: 2 Seconds	Duration: 1 hour/level
Range: Touch	Affected Area: 1 Creature
Mana: 2	Damage: N/A
Save: N/A	Save Affect: N/A
Components: V, S	Concentration: None
Material Component - None	
Somatic Component - Touching of subject	

Execution - By casting this spell, the caster is able to slow the onset of a poisons affect on a subject's body.

Affect - The spell will not detoxify the poison or reverse any ill affects that have already taken place. The onset time and duration of the poison will be slowed by a factor of 60. The poisons affects that would normally occur in a 1 round (10 second) time frame will instead occur in a 1 turn (10 minute) time frame. This generally allows ample time for administering of healing magics or anti-venoms/anidotes (if available).

Aftermath - If the enchantment is ended or dispelled, or the spells duration is exhausted, the affects will immediately resume their normal rate of pregression.

Cleric/2 - Snake Charm

Class: Cleric	Level: 2
Cast Time: 2 seconds	Duration: N/A
Range: Touch	Affected Area: 1 Creature
Mana: 2 per snake	Damage: None
Save: Charisma	Save Affect: Avoids for 1 Round
Components: V, S	Concentration: N/A
Material Component: None	
Somatic Component: Touching of subject	

Affect - Explanation/Description: When this spell is cast, a hypnotic pattern is set up which causes one or more snakes to cease all activity except a semi-erect postured swaying movement.

Adjustments - If spell is used while the snakes are peaceable, the affect wil last 2 turns (20 minutes). If the spell is used on snakes that are an agitated or angry, the affect will last 2 minutes.

Cleric/2 - Speak With Animals

Class: Cleric	Level: 2
Cast Time: 2 Seconds	Duration: 1 Round/Level
Range: Touch	Affected Area: 1 Creature or object
Mana: 2	Damage: None
Save: Dexterity	Save Affect: Avoids
Components: S	Concentration: N/A
Material Component: None	
Somatic Component: Placing a hand ot the ear as if to hear better	

Execution - This spell, the cleric is empowered to comprehend and communicate with any warm or cold-blooded animal which is not mindless (such as an amoeba). The cleric is able to ask questions, receive answers, and generally be on amicable terms with the animal. This ability lasts for 2 melee rounds for each level of experience of the cleric employing the spell. Even if the bent of the animal is opposite to that of the cleric (evil/good, good/evil), it and any others of the same kind with it will not attack while the spell lasts, If the animal is neutral or of the same general bent as the cleric (evil/evil, good/good), there is a possibility that the animal, and its like associates, will do some favor or service for the cleric. This possibility will be determined by the referee by

consulting a special reaction chart, using the charisma of the cleric and his actions as the major determinants. Note that this spell differs from speak with monsters (q.v.), for it allows conversation only with basically normal, non-fantastic creatures such as opes, bears, cats, dogs, elephants, and so on.

Cleric/2 - Spiritual Hammer

Class: Cleric	Level: 2
Cast Time: 2 Seconds	Duration: 1 Round/level
Range: 15' + 10'/level	Affected Area: 1 Creature or object
Mana: 2	Damage: None
Save: Dexterity	Save Affect: Avoids
Components: S	Concentration: High

Material Component: Hammer, mace, or flail
Somatic Component: Tossing weapon at opponent

Execution - When this spell is used, the caster may toss a medium sized weapon at an opponent, and use it to attack once per round, doing normal damage, as if the spell caster were in combat wielding it.

Affect - The attack will require a normal roll-to-hit versus the opponent's armor class. A successful hit will deal 1D6 hit-points of bludgeoning damage.

Limitations - Maintaining the spell requires high concentration on the part of the spell caster and any disruption will end the spell. The roll-to-hit will be without any strength adjustments or other special bonuses. The opponent may attack the spiritual hammer normally by making a roll-to-hit on armor class of 8. If a successful hit is made, the caster does not take damage, but the spell is ended.

Errata - If the spell caster decides to move the spiritual hammer to a different target that is within 30' of the first, it will use up one melee round to make the change. For each additional 30', another round will be used for the change.

Aftermath - When the spell is over, the weapon will rematerialize in the spell casters's hand.

Cleric/3 - Cause Critical Wounds

Class: Cleric	Level: 3
Cast Time: 3 seconds	Duration: N/A
Range: Touch	Affected Area: 1 Creature
Mana: 3	Damage: 3D10 Death Magic
Save: Dexterity	Save Affect: Avoids for 1 Round
Components: V, S	Concentration: N/A

Material Component: None
Somatic Component: Touching of subject

Execution - After the spell is complete the caster may make a roll-to-hit to touch a creature and cause 2-16 hit-points of damage.

Affect - The spell will cause opening of wounds and bleeding.

Limitations - This spell has no affect on undead creatures.

Cleric/3 – Animate Dead

Class: Cleric	Level: 3
Cast Time: 3 turns/per	Duration: Permanent (non-magical)
Range: Touch	Affected Area: Up to 7 Creatures
Mana: 3 per creature	Damage: None
Save: Dexterity	Save Affect: Avoids for 1 Round
Components: V, S, M	Concentration: N/A

Material Component: Corpses and drop of blood
Somatic Component: Dripping of blood on forehead of corpses

Execution - The casting of this spell will create an undead life force in the remains of a dead humanoid, thereby animating it and creating an undead creature under the caster's control. The creature will be animated as either a skeleton or a zombie, depending on the status of the remains.

Adjustments - The spell will not restore the subject's mental or vocal abilities. It cannot speak, be asked questions of it's former life, or guide the way through areas it occupied when it alive. The subject will be able to obey simple one-word commands such as "walk", "follow", "attack", "stay", "carry", etc. Control of the undead can not be delegated, as the creature will only recognize commands from the spell caster. If the spell caster should die or become separated from the animated dead, the creature will wander about lost, gradually becoming more and more hostile voer several weeks. Eventually, a deserted animated dead undead will attack anyone who crosses it's path.

Aftermath - After the spell is cast there is non-magical duration and there is no lingering magical enchantment that can be destroyed by enchantment dispeling or ended by command words. The spell will not hinder normal decomposition of the corpse. Using a zombie indoors will fill the area with a stench. Bringing any undead into an inhabited area will not be well received by townspeople. Zombies will eventually become skeletons as the flesh deteriorates and falls away.

Cleric/3 - Cause Blindness

Class: Cleric	Level: 3
Cast Time: 3 seconds	Duration: 1 Round/level
Range: Touch	Affected Area: 1 Creature
Mana: 3	Damage: N/A
Save: Charisma	Save Affect: Negates
Components: V, S, M	Concentration: None

Material Component: Pinch of soil
Somatic Component: Touching of a drop of holy water to each eye

Affect - This spell will cause natural creatures to temporarily go blind.

Limitations - The spell will not detroy or damage eye tissue.

Cleric/3 - Contiual Light

Class: Cleric	Level: 3
Cast Time: 1 Second	Duration: Permanent
Range: 15' + 10'/level	Affected Area: 2 inch orb
Mana: 3	Damage: None
Save: N/A	Save Affect: N/A
Components: V, S	Concentration: None

Material Component: None
Somatic Component: Clap of hands

Execution - When this spell is cast, it creates a small, brilliantly glowing 2" sphere. The spell can be cast into the air (where it will remain motionless) or on an object (in order to be moved about).

Affect - The magical orb that will effectively light a surrounding 15' radius. Although different in appearance, a light sphere gives off roughly the same amount of light as a bright torch.

Adjustments - By speaking the command words, the light can be brightened, dimmed, or turned off

Aftermath - The orb is a continual magic and, will last until is dispelled by magics that destroy continual magics. If the spell is cast onto an object, it becomes a magical item. Once cast bears no connection to the spell caster. Anyone who knows the

Limiations - A light spell cannot be cast onto living tissue nor objects or creatures already affected by continual magics. The spell might, however, be cast onto the clothing or something carried by a living or magical creature. Likewise, the spell may be cast on a container for a magical item, or an a non-magical object

Level	Number of Undead that can be created
0-2	1 Creature
3-5	Up to 2 Creatures
6-8	Up to 3 Creatures
9-11	Up to 4 Creatures
12-14	Up to 5 Creatures
15-17	Up to 6 Creatures
18-	Up to 7 Creatures

attached to the magical item.

Errata - A light sphere give off no heat and consumes no oxygen. It cannot be blown out, doused, or extinguished by normal means. A light sphere has no physical mass of its own. It cannot be touched.

Cleric/3 - Create Food and Drink

Class: Cleric	Level: 2
Cast Time: 3 seconds	Duration: N/A
Range: Touch	Affected Area: 1 Creature
Mana: 3	Damage: N/A
Save: N/A	Save Affect: N/A
Components: V, S	Concentration: N/A

Material Component: None
Somatic Component: Waving off hands over food in sweeping motion

Execution - By use of this spell the caster is able to create enough food and drink to feed 1 humanoic creature for wach level of experience of the spell caster.

Affect - The spell can be used to to create any sort of common food known to the caster. The food can be created inside unsealed containers and will be at whatever temperature as would be normal for eating.

Aftermath - Once the food is created it is for all practical purposes regular food and retains no magical nature. Magically created food is subject to all normal adversarious conditions such as spoilage, contamination, etc.

Limitations - The spell cannot be used to create foods with magical, healing, or special chemical qualities.

Cleric/3 - Create Holy Water

Class: Cleric	Level: 3
Cast Time: 3 Turns (30 min)	Duration: N/A
Range: 15'	Affected Area: 1 Vial/level
Mana: 3	Damage: N/A
Save: N/A	Save Affect: N/A
Components: V, S, M	Concentration: N/A

Material Component: Silver receptacle and pure water
Somatic Component: Clasping of hands

Exectution - By use of this spell, the caster is able to transform ordrinary water into holy water. The caster is able to create one vials worth (2 fluid ounces) per level of exerience

Restrictions - The water must be clean and free of impurities (magically created water being ideal). The water must be kept in a silbver container during the casting process..

The entire amount must be in a single container made of silver, usually some ornate container fitted with jewels. A plain silver container will suffice at lower levels of experince. As a cleric reaches higher levels of experience and larger amounts of holy water are created, the cleric must retain a more costly and finely jeweled container or risk showing disrespect to the patron diety.

Erratta - A vial of holy water is considered to be a non-magical potion. Drinking of holy water has no affect on natural creatures. It will cause 1D6 burn damage to undead creatures and is useful in the casting of many spells. See Non-Magical Game Standards for more information on holy water

Cleric/3 - Cure Blindness

Class: Cleric	Level: 3
Cast Time: 3 seconds	Duration: N/A
Range: 15'	Affected Area: 1 Creature
Mana: 3	Damage: N/A
Save: N/A	Save Affect: N/A
Components: V, S, M	Concentration: N/A

Material Component: Holy water
Somatic Component: Touching of a drop of holy water to each eye

Affect - This spell will cure most forms of blindness that are not caused by tissue damage.

Limitations - The spell will not regrow or replace lost eye tissue.

Erratta - There are many affects in the game that can cause blindness either magically, or by mental block, etc. This spell will cure all of them that are not caused by tissue damage.

Cleric/3 - Cure Disease

Class: Cleric	Level: 3
Cast Time: 3 Seconds	Duration: N/A
Range: Touch	Affected Area: 1 Creature
Mana: 3	Damage: 1D8 Death
Save: Dexterity	Save Affect: Avoids for 1 Round
Components: V, S, M	Concentration: N/A

Material Component: Mint leaf
Somatic Component: Touching of subject

Execution - This spell cause all natutral diseases to be cured from a subject's body.

Affect - All viruses, infections, and dieases are immediatedly destroyed.

Limitations - the spell will not affect lycanthropy, the contagion of undead, or any ony sort of supernatural or magical diseases. The spell will not reverse any damages or affects already taken place by the disease. The spell will not prevent the subject from contracting the same disease (or others) again.

Cleric/3 - Destroy Parasites

Class: Cleric	Level: 3
Cast Time: 1 Second	Duration: N/A
Range: Touch	Affected Area: 1 Creature
Mana: 1	Damage: 1D8 Death
Save: Dexterity	Save Affect: Avoids for 1 Round
Components: V, S	Concentration: N/A

Material Component: None
Somatic component: Touch of caster

Execution - By means of this spell, the caster is able to kill all living foreign creatures in a subject's body.

Affect - The spell will destroy and render harmless all bacterias, larva, viruses, egss and any other sorts of parasites.

Limitations - The spell will not heal or remove any sort of damage that has already been cause by an infestation. It will not reveal what infestations, if any, where actually present or if the spell was used when not needed.

Cleric/3 - Dispel Enchantment

Class: Cleric	Level: 3
Cast Time: 3 Seconds	Duration: 1 Round/Level
Range: 15' + 10'/Level	Affected Area: Variable
Mana: 3	Damage: None
Save: N/A	Save Affect: N/A
Components: V, S	Concentration: N/A
Material Component: None	
Somatic component: Snapping of fingers	

Execution - This spell can be cast in one of two forms. It may be used in sigular affect or area affect.

Singular affect - When this spell is used in singular form it will remove all magics from the the creature or item it is cast upon. Any enchantments that were affecting the subject will be destroyed. If the spell is used singularly on a continual magic, (magical creature, magical item, etc) the continual magic will be neutralized for of round for every level of experince of the spell caster.

Area casting - If this spell is used in area form it has absolutely no affect on continual magics. It will, however destroy all enchantments in the affected area, When used in this form, the spell has no duration and its affect and will not prevent further magics from being introduced.

Limiations - This spell will not affect artifacts or relics. It will not prevent a creature from casting a spell, reading a scroll, or employing a magical item. When the spell is invoked in singular form, the caster can specify any duration up to the maximum of 1 round/level, but the the duration cannot be ended early by used of command words. Unless otherwise pre-stated, the referee will assume the spell was cast for maximum duration. The spell will not reverse any magically induced damage or reverse any affects that do not have a magical duration.

Cleric/3 – Enchanted Glyph

Class: Cleric	Level: 3
Cast Time: 3 turns	Duration: N/A
Range: Touch	Affected Area: 1 Object
Mana: 1	Damage:
Save: None	Save Affect: None
Components: V, S, M	Concentration: N/A
Material Component: Holy Water	
Somatic component: Drawing of glyph with holy water on object	

Execution - By means of this spell the caster can leave a secondary spell as a trap or safeguard on an object that is triggered when the item is touched..

Glyph Type Spells:
- Cause/Heal Wound SPells
- Cause/Cure Blindness spells
- Electrical/Lightning spells
- Flame/Fire Spells
- Paralyzation spells

Affect - The secondary spell is released when the object is touched by living flesh (the touch of magical or undead creatures will not activate the glyph)

Requirements - The secondary spell must be cast immediately after this spell is cast, either by the same caster or an associate. The secondary spell must be cast before the holy water dries

Limitations - A glyph cannot be placed on a creature or a magical item. An object cannot hold more then one glyph.

Adjustments - After the glyph is in place, the caster may use a command word to temporarily disable the glyph, handle the object or move it about, then speak the command word to reinstate the glyph. There is no limit to the number of times the glyph can be suspended and reinstated.

Aftermath - The glyph will remain in affect until it is released onto a subject, the spell caster calls for the spell to end, the spell exhausts its duration, or the enchantment is dispelled.

Erratta - After the holy water dries, the glyph will be completely invisible. Creatures addected by the secondary spell from a glyph will not necessarily know where the magic has come from.

Cleric/3 - Feign Death

Class: Cleric	Level: 3
Cast Time: 3 turns	Duration: N/A
Range: Touch	Affected Area: 1 Creature
Mana: 3	Damage: None
Save: N/A	Save Affect: N/A
Components: V, S	Concentration: N/A
Material component: None	
Somatic component: Horizontal sweeping motion with the hand	

Execution - Casting this spell will casue a subject to appear dead. Once cast, the affect is physiological and cannot be magically dispelled.

Affect - The subject will seem completely lifeless. All bodily functions will cease and the flesh will take on a pale appearance and cool to room temperature. The subject will not require any food or air to be sustained.

Limitations - The spell has no affect upon unwilling subjects, and willing subject will be able to rouse themselves at any time. To maintain the the affect, the subject must make no voluntary movements. If the subject is moved about by external means, the affect is not dissapaited.

While under the spells affect, none of the subject's senses will function except hearing. The subject will not be aware of being moved or wounded unless they pick up on some audible clues as to what is occurring.

Erratta - While under the affect of the spell, the subject will experience no damage or discomfort from adverse temperature, so long as the temperature is warm enough to prevent freezing, and cool enough to not sear flesh.

Cleric/3 - Heal Critical Wounds

Class: Cleric
Level: 3
Cast Time: 3 Seconds
Duration: N/A
Range: Touch
Affected Area: 1 Creature
Mana: 3
Damage: 3D12 to undead
Save: Dexterity
Save Affect: Avoids

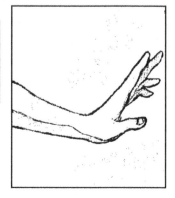

| Level | Creature Type | | | | |
	Nat	Sup-Nat	Magical	Undead	Xtra-Dim
0-2	1D4	1D6	1D8	1D10	1D12
3-8	2D4	2D6	2D8	2D10	2D12
6-10	3D4	3D6	3D8	3D10	3D12
9-11	4D4	4D6	4D8	4D10	3D12
12-14	5D4	5D6	5D8	5D10	5D12
15-17	6D4	6D6	6D8	6D10	6D12
18-20	7D4	7D6	7D8	7D10	7D12
21-	8D4	8D6	8D8	8D10	8D12

Components: V, S
Concentration: N/A
Somatic component:Touch
Material Component: None

Execution - After the spell is complete the caster may touch a creature and heal 3D12 hit-points of damage.

Affect - After the spell is complete the caster may touch a creature and heal 3D12 hit-points of damage. The spell will cause closure of large wound and cessation of heavy bleeding

Limitations - The spell will not affect creatures with a current hit-point tally of 0 or less. It the spell is relesed onto a subject with less than 1 hit-point, no healing will take place and the caster's mana will be used.

Errata - If this spell is used on an undead creature, it will cause rather then heal damage.

Cleric/3 – Holy Bolt

Class: Cleric
Level: 3
Cast Time: 3 Seconds
Duration: N/A
Range: 15' + 10'/Level
Affect Area: 1 Creature
Mana:3
Damage: Varies
Save: None
Save Affect: N/A
Components: V, S, M
Concentration: N/A

Material compnent: Holy symbol
Somatic component: Holding symbol to chest with one hand and pointing with the other.

Execution - This spell will do some damage to all creatures

Description - The spell appears as a shimmering ball of magical energy, 1' - 2' inches in diameter, that shootsforth from the caster's outstretched finger and strikesthe target creature

Affect - This spell affects different sorts of creatures in different ways depending upon the type. The more "un-natural" the creature, the greater the damage.

Cleric/3 - Locate

Class: Cleric	Level: 3
Cast Time: 3 turns	Duration: 1 round/level
Range: 60' + 10'/level	Affected Area: N/A
Mana: 3	Damage: None
Save: N/A	Save Affect: N/A
Components: V, S, M	Concentration: N/A

Material Component: Needle, pin or other tiny metal rod
Somatic Component: Placing needle on palm of hand

Affect - This spell can be used to locate a creature or item, or a type of item or creature. As the spell caster move about

Limitations - The spell will only reveal the direction and will not reveal how far away the located item or creature is from the spell caster. The needle will point directly to the tiem or creature, but will not reveal what passages need to be taken to reach it. Sometimes, the needle will point directly to a stone wal when the winding passage that needs to be taken is a different direction. The spell requires low concentration to maintain, and will be broken if the caster is wounded or cast a different spell. Aritfacts, relics and some unique creatures cannot be located.

Location by specific item or creature - If the spell is used to locate a specific item or creature, the exact item or creature must be in range of the spell or the needle will not move,

however, the spell caster can move around hoping to bring the sought after subject into range.

Location by item or creature type - The spell caster can visualize a type of itme such as stairs, wand, doorway, gold peice etc. To find a creature type, the spell caster will need to visualize a human, elf, orc, kobold, etc. The needle will point to the nearest example.

Errata - If the intended subject is not in range when the spell is cast, the needle will remain motionless. However, if the spell caster moves around before the duration expires and the intended subject comes into range, the needle will lock On and begin to point. Likewise, if the caster moves out of range of the object, or the object moves out of range of the caster, the needle will go dead. If, the item is used to locate a type and the a different creature or tiem of the sought after type comes into closer range, the needle will turn to point to the closer subject.

Cleric/3 – Obscure detection

Class: Cleric	Level: 3
Cast Time: 3 turns	Duration: 1 hour/level
Range: 60' + 10'/level	Affected Area: N/A
Mana: 3	Damage: None
Save: N/A	Save Affect: N/A
Components: V, S	Concentration: N/A

Material Component: None
Somatic Component: Touch of spell caster

Affect - This spell can be used to make a creature or item impossible to located, scry, or expose by any sort of detection spells.

Limitations - The spell will only affect one item or creature. It will not protect comrades or carried items from being detected.

Cleric/3 - Protection From Evil 15' Radius

Class: Cleric	Level: 1
Cast Time: 1 Second	Duration: N/A
Range: Touch	Affected Area: 1 Creature
Mana: 1	Damage: None
Save: None	Save Affect: N/A
Components: V, S	Concentration: N/A

Material component: Holy water
Somatic component: Sprinkling of holy water along perimeter of affected area.

Executiion - The casting of this spell will create a 30' diameter are in which undead and extra-planar creatures cannot enter.

Limitations - The spell will not affect natural or super-natural creatures. The spell will not prevent an undead from striking persons close to the edge of the affected area with a weapon, using a mental attacks, or hurling an objects into the affected area.

Cleric/3 - Remove Curse

Level: 3	Components: V, S
Range: Touch	Casting Time: 6
segments	
Duration: Permanent	Saving Throw: Special
Area of Effect: Special	

Affect - This spell will allow a creature to become free of a curse or a cursed item.

Explanation/Description: Upon costing this spell, the cleric is usually able to remove a curse - whether it be on an object, a person, or in the form of some undesired sending or evil presence. **Limtations** - The spell will not neutralized the cursed nature of an itme, but will only a creature to be rid of a cursed item.

Cleric/3 - Sanctify

Class: Cleric	Level: 3
Cast Time: 3 seconds	Duration: Permanent (non-magical)
Range: Touch	Affected Area: 1 Creature or object
Mana: 3	Damage: None
Save: N/A	Save Affect: N/A
Components: V, S, M	Concentration: N/A

Material Component: Holy symbol
Somatic Component: Touching of holly symbol to subject.
Execution - The employment of this spell will sanctify an item or the dead body of a creature.
Affect -The spell is commonly used to sanctify holy symbols after they are crafted, thereby giving them their powers over undead creatures. The spell is also often used at various appropriate rituals such as funerals.
Bodily sanctification - If the spell is used on a creatures dead body, it will prevent the creature from being later raised as an undead. If the spell is used on a slain udead creature, the remains can be sanctified, then resserected to natural living status.
Item sancitifaction - If a sanctified item is placed against the body (or passed through its non-corpreal form) it will cause 1D6 burn damage.
Sanctifying cursed items - IF the spell is used on an evilly cursed item, the itme will burst into flames and be consumed.
Restrictions - Wise use of this spell is very pleasing to a diety, while frivolous use might anger a diety. A sanctified item has the attention of the patron diety of the spell caster. It is well and good to create a holy symbol which will become a revered item that will be used ot battle evil. Using the spell to sanctify arrows in return for pay from customers, however, might anger a diety. If a cleric is approaching the limits of acceptable usage, the diety will reveal such to the cleric in a dream or a vision. Absent of such a warning, the character is safe in assuming that the spell is being used properly.

Cleric/3 - Speak with Dead

Class: Cleric	Level: 3
Cast Time: 3 Rounds	Duration: N/A
Range: Touch	Affected Area: 1 Creature
Mana: 3	Damage: None
Save: None	Save Affect: N/A
Components: V, S	Concentration: N/A

Material Component: None
Somatic Component: Slowly waving hand horizontally over corpse
Execution - This spells will temporarily restore the mental abilities of a dead person and magically enable them to hear and speak.
Affect - The spell will cause the deceased to recall any memories from while they were living, up to their time of death and what killed them (if they were aware of the cause at the time). The subject will be aware that they are dead and that they are only able to speak via the affect of outside influences (they may not necessarily know it was magics or the type of spell.
Limiations - The spell will not bring the affected creature into any sort of friendly status with the spell caster. A dead enemy is unlikely to offer any useful information. The spell will not endow the subject with any knowledge of languages beyond what they knew while they were living. The subject will have no knowledge of events that occurred after their death, nor even any concept of how much time has passed since they died.

Cleric/3 - Tongues

Class: Cleric	Level: 3
Cast Time: 3 Seconds	Duration: N/A
Range: 0	Affected Area: Self
Mana: 3	Damage: None
Save: Dexterity	Save Affect: Avoids for 1 Round
Components: S	Concentration: N/A

Material Component: None
Somatic Component: Dragging a finger across the lower lip
Affect - This spell will cause the caster to be totally articulate in all froms of non-magical conversing. The caster will be able to comprehend, speak, read and write any form of verbal or written communication. The spell will also endow the caster with the dialects and accents as may be appropriate.
Limitations - The spell will not change the tonal qualities of the spell casters voice. The caster might sound like a ntaive of a particular area, but the affect will not be aid in the impersonatation of an idividual. The enchantment will not enable the caster to cimmunicate in the grunts and body languages of animals or any creature that communicates by means other than a spoken language.
Uses - The caster might use the spell to communicate with a stranger or interrogate a prisoner.
Aftermath - The spell will end when it exhausts its duration or the enchantment is dispelled.

Cleric/4 – Create Potion of Healing

Class: Cleric	Level: 4
Cast Time: 4 Turns	Duration: N/A
Range: 0	Affected Area: 1 Creature
Mana: 4	Damage: N/A
Save: N/A	Save Affect: Avoids for 1 Round
Components: V, S	Concentration: N/A

Material Component: Mint leaf
Somatic Component: Placing the mint leaf on surface of water and gently agitating the container
Affect - This spell will transform holy water into healing potions. The spell will transform up to 1 vial (4 ounces) of holy water per level of the spell caster. The potion will heal 1D8 hit-points of damage to normal creatures.
Limitations - The entire amount must be in a single container made of silver, usually some ornate container fitted with jewels. A plain silver container will suffice at lower levels of experince. As a cleric reaches higher levels of experience and larger amounts of holy water are created, the cleric must retain a more costly and finely jeweled container or risk showing disrespect to the patron diety.
Erratta - A vial of healing potion will restore 1D8 hit-points of damage to any creature who has 0 hit-points or more. Healing potions will not affect creatures in negative hit-points. Healing potions have a shelf life of 4 weeks. For mor information on potions, consult Game-standards/magical/potions/healing.

Cleric/4 – Detect Alignment

Class: Cleric	Level: 4
Cast Time: 4 Seconds	Duration: t Round
Range: 15' + 10'/level	Affected Area: 1 Creature

Mana: 4 — Damage: None
Save: Charisma — Save Affect: Plain white aura
Components: V, S — Concentration: N/A
Material Component: None
Somatic Component: Pointing at subject

Alignment Aura Color

Color	Alignement
Gold	Lawful - Good
Silver	Neutral - Good
Copper	Chaotic - Good
Blue	Lawful - Neutral
Green	Neutral - Neutral
Red	Chaotic - Neutral
Yellow	Lawful - Evil
Orange	Neutral - Evil
Purple	Chaotic - Evil

Affect - This spell will reveal the alignment of a subject character or creature by the color of a shimmering aura that the spell creates

Limitations - It the subject is conscious, they will almost always be aware of the aura anmd know that something has occurred. The subject may or may not be knowlegable of the spell, however, and may not realize exactly what has transpired. A subject who is aware of the spell and puts up a mental block, is allowed a charisma saving throw. If the save is successful, a plain white aura is generated that designates no particular alignement.

Errata - Casting any sort of spell on a stranger, or even a friend without permission can be very offensive, even if the spell causes no damage. Unexpected use of this spell will almost certainly provoke the angst of the subject.

Cleric/4 - Detect Lie

Class: Cleric — Level: 4
Cast Time: 4 Seconds — Duration: 1 Round/level
Range: 15' + 10'/level — Affected Area: 1 Creature
Mana: 4 — Damage: N/A
Save: Charisma — Save Affect: Negates
Components: V, S — Concentration: Low
Material Component: None
Somatic Component: Placing a hand to the ear as if to hear better

Affect - By means of this spell the caster is able to pick up on minute, normally inaudible fluctuations in the subjects voice in order to tell if the subject is lying. A successful save indicates that the subject is able to mask these fluctuations so as to not reveal lies.

Limitations - The spell only reveals if the speaker *believes* the information is correct and not whether it is truly accurdate. The spell requires low concentration to maintain and can be held in affect throughout its duration as long as the caster is not wounded or does not attempt to cast a new spell or activate a magic item. The spell will not increase the caster's hearing range. To determine if the subject is speaking the truth, the caster must be able to hear the subject naturally.

Cleric/4 - Divination

Class: Cleric — Level: 4
Cast Time: 4 Seconds — Duration: Variable
Range: 0 — Affected Area: N/A
Mana: 4 — Damage: N/A
Save: N/A — Save Affect: N/A
Components: V, S, M — Concentration: High
Material Component: Holy symbol

Somatic Component: Pressing symbol to chest and bowing head

Execution - This spell is used to receive information about an area, structure, section of a dungeon, etc.

Limitations - The spell will reveal information about the history of an area, not the properties of an object. Although a diety's knowledge usually far surpasses that of a mortal, it may not be all inclusive. There may be errors and omissions in the information, although generally, most of what revealed will be correct. The percentage of inaccuracies and omissions is equal to the caster's wisdom score.

Cleric/4 - Electric Touch

Class: Cleric — Level: 4
Cast Time: 1 Second — Duration: N/A
Range: Touch — Affected Area: 1 Creature
Mana: 4 — Damage: 1D8 Death
Save: Dexterity — Save Affect: Avoids for 1 Round
Components: V, S, M — Concentration: N/A
Material compnent: Piece of silver
Somatic component: Touching of silver to flech of intended victim

Execution - After this spell is cast the next creature or metallic surface the caster touches using a hand will be subject to a buzzing voltage.

Uses - If a spell caster dips their hand into the water, the spell will be discharged and all creatures in the water within a 15' radius will suffer the damage of the spell.

Level	Electric Damage
0-3	1D10 Hit-points
4-8	2D10 Hit-points
8-11	3D10 Hit-points
12-15	4D10 Hit-points
16-19	5D10 Hit-points
20-23	6D10 Hit-points
24-27	7D10 Hit-points
28-31	8D10 Hit-points
32-35	9D10 Hit-points
36-	10D10 Hit-Points

Cleric/4 - Exorcise Mind Control

Class: Cleric — Level: 4
Cast Time: 4 turns — Duration: N/A
Range: Touch — Affected Area: 1 Creature
Mana: 4 — Damage: None
Save: N/A — Save Affect: N/A
Components: V, S, M — Concentration: N/A
Material compnent: Holy water
Somatic component: Sprinkling of holy water on subject

Execution - This spell is used to remove all mental controls and influences subject either magical or non-magical.

Limitations - The spell will not reveal if there actually was any sort of mind control taking place. It also will not reveal who or what is controlling or influencing the subject, nor will it reveal what sort of method is being used.

Cleric/4 - Gaseous Form

Class: Cleric — Level: 1 Turn/Level
Cast Time: 4 Seconds — Duration: N/A
Range: Touch — Affected Area: 1 Creature or Object
Mana: 4 — Damage: None
Save: Dexterity — Save Affect: Avoids
Components: V, S — Concentration: N/A

Material Component: drop of alcohol (wine, ale, mead, or others)
Somatic Component: Rubbing drop on flesh of subject

Execution - Once this spell is cast, the touch of the caster will transform one creature and all carried items ir one object into a billowing green gas.

Transforming Objects - If this spell is used on an object, the cloud will hang in one spot (if there is no draft), or willow about in the breeze.

Items - If an item is turned to gasesou form it will settle to the ground, making a six inch layer with its diamter relative to its physical body mass before the conversion.

Creatures - While in gaseous form, a creatureis able to float in any direction horizontally or vertically at a rate of 30 yards per round (1/10 mile per minute/6 miles per hour) relative to the surrounding air. The subject will be able to control their form so as to leak through small cracks or openings.

Senses - While is gaseos from, a creature will have multi-directional "vision" due to being able to sense the light that is passing through their gaseous body. The subject will able to "hear" by sensing the vibrations of in the air. The subject can speak, but only in a hollow, whipery voice.

Spell casting - A subject will not be able to cast spells while in gaseous from since the voice will be distorted and not effective for magical use, nor will the subject have hands for somatic gestures or materials for components

Erratta - Heavy winds over 5 miles per hour can move the cloud about, but will not cause it to disperse.

Aftermath - When the spell exhausts its duration or the enchantment is magically dispelled, the object or creature will solidify. If the creature or item is in the air, it will fall to the earth and suffer fall damage, the anount depending on the height of the fall. See Game-standards-non-magical/falling

Cleric/4 - Lower Water

Class: Cleric	Level: 4
Cast Time: 4 turns	Duration: N/A
Range: Touch	Affected Area: 10' x 10' x 10'/level
Mana: 4	Damage: None
Save: N/A	Save Affect: N/A
Components: V, S, M	Concentration: N/A

Material compnent: Holy symbol
Somatic component: Touchin of holy symbol to watrs surface

Affect - The casting of this spell will remove massive anounts of water, up to 1000 cubic feet per level of experince of the spell caster.

Limitations - The spell will only affect the water and will not eliminate any objects or creatures in the water.

Cleric/4 - Neutralize Poison

Mage/Evocation	Level: 3
Cast Time: 1 segment	Duration: 1 round/level
Range: Touch	Affected Area: 1 Creature or item
Mana:3	Damaage: N/A
Save: Charisma	Save Affect: Negates
Components: V, S	

Material Component: None
Somatic Component: None

Affect - This spell causes all poisons inside a single creature to become inert and harmless. If the spell is used on person suffering the effects of poison, the poison affects will cease immediately. All poisons and venoms in the subject will be affected regardless if they deal damage, or only paralyzation.

Limitations - This spell will not heal damage already incurred from a poison. Only one item or creature will be affected per spell. The spell cannot be used to neutralize an entire quiver of poison arrows, or an entire swarm of poison insects.

Erratta - . If the spell is used on a venmous creature, it will neutralize the venoms thereby rendering the creature non-poisonous until the creature can secrete new poison. The spell will not cause venoms or poisons to change color or consitency. After being neutralized, the poison retains no magical nature from this spell, and magical dispelling will not restore the poison. If the spell is used to neutralize a venomous creature, the effects are temporary, since the magic will not alter a creatures poison

Level	Fire Damage
0-3	1D6 Hit-points
4-7	2D6 Hit-points
8-11	3D6 Hit-points
12-15	4D6 Hit-points
16-19	5D6 Hit-points
20-23	6D6 Hit-points
24-	7D10 Hit-points

producing capabilities.

Cleric/4 - Pennance

Class: Cleric	Level: 4
Cast Time: 4 Rounds	Duration: N/A
Range: Touch	Affected Area: 1 Creature
Mana: 4	Damage: None
Save: N/A	Save Affect: N/A
Components: V, S, M	Concentration: N/A

Material Component: Holy water
Somatic Component: Sprinkling of holy water on subject

Affect - This spell is used to resolve any acts or situations that myay have caused a subject to fall into disfavor with their diety.

Execution - The spell will give the caster exacting knowledge of what sort of transgression has taken place and what sort of penance the diety requires for atonement. The spell will only function if the subject has freely agreed to accept the spell caster's help. Naturally, the spell caster may charge a fee for this service

Erratta - A penance may consist of performing a service, paying a large tithe, or some other sort of scrifice. It is rare for an offense to become so great that the relationship with the diety is irrepairable. Therefree will determine what sort of penance, if any, is appropriate. Once the spell is cast and the penance is given, it falls to the subject, not the caster, to satisfy it. To receive atonement, the subject must meet the pennance as well as meeting any obligation to the spell caster for the casting of the spell. A subject need not be of the same diety nor even the same alignement to use this spell to seek penance.

Limitations - Woe to the spell caster who falsifies the penance a diety has perscribed, or attempts to alter the terms of payment for the spell after it has been cast

Cleric/4 - Pillar of Fire

Class: Cleric	Level: 4
Cast Time: 1 Second	Duration: N/A
Range: Touch	Affected Area: 1 Creature
Mana: 1	Damage: 1D6/4 Levels
Save: Dexterity	Save Affect: ½ damage
Components: V, S, M	Concentration: N/A
Material Component: Bit of sulphur	
Somatic Component: Tossing of sulphur	

Execute - This spell creates a massive pillar of flame that is 30' wide and 60' high.

Description - The column of fire will be 30' in diameter and up to 90' high (space permitting). The light from the flames will be intense but not blinding. The roar from the flames will be loud but not defeaning

Limiations - A flame strike can only be cast vertically

Side Affects - The flames will ignite all combustible items within the affected area, but will not surpass the 30' diameter or 90' height.

Cleric/4 – Rejuvenate

Class: Cleric	Level: 4
Cast Time: 4 turns	Duration: N/A
Range: Touch	Affected Area: 1 Creature
Mana: 4	Damage: None
Save: N/A	Save Affect: N/A
Components: V, S, M	Concentration: N/A
Material compnent: Holy water	
Somatic component: Sprinkling of holy water on subject	

Affect - This spell will heal all hit-points of damage to a subject, as long as they are alive, even if they have slipped into negative hit-points.

Limitations - The spell will not replace hit-pointslost due to experience-level-drainange unless the experience levels are restored first. This spell has no affect on undead creatures

Cleric/4 – Silence 15' Radius

Class: Cleric	Level: 4
Cast Time: 4 Seconds	Duration: N/A
Range: Touch	Affected Area: 1 Creature
Mana: 1	Damage: 1D8 Death
Save: Dexterity	Save Affect: Avoids for 1 Round
Components: V, S	Concentration: N/A
Material Component: N/A	
Somatic Components: Finger to the lips as if to silence	
Material Component: Feather	

Execution - Casting this spell will stop all sound causing vibrations in a 15 foot radius of the spell point of origin.

Affect - Creatures and objects inside the affected area will be incapable of speaking alound, communicating verbally, or casting spells with verbal components, os using magic items that require command words. Missle weapons fired into the affected area will alnd silently. Creatures struck by missles inside an affected area will be unable to cry out or sound an alarm.

Limitations - The point of origin cannot be moved after the spell has been cast, nor can the spell be cast onto a creature or item in order to be moved about. If the spell caster is inside the affected area, they will be unable to speak the command words to end the spell.

Uses - A party passing through a silenced area cannot be heard by an enemy, but also cannot communicate with each other verbally.

Aftermath - The spell will run until it exhausts its duration, the enchantment is dispelled, or the spell caster speaks the command words for the spell to end (from outside the circle).

Cleric/5 - Commune

Level: 5	Components: V, 5, M
Range: 0	Casting Time: 1 turn
Duration: Special	Saving Throw: None
Area of Effect: Special	

Explanation/Description: By use of a commune spell the cleric is able to contact his or her divinity - or agents thereof - and request information in the form of questions which can be answered by a simple "yes" or "no". The cleric is allowed one such question for every level of experience he or she has attained. The answers given will be correct. It is probable that the **referee** will limit the use of commune spells to one per adventure, one per week, or even one per month, for the "gods" dislike frequent interruptions. The material components necessary to a commune spell are the cleric's religious symbol, holy/unholy water, and incense.

Cleric/5 – Continual Glyph

Class: Cleric	Level: 5
Cast Time: 1 Second	Duration: Permanent
Range: Touch	Affected Area: 1 Creature
Mana: 5	Damage: Varies
Save: Varies	Save Affect: Varies
Components: V, S	Concentration: N/A
Material Component	
Somatic Component	

Execution - By means of this spell the caster can leave a secondary spell as a trap or safeguard on an object that is triggered when the item is touched..

Glyph Type Spells:
  Cause/Heal Wound SPells
  Cause/Cure Blindness spells
  Electrical/Lightning spells
  Flame/Fire Spells
  Paralyzation spells

Affect - The secondary spell is released when the object is touched by living flesh (the touch of magical or undead creatures will not activate the glyph). After the secondary affect is discharged, the glyph will re-arm itself in the course of 1 round and discharge again the next time it is touched.

Requirements - The secondary spell must be cast immediately after this spell is cast, either by the same caster or an associate. The secondary spell must be cast before the holy water dries

Limitations - Once a glyph is discharged on a creature, it will not discharge on the same same creature again as long as physical contact with the glyphed area is maintained. Once the glyph is in place, it bears no connectin to either spell caster and anyone who knows the proper command words can control it. (specially chose byt the glyph caster at cast time) can control it. The glyph can be created to have no deactivating or dissoliving command words. A glyph cannot be placed on a creature or a magical item. An object cannot hold more then one glyph.

Adjustments - After the glyph is in place, anyone who knows the proper command words can temporarily disable the glyph, handle the object or move it about, then speak the command word to reinstate the glyph. There is no limit to the number of times the glyph can be suspended and reinstated.

Aftermath - The glyph will remain in affect until it is removed by a destroy magic affect or the command word is spoken to dissolve it.

Erratta - The command words to control the glyph can be any of the spell caster's choosing. The glyph spell caster may elect to not include dsable/reinstate command words, dissolution command words, or both. After the holy water dries, the glyph will be completely invisible. Creatures affected by the secondary spell from a glyph will not necessarily know where the magic has come from.

Cleric/5 – Create Potion of Extra Healing

Class: Cleric	Level: 4
Cast Time: 4 Turns	Duration: N/A
Range: 0	Affected Area: 1 Creature
Mana: 4	Damage: N/A
Save: N/A	Save Affect: Avoids for 1 Round
Components: V, S	Concentration: N/A

Material Component: Mint leaf
Somatic Component: Placing the mint leaf on surface of water and gently agitating the container

Affect - This spell will transform holy water into healing potions. The spell will transform up to 1 vial (4 ounces) of holy water per level of the spell caster into potions of extra-healing. The potion will heal 2D10 hit-points of damage to normal creatures.

Limitations - The entire amount must be in a single container made of silver, usually some ornate container fitted with jewels. A plain silver container will suffice at lower levels of experince. As a cleric reaches higher levels of experience and larger amounts of holy water are created, the cleric must retain a more costly and finely jeweled container or risk showing disrespect to the patron diety.

Erratta - A vial of extra healing potion will restore 2D10 hit-points of damage to any creature who has 0 hit-points or more. Healing potions will not affect creatures in negative hit-points. Healing potions have a shelf life of 4 weeks. For mor information on potions, consult Game-standards/magical/potions/healing.

Cleric/5 – Create Holy Symbol

Class: Cleric	Level: 5
Cast Time: 1 Second	Duration: Permanent
Range: Touch	Affected Area: 1 Creature
Mana: 5	Damage: 1D8 Death
Save: Dexterity	Save Affect: Avoids for 1 Round
Components: V, S	Concentration: High

Material Component: Finely crafted symbol
Somatic Component: Sprinkling of holy water onto symbol

Affect - This spell will endow a properly crafted piece of jewelery into a holy symbol

Limitations - The spell should inly be used on items that have finely crafted out of precious metals and stones. The higher the level of the intended user, the greater the value and the quality must be. Using the spell on a crude symbol would be displeasing to the patron diety.

Cleric/5 – Depetrification

Class: Cleric	Level: 5
Cast Time: 5 Rounds	Duration: Permanent
Range: Touch	Affected Area: 1 Creature
Mana: 5	Damage: None
Save: None	Save Affect: N/A
Components: V, S, M	Concentration: N/A

Material Component: Holy water
Somatic Component: Sprinkling of holy water on subject

Affect - This spell will restore one item, or one creature and all carried items from stone back into their previous forms.

Limitations - The spell will only affect those stone objects that were pretrified and will not affect natural stonework such as a statue.

Cleric/5 – Destroy Mind Control

Level: 5	Components: V, S, M
Range: Touch	Casting Time: 1 turn
Duration: Permanent	Saving Throw: None
Area of Effect: One person	

Explanation/Description: This spell is used by the cleric to remove the onus of unwilling or unknown deeds from the person who is the subject of the atonement. The spell will remove the effects of magical alignment change as well. The person for whom atonement is being made must be either truly repentant or not in command of his or her own will so as to be able to be repentant. Your **referee** will judge this spell in this regard, noting any past instances of its use upon the person. Deliberate misdeeds and acts of knowing and wiliful nature cannot be atoned for with this spell. The material components of this spell are the cleric's religious symbol, prayer beads or wheel or book, and burning incense.

Cleric/5 – Disperse Evil

Class: Cleric	Level: 5
Cast Time: 5 Rounds	Duration: 1 Round/Level
Range: o	Affected Area: 15' + 10'/level
Mana: 5	Damage: None
Save: Charisma	Save Affect: Negates
Components: V, S, M	Concentration: N/A

Material Component: Holy water and holy symbol
Somatic Component: Pouring of holy water on holy symbol

Affect - This spell will cause all undead and extra-planar creatures to immediately flee the area. They will move away from the spell caster until either they have left the affected area or the duration of the spell is exhausted.

Limitations - The spell will not affect natural or super-natural creatures. The spell will not prevent the affected creatures from returning after the spell has ended. The spell requires high concentration on the part of the caster to maintain. Any interrruption or distraction will immediately cancel the affect.

Cleric/5 - Insect Plague

Class: Cleric	Level: 5
Cast Time: 1 Second	Duration: Permanent
Range: Touch	Affected Area: 1 Creature
Mana: 5	Damage: 1D8 Death
Save: Dexterity	Save Affect: Avoids for 1 Round
Components: V, S	Concentration: High
Material Component	
Somatic Component	

Execution- This spell will create a horde of creeping, hopping, and flying insects swarm in a thick cloud Creatures within the insect plague sustain 1 hit point of damage for each melee round they remain in it due to the bites and stings of the insects, regardless of armor class. Persons inside the swarm will not be able to muster the concentration necessary to cast spells or activate magical items

Affect - The swarm of insects will obscure vision, limiting it to 30'. The insects swarm in an area which centers around a point of origin.

Limitations - The spell can only be cast upon a fixed point and once the spell is cast the point of origin cannot be moved about. The spell cannot be cast upon a creature or object in order to be moved about. If the spell caster moves our of range, the spell will end.

Erratta - Heavy smoke will drive off insects within its bounds. Fire will also drive insects away; a wall of fire in a ring shape will keep the insect plague outside its confines, but a fire ball will simply clear insects from its blast area for 1 turn. Lightning and cold/ice act likewise.

Aftermath - When the spell exhausts its duration, the insects will disperse. If the spell castermoves out of range or speaks the command words calling for the spell to end, the affect is dispelled. Likewise, enchantment dispelling will cause the spell and affect to end prematurely.

Cleric/5 - Raise Dead

Class: Cleric	Level: 5
Cast Time: 5 Rounds	Duration: N/A
Range: 15' + 10'/level	Affected Area: 1 Dead creature
Mana: 5	Damage: None
Save: N/A	Save Affect: N/A
Components: V, S	Concentration: N/A
Material Component: Holy water	
Somatic Component: Sprinkling of holy water on subject	

Execution - This spell will bring a character back from the brink of death and place them at -9 hit-points.

Time Limitations - The spell must be used within a strict time frame, within a number of minutes equal to the subject's contsitution or the spell caster's level of experience, which ever is lesser.

System Shock - Once the spell is cast, the recipient must make a system shock roll on percentile dice less than or equal to the subjects constitution score/ A successfule percentile roll indicates that the recipient is restored to life. A failed roll indicates that subject was restored, but died again from the shock. The mana required for the spell will be used in either event.

Poison - If the subject was killed from poison and not all the poison damage was delivered, the poison will need to be

netralized prior to the casting of this spell. If it is not, the subject will start to receive the remainder of the poison damage as soon as they are raised and will die again.

Undead - If the spell is to be used to raise an undead creature which has been killed, the body will need to be sancitified before being raised. If the body is not sanctified, the spell will default to restoring the creatures more recent undead life force rather than the earlier natural life force. In this case, the undead creature is immediately restored to full hit-points.

Cleric/5 - Regenerate

Class: Cleric	Level: 5
Cast Time: 1 Second	Duration: N/A
Range: 15' + 10'/level	Affected Area: 15' Radius
Mana: 4	Damage: 2D8
Save: N/A	Save Affect: N/A
Components: V, S	Concentration: N/A
Material Component: Drop of trolls blood	
Somatic Components: Placing of blood onto affected area	

Affect - This spell will cause a natural creature to regrow lost limbs and members that have been amputated. As the limb is regrown, an amount of hit-points equal to those lost by the amputation will be retored. The regrowth of the member will take place at 1 hit-point per round.

Limitations - The spell will not regrow area which have been burned by fire or acid or extreme heat. The spell will only affec one bodily area. If multiple limbs or members were lost, multiple spells must bew used.

Erratta - The spell has no magical duration. Once the regrowth has started, the affect is physiological and cannot be halted by command words or enchantment dispelling. The replacement will be an exact duplicate of the original. No scars, loss of strength, or other detrimental affects will be retained.

Cleric/5 - Scry

Class: Cleric	Level: 5
Cast Time: 5 rounds	Duration: 1 Round/level
Range: 1 mile/level	Affected Area: 15' Radius
Mana: 4	Damage: None
Save: None	Save Affect: N/A
Components: V, S, M	Concentration: High
Material Component: Holy water	
Somatic Components: Pouring of holy water into saucer or onto flat, recessesed surface where it will not run off or drain away.	

Affect - This spell will enable the caster to view a creature of object and the area of 15' radius around it.

Descripton - At the start of the spell, the holy water is poured out. As casting takes place, the reflective surface of the water becomes sharper until the it becomes mirror like. As the spell concludes, the reflection will haze and be replaced by an image of the intended subject (if the scry is successful)

Limitations - An object or creature in a hermetically sealed area cannot be scryed. Only one creature or item can be scryed per casting of the spell. There is no audio reception accompanying the image. The spell will not always function. The percentile chance of making a successful connection is dependent on the caster familiarity with the subject (see magical standards/scrying) Although no saving throw is allowed, there are game factors which can prevent a subject from being scryed.

Erratta - The scry image is visible to anyone who is close enough to view the pool of holy water. Although the subject of the spell cannot be changed, the caster can move the viewpoint around so that the different sides of the subject can be seen.

Cleric/5 - True Seeing

Class: Cleric | Level: 5
Cast Time: 5 Rounds | Duration: N/A
Range: 0 | Affected Area: 15' Radius
Mana: 5 | Damage: None
Save: N/A | Save Affect: N/A
Components: V, S, M | Concentration: N/A

Material Component: Water droplets
Somatic Components: Tilting back the head and placing a drop of water on each eye, then looking in the direction of the intended point of origin.

Execution - This spell will allow the caster to gain a heightened awareness of items and creatures in the affected area.

Affect - The caster will be aware of all doors, traps, invisibile or magically disguised, or magically altered creature and items within the affected area. Creatures that have been physically altered, even if no residual magic remains, will be obvious

Limitations - The spell will not be affected onm objects outside the affected area, even if they are in the spell caster's line of sight.

Cleric/6 - Aerial Servant

Class: Cleric | Level: 6
Cast Time: 6 Rounds | Duration: N/A
Range: 0 | Affected Area: 1 Arial Servsnt
Mana: 6 | Damage: 2D8
Save: N/A | Save Affect: N/A
Components: V, S, M | Concentration: N/A

Material Component: Drop of trolls blood
Somatic Components: Placing of blood onto affected area

Affect - This spell summons a continual magic to create a magical creature that is an invisible aerial servant (see Creature Manual) to do the bidding of the spell caster. The servant is able to obey moderately complex commands such as "take this pitcher, go to the stream and fill it with water, and return" or "open this bottle, fly over the three orcs down the road, and pour the contents on their heads"

Limitations - The creature will not fight. It can not lift more than 10 pounds. It will not obey any order that will place it in grave danger. It will be of the same alignment

Aftermath - The spell will bind the creature to the spell caster for 1 hour per level of experince of the spell caster, after which the duration of the control is exhausted. Prior to the maximum control time the arial servant can be dimissed if it is ordered to do something that its limitations will not allow it to comply with, the spell caster speaks the command words ending the binding enchantment, or if the controlling enchantment is dispelled.

Cleric/6 - Animate Object

Class: Cleric | Level: 6
Cast Time: 6 Rounds | Duration: N/A
Range: 15' + 10'/level | Affected Area: Up to 1lb (10gpw)/level
Mana: 6 | Damage: N/A
Save: N/A | Save Affect: N/A
Components: V, S, M | Concentration: N/A

Material Component: Object ot be animated
Somatic Components: Pointing at object with one hand while making a swirling motion with the other hand.

Affect - This spell enchants an inanimate objects giving it with mobility and a semblance of life. The parts of the object that normally stiff and inflexible become supple and bendable as if constructed of muscle tissue. The object will be able to obey simple one-word commands such as "walk", "follow", "attack", "stay", "carry", etc.

Limitations - Control of the object can not be delegated, as the creature will only recognize commands from the spell caster. Magical items are not affected. The spell cannot be cast on spereated object to have them act together in unison as if connected. A pile of coins cannot function as one object. Interconnected objects, however, such as link in a length of chain can be made to work together as one. An objects movement is limited by its configuration. A rug can only squirm across the floor. A rope or stick can slither about like a snake. A three legged stool can walk about but not attack. A piece of furniture with 4 or more legs can rise up on 3 of them (the minimum number of pointed limbs to provide a stable foundation for striking) and hit with the remaining legs. An object with "feet" such as a suit of amror or a statue can walk on two limbs since the shape of its feet afford more stability then the ends of furniture legs.

Erratta - The object can be of any material whatsoever - wood, metal, stone, fabric, leather, ceromic, glass, etc. Most objects that can walk will have a movement rate of 5 mph (25ypr)

Cleric/6 - Blade Barrier

Class: Cleric | Level: 6
Cast Time: 6 Rounds | Duration: 1 Round/level
Range: 15' + 10'/level | Affected Area: 900 square feetl
Mana: 6 | Damage: 1D8 per 6 levels
Save: None | Save Affect: N/A
Components: V, S, M | Concentration: None

Material Component: Dagger

Level	Cutting Damage
0-5	1D8 Hit-points
6-11	2D8 Hit-points
12-17	3D8 Hit-points
18-23	4D8 Hit-points
24-29	5D8 Hit-points
30-35	6D8 Hit-points
36-	7D8 Hit-points

Somatic Components: Flipping blade into air to send it twirling.

Affect - This spell creates ic employs this spell to set up a wall of circling, razor-sharp blades that whirl and flash in endless movement around an immobile point. Any creature which attempts to pass through the blade barrier suffers cutting damage.

Adjustments - The spell can be cast as a flat wall square wall upt 30' x 30', or curved to encircle an area, or in a semisphere to guard agaist an arial attack. The spell caster is able to speak command words that cause the blades to stop momentarily, in order to allow someone to step through, then speak the command words to set them in motion again.

Limitations - Once the spell is cast, the size, shape and location of the barrier cannot be changed. The twirling of the blades can only be paused for the entire barrier and not for a small part of it.

Erratta - Although the blades are magically created and their movement is magically inducedm, the cutting damage they cause is for all practical purpose no magical as if a normal edged wepon were used.

Aftermath - The barrier will remain until the spell exhausts its duration, the enchantment is dispelled, or the caster speaks the command words calling for the spell to end.

Cleric/6 – Call Lightning

Level	Electrical Damage
0-5	1D10 Hit-points
6-11	2D10 Hit-points
12-17	3D10 Hit-points
18-23	4D10 Hit-points
24-29	5D10 Hit-points
30-37	6D10 Hit-points
38-	7D10 Hit-points

Erratta - A vial of healing potion will restore 3D12 hit-points of damage to any creature who has 0 hit-points or more. Healing potions will not affect creatures in negative hit-points. Healing potions have a shelf life of 4 weeks. For mor information on potions, consult Game-standards/magical/potions/healing.

Cleric/6 - **Find The Path**

Class: Cleric	Level: 6
Cast Time: 4 Turns	Duration: 1 Turn/Level
Range: 0	Affected Area: N/A
Mana: 6	Damage: N/A
Save: N/A	Save Affect: Avoids for 1 Round
Components: V, S, M	Concentration: N/A

Material Component: Needle
Somatic Component: Placing the mint leaf on surface of water and gently agitating the container

Affect - This spell will reveal the shortest, most direct route that he or she is seeking, be it the way to or from or out of a locale. The locale can be outdoors or underground, a trap or even a maze spell. The spell will enable the cleric to select the correct direction which will eventually lead him or her to egress, the exact path to follow (or actions to take), and this knowledge will persist as long as the spell lasts, i.e. 1 turn for each level of experience of the cleric casting find the path. The spell frees the cleric, and those with him or her from a maze spell in a single melee round and will continue to do so as long as the spell lasts. The material component of this spell is a set of divination counters of the sort favored by the cleric - bones, ivory counters, sticks, carved runes, or whatever. The reverse, lose the path, makes the creature touched totally lost and unable to find its way for the duration of the spell, although it can be led, of course.

Cleric/6 - **Heal**

Class: Cleric
Level: 3
Cast Time: 3 Seconds
Duration: N/A
Range: Touch
Affected Area: 1 Creature
Mana: 6
Damage: Special to undead
Save: Dexterity
Save Affect: Avoids
Components: V, S
Concentration: N/A
Somatic component: Touch
Material Component: None

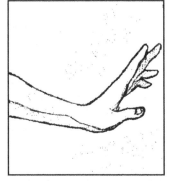

Affect - This wll wipe away disease, parasites, and injuries in the next creature the spell caster touches and heal them to within 1D4 total hit-points. If this spell is used on an undead creature it will reduce the undead creature to 1D4 hit-point.
Execution - After the spell is complete the caster may touch a creature and heal 3D12 hit-points of damage.
Affect - After the spell is complete the caster may touch a creature and heal 3D12 hit-points of damage. The spell will cause closure of large wound and cessation of heavy bleeding
Limitations - The spell will not affect creatures with a current hit-point tally of 0 or less. It the spell is relased onto a subject

Class: Cleric	Level: 6
Cast Time: 5 Rounds	Duration: N/A
Range: 15' + 10'/level	Affected Area: 30' wide x 60' high
Mana: 6	Damage: 1D10 per 6 levels
Save: Dexterity	Save Affect: ½ damage
Components: V, S	Concentration: N/A

Material Component: Piece of silver
Somatic Component: Holding sivler piece in the air with one hand and pointing towards point of origin with other

Execution- This spell creates a massive network of lightning that is 30' wide and 120' high.
Description - The affected area will be 30' in diameter and up to 120' high (space permitting
Limitations - A flame strike can only be cast vertically
Side Affects - The flash from the light will blind any who do not cover their eyes or turn their head for 1-4 rounds. The thunder clap will defean any who do not cover their ears for 5-8 rounds. The will melt all metals within the affected area that fail a savig throw.

Cleric/6 - Create Potion of Intensive Healing

Class: Cleric	Level: 4
Cast Time: 4 Turns	Duration: N/A
Range: 0	Affected Area: 1 Creature
Mana: 4	Damage: N/A
Save: N/A	Save Affect: Avoids for 1 Round
Components: V, S	Concentration: N/A

Material Component: Mint leaf
Somatic Component: Placing the mint leaf on surface of water and gently agitating the container

Affect - This spell will transform holy water into healing potions. The spell will transform up to 1 vial (4 ounces) of holy water per level of the spell caster. The potion will heal 3D12 hit-points of damage to normal creatures.
Limitations - The entire amount must be in a single container made of silver, usually some ornate container fitted with jewels. A plain silver container will suffice at lower levels of experince. As a cleric reaches higher levels of experience and larger amounts of holy water are created, the cleric must retain a more costly and finely jeweled container or risk showing disrespect to the patron diety.

with less than 1 hit-point, no healing will take place and the caster's mana will be used.

Errata - If this spell is used on an undead creature, it will cause rather then heal damage. The undead creature will be redused to 1d4 hit-points

Cleric/6 - **Part Water**

Level: 6	Components: V, S, M
Range: 2"/level	Casting Time: 7 furn
Duration: 7 turn/level	Saving Throw: None
Area of Effect: Special	

Explanation/Description: By employing a part water spell, the cleric is able to cause water or similar liquid to move apart, thus forming a trough. The depth and length of the trough created by the spell is dependent upon the level of the cleric, and a trough 3' deep by 1' by 2" (20' or 20 yards) is created per level, i.e. at 12th level the cleric would part water 36' deep by 12' wide by 24" (240' or 240 yards) long. The trough will remain as long as the spell lasts or until the cleric who cast it opts to end its effects (cf. dispel magic). The material component of this spell is the cleric's religious symbol.

Cleric/6 - **Power Surge**

Class: Cleric	Level: 6
Cast Time: 7 rounds	Duration: 20 hours
Range: 0	Affected Area: 1 Magical Creature/Item
Mana: 7	Damage: None
Save: N/A	Save Affect: N/A
Components: V, S	Concentration: N/A

Material Component: Holy symbol
Somatic Component: Rubbing of holy symbol then touching it to creature

Execution-This spell will temporarily raise a creatures maximum attainable hit-points by 20 points.

Limitations- This spell will not raise the current hit-point tally, healing spells or other magics must be used to realize the new maximum. This spell cannot be recast on the same creature for additional increases, nor it can it be combined with other magics to raise a character's maximum hit-points.

Erratta – Although magically induced, the affect is non-magical and cannot be dispelled or ended by the use of command words.

Aftermath – After the spell is cast, the affect will begin to erode until the affect is goneat The character's

Cleric/6 - **Speak With Monsters (Alteration)**

Level: 6	Components: V, S
Range: 3" radius	Casting Time: 9segments
Duration: I round/level	Saving Throw: None

Explanation/Description: When cast, the speak with monsters spell allows the cleric to converse with any type of creature which has any form of communicative ability. That is, the monster will understand the intent of what is said to it by the cleric. The creature or creatures thus spoken to will be checked by your **referee** in order to determine reaction. All creatures of the same type as that chosen by the cleric to speak to can likewise understand if they are within range. The spell lasts for 1 melee round per level of experience of the cleric casting it, and during its duration conversation can take place as the monster is able and desires.

Cleric/6 - **Stone Tell (Divination)**

Level: 6	Components: V, S, M
Range: Touch	Costing Time: 7 turn
Duration: 7 turn	Soving Throw: None
Area of Effect: One cubic yard of stone	

Affect - When the cleric casts a stone tell upon an area, the very stones will speak and relate to the caster who or what has touched them as well as telling what is covered, concealed, or simply behind the place they are. The stones will relate complete descriptions as required. The material components for this spell are a drop of mercury and a bit of clay.

Cleric/6 - **Word Of Recall (Alteration)**

Level: 6	Components: V
Range: 0	Casting Time: ? segment
Duration: Special	Saving Throw: None
Area of Effect: Special	

Explanation/Description: The word of recall spell takes the cleric instantly back to his or her sanctuary when the word is uttered. The sanctuary must be specifically designated in advance by the cleric. It must be a well known place, but it can be any distance from the cleric, above or below ground. Transportation by the word of recall spell is infallibly safe. The cleric is able to transport, in addition to himself or herself, 250 gold pieces weight cumulative per level of experience. Thus, a 15th level cleric could transport his or her person and 3,750 (375 pounds) gold pieces weight in addition; this extra matter can be equipment, treasure, or living material such as another person.

Cleric/7 – **Destroy Continual Magic**

Class: Cleric	Level: 7
Cast Time: 7 rounds	Duration: Permanent
Range: 0	Affected Area: 1 Magical Creature/Item
Mana: 7	Damage: Avoids for 1 Round
Save: Dexterity	Save Affect: N/A
Components: V, S	Concentration: N/A

Material Component: Item or creature
Somatic Component: Rubbing of holy symbol then touching magical item/creature

Affect - This spell will completely destroy all magical enchantments and continual magics on one creature or item.

Limitation - The spell will not affect magics that are affecting an area which the creature or objects happens to be in. For example, using the spell on a magical item that is inside a magically silenced room will not dispel the magics causing the silence.

Erratta - The spell will not destroy or change the appearance of the item or creature, only render it magically inert. A magical creatures will be immediately rendered lifeless. It should be noted that there are creatures in the game that are creted by magics that are not magical creatures. Some creatures with natural, supernatural, undead, and even extra-planar life forces can be create with magics, but are not affected by this spell.

Cleric/7 - **Holy Word**

Class: Cleric	Level: 7
Cast Time: 7 Rounds	Duration: 1 Day/level (non-magical)
Range: Touch	Affected Area: N/A
Mana: 7	Damage: None
Save: Dexterity	Save Affect: Avoids for 1 Round
Components: V, S, M	Concentration: None

Material Component: Holy symbol
Somatic Component: Touching of holy symbol to creature

Affect - This spell will drive off extra-planar creatures of a diametrically opposite alignment, forcing them to return to their own plane of existence.

Limitations - The caster is unable to use the spell on a creature that does not have an opposing alignment. A good aligned spell caster can affect all three evil alignments (chaotic, neutral, evil) while an evil aligned spell caster can affect all good alignements. A lawful can affect all chaotics (good, neutral, evil), while a chaotic can affect all lawfuls. Neutral-neautral aligned spell casters cannot make effective use of this spell.

Aftermath - The spell does not have a magical duration that can be dispelled or ended with a command word. An extra-planar creature that is banished in this way will be unable to re-enter the prime material plane for 1 day for each experience level of the spell caster.

Cleric/7 – Miracle

Class: Cleric	Level: 7
Cast Time: 7 turns	Duration: Varies
Range: Varies	Affected Area: Varies
Mana: 70	Damage: Varies
Save: Varies	Save Affect: Varies
Components: V, S, H	Concentration: Varies

Material Component: Item or creature
Somatic Component: Rubbing of holy symbol then touching magical item/creature

Affect - This spell can be used to beseech a patron diety for spell like affect.

Limitations - The frequent or fivilous use of this spell is likely to be frowned upon by a diety. The precentle odds of the spell having any affect are equal to the caster's modified wisdom score.

Erratta - Adjudication of this spell is largely a judgement call on the part of the refee since it's uses can be so varied. As a rule of thumb, it can be used to produce magics roughly equivalent in game affect as nearly any 6th level spell or lower. This spell differs greatly from a wish in that it is less powerful (being 7th leve instead of 9th) but is not as easily comfounded by the "path of least resistance" stipulation that applies to wishes. This spell is interpreted by the deity based more on intent of the caster then exact wording of the request. If the spell caster's request exceeds the magic capacity of the spell, usually a lesser, toned result will be obtained instead.

Cleric/7 - Restortion

Class: Cleric	Level: 7
Cast Time: 7 Rounds	Duration: 1 Day/level (non-magical)
Range: Touch	Affected Area: N/A
Mana: 7	Damage: None
Save: Dexterity	Save Affect: Avoids for 1 Round
Components: V, S, M	Concentration: None

Material Component: Holy symbol
Somatic Component: Touching of holy symbol to creature

Affect - This spell will restore experience points which have been drained away.

Limitaions - The spell will only restore the creature to the experince points that were had when the loss took place, and will not add points lost to the current tally. (See Experience loss/restoreation for more information.

Cleric/7 - Resurrection

Class: Cleric	Level: 7
Cast Time: 7 Rounds	Duration: 1 Day/level (non-magical)
Range: Touch	Affected Area: N/A
Mana: 7	Damage: None
Save: Dexterity	Save Affect: Avoids for 1 Round

Components: V, S, M	Concentration: None

Material Component: Holy symbol
Somatic Component: Touching of holy symbol to creature

Affect - This spell will The cleric employing this spell is able to restore life and complete strength to the person he/she bestows the resurrection upon. The person can have been dead up to 10 years cumulative per level of the cleric casting the spell, i.e. a 19th level cleric can resurrect the bones of a person dead up to 190 years. See raise dead for limitations on what persons can be raised. The reverse, destruction, causes the victim of the spell to be instantly dead and turned to dust. Destruction requires a touch, either in combat or otherwise. The material components of the spell are the cleric's religious symbol and holy/unholy water. Employment of this spell makes it impossible for the cleric to cast further spells or engage in combat until he or she has had one day of bed rest for each level of

experience of the person brought back to life or destroyed.

Cleric/7 - Symbol

Level: 7	Components: V, S, M
Range: Touch	Costing Time: 3
segments	
Duration: 1 turn/level	Saving Throw: Neg.
Area of Effect: Special	

Explanation/Description: The cleric costing this spell inscribes a symbol in the air or upon any surface, according to his or her wish. The symbol glows for 1 turn for each level of experience of the cleric casting it. The particular symbol used can be selected by the cleric at the time of casting, selection being limited to:

HOPELESSNESS - Creatures seeing it must turn back in de ection and/or surrender to capture or attack unless they save versus magic. Its effects last for 3 to 12 turns.

PAIN - Creatures affected suffer -4 on "to hit" dice and -2 on dexterity ability score due to wracking pains. The effects last for 2-20 turns.

PERSUASION - Creatures seeing the symbol become of the some alignment as and friendly to the cleric who scribed the symbol for from 1 to 20 turns unless a saving throw versus magic is made.

The material components of this spell are mercury and phosphorus. (cf. eighth level magic-user symbol spell.)

Cleric/7 - Wind Walk (Mass gasous form)

Class: Cleric	Level: 7
Cast Time: 7 Rounds	Duration: 1 Mintue/Level
Range: 0	Affected Area: 15'
Mana: 7	Damage: None
Save: Dexterity	Save Affect: Leaves affected area
Components: V, S, M	Concentration: None

Material Component: Holy symbol
Somatic Component: Touching of holy symbol to creature

Affect - This spell will transform all creatures and items in a 15' radius into a large singular billowing green gas

Creatures - While in gaseous form, a creatureis able to float in any direction horizontally or vertically at a rate of 30 yards per round (1/10 mile per minute/6 miles per hour) relative to the surrounding air. The subject will be able to control their form so as to leak through small cracks or openings. Affected creatures will have multi-directional "vision" due to being able to sense the light that is passing through their gaseous body. The subject will able to "hear" by sensing the vibrations of in the air. The subject can speak, but only in a hollow, whipery voice. Subjects will not be able to cast spells while in gaseous from since the voice will be distorted and not effective for magical use, nor will the subject have hands for somatic gestures or materials for components

Erratta - Heavy winds over 5 miles per hour can move the cloud about, but will not cause it to disperse.

Aftermath - At any time during the duration the caster can rematerialize from the cloud, then can select when and in what order the other creatures and items are materialized. When the spell exhausts its duration or the enchantment is magically dispelled, the object or creature will solidify. If the creature or item is in the air, it will fall to the earth and suffer fall damage, the anount depending on the height of the fall. See Game-standards-non-magical/falling

Druid Spells

Druidic spells deal in the use and manipulation of the elements and natural objects and forces.

Druid/1 - Enchanted Flame

Class: Druid	Level: 1
Cast Time: 1 Second	Duration: 1 hour/level
Range: 15' + 10'/level	Affected Area: 6" surface area
Mana: 1	Damage: 1D6
Save: Dexterity	Save Affect: ½ damage
Components: V, S, M	Concentration: None

Material Comp: Bit of sulphur
Somatic Comp: Snap of fingers

Execution - The spell will cause any non-living, non-magical surface to erupt in to flame.

Affect - The flame created will be roughly the same size and intensity as a normal torch flame. It will produce the same heat and can be used to ignite other combustibles. The enchanted flame cannot be extinguished by being blown out, doused, or smothered, however any other fires that it is used to start are subject to those adversarial conditions.

If the spells is cast on item that is in direct contact with the flesh of a creature it will cause 1D6 hit-points of burn damage every turn that it remains in contact with the creatures skin. (Dexterity saving throw ½ damage)

Aftermath - The flame from the spell will be immediately extinguished if the enchantment is dispelled or the caster speaks the command word calling for the spell to end. After the spell exhausts its duration, the flame will begin to shrink and, voer the course of 1 round (10 seconds) go out completely if burnable fuels are not added. If the fire is fed after the spell has ended, it will be considered to be a normal fire with no magical natures.

Druid/1 - Enchanted Light

Class: Cleric	Level: 1
Cast Time: 1 Second	Duration: N/A
Range: Touch	Affected Area: 1 Creature
Mana: 1	Damage: 1D8 Death
Save: Dexterity	Save Affect: Avoids for 1 Round
Components: V, S	Concentration: N/A

Material component: None
Somatic component: Snap of fingers

Execution - The spell can be cast into the air (where it will remain motionless) or on an object (in order to be moved about).

Affect - When this spell is cast, it creates a small, brilliantly glowing 2" sphere that will effectively light a surrounding 15' radius. Although different in appearance, a light sphere gives off roughly the same amount of light as a bright torch.

So long as the spell is in range, the caster may control the intensity of the light. By speaking command words, the caster can call upon the light to go black, brighten to full intensity, or any shade in between.

A light sphere give off no heat and consumes no oxygen. It cannot be blown out, doused, or extinguished by normal means. A light sphere has no physical mass of its own. It cannot be touched. If the spell is cast on an object and the object is cracked or broken, the light will be immediately extinguished.

Likewise, if the enchantment is dispelled, the light will immediately go dark.

Limitations - A light spell cannot be cast onto living tissue of magical objects or creatures. The spell might, however, be cast onto the clothing or something carried by a living or magical creature. Lkiewise, the spell may be cast on a container for a magical item, or an a non-magical object attached to the magical item.

Aftermath - After the spell exhasts its duration, the light will begin to dim. Over the course of one round (10 seconds) the light will continue to darken until it is completely extinguished.

Druid/1 - Enchanted Spring

Class: Druid	Level 1
Cast Time: 10 minutes	Duration: 1 Turn/Level
Range: Touch	Affected Area: 1" spot
Mana: 1	Damage: N/A
Save: N/A	Save Affect: N/A
Components: V, S	Concentration: None

Material Comp: None
Somatic Comp: Touching the ground with extended finger

Execution - The druid will conclude the casting of the spell by touching the ground. This will cause a small spring of water to erupt from the enchanted area. The water will be a ½ stream under light pressure that will cause the water to geyser up and make a 1 foot arc before falling back to the ground.

Affect - The water will be pure and drinkable and can be drank from the spring, or caught in a container.

Aftermath - The water, once created, is for all intents and purposes, normal water. Ending of the enchantment will not cause the spring to stop creating water, but will not cause the water that already exists to vanish

Druid/1 - Entanglement

Class: Druid	Level 1
Cast Time: 1 Round	Duration: 1 Turn/Level
Range: Touch	Affected Area: 1" spot
Mana: 1	Damage: None
Save: Dexterity/Strength	Save Affect: Avoids/Escapes
Components: V, S	Concentration: None

Material Comp: None
Somatic Comp: Waving the fingers of one hand in the air whle pointing to the spells intended point of origin with the other.

Execution - The spell will cause an immediate growth spurt in any sort of grasses or vegetation.

Affect - The affected vegeatation will grow into vine-like stands with clinging tendrils that will rise up and ensnare persons standing in the affected area. Creaures that attempt to dive away are permitted a dexterity saving throw. Without a successful save, the victims will be unable to attack, flee, or cast spells, or use magical items that with an activation requiring concentration.

Aftermath - Once a creature is ensnared, they are permitted a strength saving throw in an attempt to break free. The spell is simple in nature and cannot be worked so that it will only capture the druid's enemies. Any creatures that enter the affected area (except for the spell caster) will be ensnared. The druid will not be able to choose and release particular victims without ending the enchantment and releasing all victims.

Druid/1 – Grow Plant of healing

Class: Druid	Level 1
Cast Time: 10 minutes	Duration: N/A
Range: Touch	Affected Area: 15' Radius
Mana: 1	Damage: 2D8

Save: None	Save Affect: N/A
Components: V, S, M	Concentration: N/A

Material Comp: Leaf and handful of soil
Somatic Comp: Mounding of soil and placing stem of leaf in soil

Execution - As the druid casts the spell, the plant will grow, bear 1-4 pieces of fruit, then wither away.

Affect - The fruit will be smooth skinned, purple (resembling an eggplant) and will be approxiamately the size of a lemon. Any natural creature who eats the fruit will receive sustenance equal to a normal sized human meal and the medicinal properties will heal 1-8 Hit-points of damage.

Aftermath - Once the spell casting is complete, the fruit itself retains no magical nature. The fruit will keep at room temperature for 3 days (5 days in stored at less then 60 degree). After the fruit gets old, it will lose its healing properties. If the fruit is frozen or smashed, it expires immediately.

Druid/1 - Pass Without Trace

Class: Druid	Level: 1
Cast Time: 1 Second	Duration: 1 hour/level
Range: Touch	Affected Area: 1 Creature/Level
Mana: 1	Damage: N/A
Save: N/A	Save Affect: N/A
Components: V, S	Concentration: None

Material Component - Leaf ashes
Somatic Component - Sprinkling of ash on feet of subjects

Execution - The spell will prevent affected creatures from leaving any discernable trail.

Affect - When this spell is cast, the recipient can move through any type of terrain - mud, snow, dust, etc. - and leave neither footprint nor scent. Thus, tracking a person or other creature covered by this enchantmen is impossible.

Aftermath - The trail (or lack of trail) has no magical properties. The dweomer on the feet of the subjects remains enchanted until it exhausts its duration, is dispels, or the caster speaks the command word calling for the affect to end.

Druid/1 - Slow Poison

Class: Druid	Level: 1
Cast Time: 1 Second	Duration: 1 hour/level
Range: Touch	Affected Area: 1 Creature
Mana: 1	Damage: N/A
Save: N/A	Save Affect: N/A
Components: V, S	Concentration: None

Material Component - None
Somatic Component - Touching of subject

Execution - By casting this spell, the caster is able to slow the onset of a poisons affect on a subject's body.

Affect - The spell will not detoxify the poison or reverse any ill affects that have already taken place. The onset time and duration of the poison will be slowed by a factor of 60. The poisons affects that would normally occur in a 1 round (10 second) time frame will instead occur in a 1 turn (10 minute) time frame. This generally allows ample time for administering of healing magics or anti-venoms/anidotes (if available).

Aftermath - If the enchantment is ended or dispelled, or the spells duration is exhausted, the affects will immediately resume their normal rate of pregression.

Druid/1 - Water Breathing

Class: Druid	Level: 1 - Necromancy
Cast Time: 1 Second	Duration: 1 hour/level
Range: Touch	Affected Area: 1 Creature
Mana: 1	Damage: None
Save: N/A	Save Affect: N/A
Components: V, S, M	Concentration: N/A

Material component - Fish gill
Somatic component - Placing of gill on neck of subject

Execution - When this spell is cast, the fish gill that is used as the material component will grow into place and begin to function. The gill will grow to a size proportional for the subject's body, and an identical gill will grow on the other side of the subject's neck.

Affect - The gill will function as a normal fishes gill, pulling tiny air bubbles from the water and oxygenating the blood. If the subject is breathing water that is heavily polluted, the breathing will become labored and difficult, possibly forcing the subject to periodically return to the surface or move to clearer waters.

Aftermath - Once the spell is cast, the affect is non-magical in nature and cannot be magically dispelled or called to end early by use of command words. After the affect exhausts its duration, the gills will begin to lose their effectiveness and, over the course of a turn (10 minutes) will stop functioning completely and fall away from the subject's body.

Druid/1 - Water Walking

Class: Druid	Level: 1 - Necromancy
Cast Time: 1 Second	Duration: 1 hour/level
Range: Touch	Affected Area: 1 Creature
Mana: 1	Damage: 1D8 Death
Save: Dexterity	Save Affect: Avoids for 1 Round
Components: V, S	Concentration: N/A

Material component - Drop of oil
Somatic component - Rubbing of oil on bottoms of feet ir shoes.

Execution - Even though the somatic gestures of the spell involve only the touching of the feet, the affect is spread over the entire body and will the subject and all carried items to be totally repulsed by water.

Affect - The subject will be able to walk, sit, or lie upon the waters surface as if it were solid terrain. Any items that are dropped will lie on the waters surface as if dropped onto the ground. Missle weapons fired down towards the water will be deflected as if fired at solid ground. Anything picked up by the subject immediately gains the same benefit, even if held for only a moment

Weight is not a a factor in the spell, although the strength required to lift an object and hold it above the waters surface is requires the same strength as it if were carried above the ground.

Turbulent waters, or waves are difficult to walk on and may require a dexterity saving throw or ability roll to retain the subjects footing.

Aftermath - The affect is immediately ended if the enchantment is dispelled or the spell caster speaks the command word for the spell to end. After the spell exhausts its duration, the subject will begin to sink and, oever the course of 1 turn (10 mintes) the affect will be lost completely.

Druid/2 - Dragon Skin

Class: Druid	Level: 2
Cast Time: 2 Seconds	Duration: 1 round/level
Range: Touch	Affected Area: 1 Creature
Mana: 2	Damage: N/A
Save: N/A	Save Affect: N/A
Components: V, S, M	Concentration: N/A

Material Component: Bit of Dragon leather

Somatic Component: Rubbing leather onto subject's skin

Dragon Skin Bonus to Armor Class

| | | Level | Dragon Leather |
			Armor Class Bonus
1	Yellow, Violet, Orange		+1
2-3	Red, Green, Blue		+2
4-6	White		+3

Execute - The spell is used to make the subject's skin more string and less vulnerable to damage, thereby improving the character's armor class.

Affect - The amount of protection available depends on the experience level of the caster. The color and texture of the subject's skin will not change, nor will the feel or sensitivity.

Aftermath - After the spell is cast, the affect is physiological and cannot be magically dispelled or ended early by command words.

Druid/2 – Fire Touch

Class: Druid	Level 2
Cast Time: 1 Second	Duration: N/A
Range: 15' + 10'/level	Affected Area: 15' Radius
Mana: 1	Damage: 1D6 to 10D6
Save: Dexterity	Save Affect: N/A
Components: V, S, M	Concentration: N/A
Somatic Comp: Crumbling sulfur in palm, then touching	
Material Comp: Bit of sulfur	

Execution - After casting this spell, the touch of the spell caster will cause an area of the subject's body to burst into flames.

Affect - The flames will cause 1D6 points of energy damage for each level of experience of the caster, up to a mximum of 10D6.

Level	Fire Damage
1	1D6 Hit-points
2	2D6 Hit-points
3	3D6 Hit-points
4	4D6 Hit-points
5	5D6 Hit-points
6	6D6 Hit-points
7	7D6 Hit-points
8	8D6 Hit-points
9	9D6 Hit-points
10-	10D6 Hit-points

Druid/2 – Fly

Class: Druid	Level 2
Cast Time: 2 Seconds	Duration: 1 hour/level
Range: Touch	Affected Area: 1 Creature
Mana: 2	Damage: N/A
Save: N/A	Save Affect: N/A
Components: V	Concentration: N/A
Material component: Feather	
Somatic Component: Sticking quill into back of subject	

Execute - When this spell is cast, when the quill of a feather is stuck into the bare skin of a subject it will divide and grow into a proportional pair wings.

Affect - The wings will be capable of lifting the subject off the ground and flying them about.

Limitations - Unless a specific duration is stated at the start of the spell, the referee will assume that the spell is cast to run for maximum duration. Cutting away the wings prematurely will cause

2-40 (2D20) hit-points of damage to the subject. Flying is difficult to learn and can cause damage if done badly. Consult the section of flying for more information.

Aftermath - When the spell exhausts its duration the wings will start to shrink and lose strength, forcing the subject to land. After one round (10 seconds) the wings will wither and fall away from the subject's body. The spells affect is physiological and cannot be magically dispelled and cannot be ended by a command word from the caster.

Druid/2 – Shape Wood

Class: Druid	Level 2
Cast Time: 1 Second	Duration: N/A
Range: 15' + 10'/level	Affected Area: 15' Radius
Mana: 1	Damage: 1D6 to 10D6
Save: Dexterity	Save Affect: N/A
Components: V, S, M	Concentration: N/A
Somatic Comp: Crumbling sulfur in palm, then touching	
Material Comp: Bit of sulfur	

Execution - The casting of this spell will make wood soft and plyable in the spell casters hands.

Affect - The spell will allow the druid to shape wood in any form desired.

Aftermath - While the spells duration is in affect the caster can shape the wood, cause it to solidify, then soften again as many times as is desired. When the spell exhausts its duration, the wood begin to harden. By the end of one turn, the affected wood will be entirely hardened

Druid/3 – Minor Morph

Class: Druid	Level 2
Cast Time: 1 Second	Duration: 1 turn (10 minutes)/level
Range: 0	Affected Area: self
Mana: 4	Damage: 1D6 to 10D6
Save: N/A	Save Affect: N/A
Components: V, S. M	Concentration: N/A
Material Comp: Bit of chameleon skin	
Somatic Comp: Rubbing the chameleon skin on flesh	

Execution - This spell will allow the druid to assume the form of any creature they have touched personally.

Affect - The spell will allow the druid to assume the shape of any natural creature of any size up to twice the caster's body weight or as small as ½ the casters body weight. The caster's body will take on the strength, dexterity, and comeliness of the duplilcated creature, however the caster's constitution and number of hit-points will remain the same. Any specialized glands such as those that would produce venoms, webbings, etc will not be reproduced. The characters clothing and any carried items will be transformed into part of the new bodyAny of the

Aftermath - When

Druid/3 – Tree Pass

Class: Druid	Level 2
Cast Time: 2 Seconds	Duration: 1 hour/level
Range: Touch	Affected Area: 1 Creature
Mana: 2	Damage: N/A

Save: N/A   Save Affect: N/A
Components: V   Concentration: N/A
Material component: Tree
Somatic Component: Placing palm flat against a tree trunk
Execute - When this spell is cast, when the quill of a feather is stuck into the bare skin of a subject it will divide and grow into a proportional pair wings.

Druid/4 – Flame Strike

Class: Cleric   Level: 4
Cast Time: 1 Second   Duration: N/A
Range: Touch   Affected Area: 1 Creature
Mana: 1   Damage: 1D6/4 Levels
Save: Dexterity   Save Affect: Avoids for 1 Round
Components: V, S   Concentration: N/A
Material Component: Bit of sulphur
Somatic Component: Tossing of sulphur

Flame Strike Damage

Level	Fire Damage
1-4	1D6 Hit-points
5-8	2D6 Hit-points
9-12	3D6 Hit-points
13-16	4D6 Hit-points
17-20	5D6 Hit-points
21-	6D6 Hit-points

rough ground

Druid/7 – Entangled Forrest

Class: Cleric
Level: 4
Cast Time: 1 Second
Duration: N/A
Range: Touch
Affected Area: 1 Creature
Mana: 1
Damage: 1D6/4 Levels
Save: Dexterity
Save Affect: Avoids for 1 Round
Components: V, S
Concentration: N/A
Material Component: Bit of sulphur
Somatic Component: Tossing of sulphur

Mage Spells

Mage/1A - Affect Fires

Mage/Alteration	Level: 1
Cast Time: 1 Second	Duration: 1 round/level
Range: 15' + 10'/level	Affected Area: 30' diameter
Mana: 1	Damage: None
Save: None	Save Affect: N/A
Components: V, S, M	Concentration: None
Material Comp: Fire	
Somatic Comp: Rubbing of fingers together	

Execution - This spell enables the caster to control the size, brightness, heat, and intensity of fire.

Affect - The spell can reduce the fire from the size of a lit match to the 30' diameter bonfire, or any size in between, or snuff the fire out.

Limitations - The size, heat and brightness of the fire must be always be consistent with each other. A match size fire cannot be made to produce the brightness and heat of a bonfire. Likewise, a bonfire cannot be created without the heat and brilliance that accompany it. The spell caster can only control the flames in the area of affect, and not flames caused from fires that have been started and moved outside the area of affect.

Adjustments - While the caster is in range of the spells poit of origing, the caster can speak command words to change the size of the fire after the spell casting is completed.

Aftermath - The enchantment is ended if the fire is extinguished either by command words from of the spell caster or by normal means. When the spell exhausts its duration, all fires will return to their normal composure based on normal factors such as availability of air, fuel, etc.

Mage/1A - Amplify

Mage/Alteration	Level: 1
Cast Time: 1 Second	Duration: 1 Minute/Level Range: 15' + 10'/level
	Affected Area: Target creature/object
Mana: 1	Damage: None
Save: None	Save Affect: N/A
Components: V, S, M	Concentration: N/A
Material Comp: None	
Somatic Comp: Cupping the hand to mouth as if to shout	

Execution - Casting this spell will cause any sounds emanation from a single creature or object to be amplified by a factor of 10 times.

Item - If the spell is cast on an object, any sounds made by using or striking the object will be greatly amplified. Normally queit and unoticable sounds will be loud and obvious, such as the unsheating of a sowrd or the twang of a bow string, the striking of a stone against another boject, etc.

Creature - If the spell is cast upon a creature, all vocal sounds and bodily noises will be affected. A subject may still use verbal command words to cast spells and activate magical items, but the volume of the speaking voice will be very loud. Sounds such as the snap fo fingers, clap of hands, etc will all be increased in volume.

Errata - Loud noises will also be proportionaltely increased. The voice from the shout of an affected subject would be defeaning. The clash of an affected sword against a shield would be thundering. The blowing of an affected horn would be ear peircing.

Mage/1A - Enlarge/Shrink Object

Mage/Alteration	Level: 1
Cast Time: 1 Second	Duration: 1 turn (10 minutes)/level
Range: 15' + 10'/level creature/object	Affected Area: Target
Mana: 1	Damage: None
Save: None	Save Affect: N/A
Components: V, S, M	Concentration: N/A
Material Comp: Object to be enlarged	
Somatic Comp: Touching of object	

Object Size/Weight - Increase/Decrease

Caster Level	Object Size	Max Decrease	Max Increase
1	50 lbs	1/2 (-50%)	x 1½ (+50%)
2	100 pounds	1/4 (-75%)	x 2 (+100%)
3	150 pounds	1/6 (-83.5%)	x 2½ (+150%)
4	200 pounds	1/8 (-87.5%)	x 3 (+200%)
5	250 pounds	1/10 (-90%)	x 3½ (+250%)
6-	300 pounds	1/12 (-92.25%)	x 4 (+300%)

Execution - This spell will cause a touched object to instantly growing in size and weight, up to four times its normal size. If the spell is used on a fluid of gas, it has a 30' diameter affected area.

Adjustments - After the spell is cast, the caster can touch the subject again and speak the command words altering the subject agains. The change can be repeated as long as the new size is within the stated limits and the spells duration has not expired.

Limitations - The spell can be used to affect objects of natural size of up to 50 pounds per level of experience of the caster. Spells cannot be combined on a pariticular item to leap frog past the spells size limitations.

Mage/1A - Fool's Gold

Mage/Alteration	Level: 1
Cast Time: 1 Round	Duration: 1 hour/level
Range: 15' + 10'/level	Affected Area: 30' diameter
Mana: 1	Damage: None
Save: None	Save Affect: N/A
Components: V, S, M	Concentration: None
Material Comp: Fire	
Somatic Comp: Rubbing of fingers together	

Execution - This spell will temporarily convert common metals to precious metals.

Affect - The spell will affect one piece of metal or multiple pieces. If the spell is cast on a piece of metal that is larger then the area of affect, only part of the metal will be changed.

Limitations - Magical metals and extremely hard metals such as Adamanite, Mithiral, and Titanium are not affected by this spell. All affected metals will be changed to the same precious metal and can be changed only once per spell.

Adjustments - While the caster is in range of the spells poit of origing, the caster can speak command words to change the size of the fire after the spell casting is completed.

Aftermath - The enchantment is ended if an affected piece is cute, bent, severed or otherwise disrupted. The affect ends it is magically dispelled, the spell exhausts its duration, or the caster speaks the command words calling for the spell to end.

Mage/1A - Mend

Mage/Alteration	Level: 1
Cast Time: 1 Turn	Duration: N/A
Range: Touch	Affected Area: 1 object
Mana: 1	Damage: N/A
Save: N/A	Save Affect: N/A
Components: V, S, M	Concentration: N/A

Material Comp: Pieces of broken or damaged object
Somatic Comp: Fitting of pieces back together and rubbing finger tips over cracks or areas of missing parts.

Execution - This spell repairs small breaks in objects.

Affect - The spell will weld a broken ring, chain link, medallion or slender dagger, providing but one break exists. Ceramic or wooden objects with multiple breaks can be invisibly rejoined to be as strong as new. A hole in a leather sack or wineskin is completely repaied.

Limitations - If the spell is used to physically repair broken magical items but will not restore their magical nature.

Mage/1A - Purify Food and Drink

Mage/Alteration	Level: 1
Cast Time: 1 Second	Duration: N/A
Range: Touch	Affected Area: 1 pound/level
Mana: 1	Damage: N/A
Save: None	Save Affect: N/A
Components: V, S	Concentration: N/A

Material Comp: None
Somatic Comp: Clasping of hands

Execution - By invoking this spell, the caster it able purify one pound (10 gold piece weight) of food and rink per level of experience of the caster.

Affect - Any poison, spoilage, staleness, disease, parasites, impurities, or other contaminates will be completely neutralized.

Limitations - Casting the spell will reveal to the caster whether or not the food was contamintated prior to the magic. The spell will not alter the type, natural taste, or quality of preperation of the food. The spell will not warm or coll the food to any desired eating temperature

Mage/1A - Silence

Mage/Alteration	Level: 1
Cast Time: 1 Second	Duration: 1 Round/Level
Range: Touch	Affected Area: 1 Creature or object
Mana: 1	Damage: None
Save: Dexterity	Save Affect: Avoids for 1 round
Components: S	Concentration: N/A

Material Component: None
Somatic Component: Placing a finger upright against the lips, then touching the intended subject

Execution - This spell will immediately silence all emanations of sound from a creature or object.

Uses - The spell might be used to silence an alarm, cause a missle to strike without noise, stop a spell-caster from using spells with somatic components.

Mage/1C - Create Water

Mage/Conjuration	Level: 1
Cast Time: 1 Second	Duration: N/A
Range: 15'	Affected Area: 4 Gallons/Level
Mana: 1	Damage: N/A
Save: N/A	Save Affect: N/A
Components: V, S	Concentration: N/A

Material Comp: None
Somatic Comp: Squeezing of the fist as if to wring water from a cloth

Execution - Casting this spell creates water that is pure and drinkable. The water can be created inside a single open container, or create in the air to raind down on an object or creature.

Limitations - The spell cannot be used to create water inside a living creature or inside any sealed container or space.

Aftermath - Once created, the water retains no magical nature and is subject to normal adversaious conditions such as freezon, spillage, evaporation, freezing, etc.

Mage/1C - Enchanted Light

Mage/Conjuration	Level: 1
Cast Time: 1 Second	Duration: N/A
Range: 15' + 10'/level	Affected Area: 15' Radius
Mana: 1	Damage: None
Save: None	Save Affect: N/A
Components: V, S	Concentration: N/A

Material component: None
Somatic component: Snap of fingers

Execution - The spell can be cast into the air (where it will remain motionless) or on an object (in order to be moved about).

Affect - When this spell is cast, it creates a small, brilliantly glowing 2" sphere that will effectively light a surrounding 15' radius. Although different in appearance, a light sphere gives off roughly the same amount of light as a bright torch.

Adjustments - So long as the spell is in range, the caster may control the intensity of the light. By speaking command words, the caster can call upon the light to go black, brighten to full intensity, or any shade in between.

Limitations - A light spell cannot be cast onto living tissue of magical objects or creatures. The spell might, however, be cast onto the clothing or something carried by a living or magical creature. Lkiewise, the spell may be cast on a container for a magical item, or an a non-magical object attached to the magical item.

Aftermath - After the spell exhasts its duration, the light will begin to dim. Over the course of one round (10 seconds) the light will continue to darken until it is completely extinguished. If the spell is cast on an object and the object is cracked or broken, the light will be immediately extinguished. Likewise, if the enchantment is dispelled, the light will immediately go dark.

Errata - A light sphere give off no heat and consumes no oxygen. It cannot be blown out, doused, or extinguished by normal means. A light sphere has no physical mass of its own. It cannot be touched.

Mage/1C - Floating Platform

Mage/Conjuration	Level: 1
Cast Time: 1 Second	Duration: 1 turn/level
Range: 15'	Affected Area: Up to 10' x 10' square
Mana: 1	Damage: None
Save: None	Save Affect: N/A
Components: V, S	Concentration: None

Material Comp: None
Somatic Comp: Holding on hand flat open horizontally while making a swirling motion over it with the extended finger of the other hand

Execution - This spell create a horizontal wall of force that can be used as a platform or to carry items, or injured persons.

Affect - The platform is a flat opaque white in color and is always square or rectangular in shape. It is strictly 2-dimensional and does not have a thickness. It is solid to the touch, and any object or creature falling on it from the height will have the fall adjudicated as if the the surface were solid stone.

Limitations - The platform supports a weight of 100 pounds (1000 gold piece weight) plus and additional 10 pounds (100 gpw) per level of the spell caster. If the weight limit of the platform is exceeded it will lower to the ground and remain until the load is lightened or the spell ends.

Adjustments - The spell is cast and controlled thereafter by command words to be a set to any size diameter up to 10' diameter, or to adjust size depending on available space. Also, it can be commanded to hover at a certain height from just off the ground, up to 10' off the ground, or it can be commanded to automatically adjust height to avoid object or accommodate overhead clearance. The platform can be commanded to remain stationary, or to follow the spell caster at specified distance up to 15' away.

Aftermath - The platform will not be dispelled if the caster is away, however, it cannot be controlled by the spell caster's command words unless the caster is withing range. The spell will remain in affect until the caster speaks the command words for the spell to end, the enchantment is dispelled, or the spell exhausts its duration. When the spells duration has been exhausted, the platform will lower to the ground and dissolve.

Mage/1C - Smoke Cloud

Mage/Conjuration	Level: 1
Cast Time: 1 Second	Duration: 1 round/level
Range: 15' + 10' level	Affected Area: 30' diameter cloud
Mana: 1	Damage: None
Save: None	Save Affect: N/A
Components: V, S, M	Concentration: Low

Material Comp: Pinch of ash
Somatic Comp: Holding the ash between the fingers and binging it to the mouth, then blowing it towards the intended point of origin
Execution - This spell will create a billowing cloud of white smoke
Description - The cloud is extremely opaque and can be cast to be a flat white, black, or any shade of gray in between. Even creatures on the very edges cannot see or be seen from the outside.
Affect - All creatures inside the cloud will be unable to see so long as they remain inside. Creatures leaving the cloud must make a dexterity saving throw. A successful roll indicate the cloud was exited. A failed dexterity saving throw indicates the creature has stumble and taken 1D4 damage the referee may adjust higher for large creatures). While a creature is inside the cloud all rolls-to-hit are at a -4 penalty due to lack of visual contact with the target.
Adjustments - The cloud can be moved about at 6 mph (30ypr), relative to the surrounding air, so long as it remains within the spells range from the spell caster.
Limitations - Once the cloud is created, the color can not be changed. The cloud will be roughly sphereical in shape, and cannot be made to form special shapes. Breathing the clouds vapors has no detrimental affects. If the spells range is exceeded the cloud will disperse and the spell will be ended. Maintaing the enchantment requires low concentration. If the caster attempts a new spell, activates a magical item, or is wounded, the spell is destroyed.
Aftermath - When the spell is ended the cloud will disperse and dissapear.

Mage/1D - Comprehend

Mage/Divination	Level: 1
Cast Time: 1 Second	Duration: 1 Round/level
Range: 0	Affected Area: Self
Mana: 1	Damage: None
Save: None	Save Affect: N/A
Components: S	Concentration: N/A

Material Comp: N/A
Somatic Comp: Placing a hand to an ear as if to hear better
Execution - This spell will enable the caster to understand the speech or utterances of a single creature.
Limitaions - The enchantment will not endow the spell caster with the ability to speak, read, write, nor even comprehend any particular language. Any sort of communicatin with the affected creature will bo one way. The caster will not be able to comprehend other creature speaking the same langue/
Uses - The spell is often used to eavesdrop on other creatures.

Mage/1D - Detect Creature

Mage/Divination	Level:1
Cast Time: 1 Second	Duration: N/A
Range: 15' + 10'/level	Affected Area: 15' Radius
Mana: 1	Damage: None
Save: None	Save Affect: N/A
Components: S	Concentration: N/A

Material Comp: N/A
Somatic Comp: Placing a hand to an ear as if to hear better
Execution - This spell will cause all creatures within the affected area to become obvious to the spell caster.
Affect - Even invisible creatures will be obvious to the user and the caster may strike them normally or target a spell or magical item. The spell will reveal the number, class (natural, super-natural, plant, undead, magical, or extra-planar), and the location of the creatures
Limitaions - The spell will only reveal the number, general class (natural, super-natural, plant, undead, magical, or extra-planar), and the location of the creatures. It will not reveal the appeance, size, powers of a creature, The spell will not detect if a creature is disguised or magically transformed in some way, or acting under the influence of a spell.
Uses - The spell is affected means of discovery if there are creatures hiding in wait, or invisible, waiting to attack.

Mage/1D - Detect Magic

Mage/Divination	Level:1
Cast Time: 1 Second	Duration: N/A
Range: 15' + 10'/level	Affected Area: 15' Radius
Mana: 1	Damage: None
Save: None	Save Affect: N/A
Components: S	Concentration: N/A

Material comp: None
Somatic Comp: A sweeping horizontal seeping motion of the arm
Execution - this spell will cause all magical items, magical creatures, and any other continual magics in the affected area to begin to visibly glow.
Affect - The brightness of the glow will give the spell caster a relative idea of the power of the magic. Aritfacts and relics will make a brief, brilliant flash, then return to normal.
Limitaions - Enchantments are not affected. The spell will not reveal what sort of continual magics are present, how they can be

used, or whether they are cursed, mechanically trapped, or magially protected.

Aftermath - The enchantment is ended when the spell exhausts its duration, the caster speaks the command words calling for the spell to end, or the enchantment is dispelled.

Mage/1D – Identify

Mage/Divination	Level: 1
Cast Time: 1 Segment	Duration: N/A
Range: Touch	Affected Area: One object
Mana: 1	Damage: None
Save: N/A	Save Affect: N/A
Components: V, S	Concentration: N/A

Material comp: Item to be identified
Somatic Comp: Holding, wielding, using, reading, or tasting the item as normal for the items usage.

Execution - This spell will enable the caster to have a percentile chance equal to their modified intelligence score of learning the most basic uses and the steps necessary to activate a magical item.

Requirements - To cast the spell , the item must be held or worn as would be normal for the items use. A belt or girdle must be fastened about the waist, gloves must be placed on the hands, a cloak draped over the shoulders, a potion tasted, a handweapon wielded, etc. Any consequences brought about by use of the itme fall on the spell caster in fill measure.

Limitations - The percentile roll from the first casting of the spell on a particular item is all inclusive. If the roll is missed the caster will not receive a new roll if the spell is cast again on the same item (although a different spell caster might get better results).

The spell will not reveal detailed information about an item such as; the number of remaining charges, the damage it causes, the range, etc.

Mage/1E – Enchanted Lock

Mage/Enchantment	Level: 1
Cast Time: 1 segment	Duration: 1 day/level
Range: Touch	Affected Area: 30'/level
Mana: 1	Damage: N/A
Save: N/A	Save Affect: N/A
Components: V, S	Concentration: None

Material Component: None
Somatic Component: Twisting motion of wrist

Execution - Casting this spell will freeze into place any non-living and non-magical obstruction to a portal or doorway.

Affect - The obstruction can be a boulder over a cave entrance, a curtain over a window, a cork in a bottle, etc. The spell will affect any size portal up to 30 feet in diameter. Affected objects will remain locked in place until the spell caster speaks a command word calling for the spell to end, the object is destroyed, or the spell is boken by magicall dispelling.

Limitations - The spell will not proctect the obstructing item from being destroyed by normal means. A woood door can be burned, a glass window can be shattered, a bottle can be broen, etc. A wizard lock will not prevent entering or exiting by other openings. If the door on a cottage is wizard locked, entrance might still be gained via a window or the chimney.

Adjustments - The spell caster can temporarily deactivate the spell by speaking the command words to suspend the spell, then later speaking the command words to reinstate it

Mage/1E – Enchanted Mouth

Mage/Enchantment	Level: 1
Cast Time: 1 Turn	Duration: 1 Day/level
Range: Touch	Affected Area: 1 Object
Mana: 1	Damage: N/A
Save: None	Save Affect: N/A
Components: V, S	Concentration: None

Material Comp: None
Somatic Comp: Cupping the hands around the mouth and speaking toward the targeted object.

Execution - This spell causes a inanimate object to deliver a prescribed message or saying.

Affect - The message can be in any language that the spell caster can speak. If cast on a statue or painting, the mouth of the face will move in time with the speaking of the words. The spell caster can speak the message or have a comrade speak it. The volume of the playback of the message can be raised up to 4 times the loudness of when the message was spoken. The message can be up to one round (10 seconds) in length for each level of expience of the spell caster.

Activation - The spell can be set to go off when touched, or if a creature passes within a certain distance of the enchanted object. The spell can be set to be activated by a certain creature class (natural, plant,super-natural,undead,extra-planar), or by anyone except the spell caster.

Limitations - The enchantment will not facilitate the use of an unknown language nor even a particular dialect or drawl. The tonal qualities of the voice will remain the same (aside for the ability to increase the volume). Only one message may be recorded, and an object can only be affect by one enchanted mouth spell. This spell can not be used on creatures or magical items. The mouth cannot be used to cast a spell even if it has only verbal components.

Adjustments - After the spell is cast, if in range of the affected object, the caster may speak the command words to change the message, change the activation, or call for the spell to end.

Aftermath - The spell is ended when the caster speaks the command words calling for the spell to end, the

Mage/1E – Enchanted Stone

Mage/Enchantment	Level: 1
Cast Time: 1 round	Duration: N/A
Range: 120 yards	Affected Area: One small stone
Mana: 1	Damage: 2D6
Save: Dexterity	Save Affect: Misses
Components: V, S	Concentration: N/A

Material Comp: Stone
Somatic Comp: Closing fist around stone, then throwing at intended target.

Execution - When this spell is cast, the caster is able to pick up and throw a stone and strike without fail to do an abnormal amount (2D6) of bludgeon damage.

Affect - The stone will strike, without fail the target and deliver the damage.

Limitations - The must be small enough to be held in the spell caster's hand. The stone will not dodge obstrustions or go around corners (other then the dropping arc as occurs with a normal throw). The spell caster must have a normal trajectory for the stoen.

Erratta - The magical nature of the stone is ended the moment the stone leaves the caster's hand. The spell only serves to set the velolcity and the direction fo the stones travel and does not have a riesidual magical affect.

Mage/1E - Feather Fall

Mage/Enchantment	Level: 1
Cast Time: 1 Segment	Duration: 1 Round/level
Range: 15' + 10'/level	Affected Area: 500 pounds/level
Mana: 1	Damage: N/A
Save: None	Save Affect: N/A
Components: V	Concentration: Low
Material Comp: None	
Somatic Comp: None	

Execution - This spell will slow the descent of falling objects or creatures to a slow 1 foot per second (10 feet per round).

Limitations - The enchantment will not later the subjects actual mass. A person trying to catch a slowly falling boulder will have to get out from under or be crushed beneath its weight.

Errata - The spell will affect any sort of movement, but will not change the subjects inertia. A boulder fired from a catapult will be slowed to 10 feet/round but it travel the same distance and cause as much damage when it arrives. It is possible for other objects or creatures to ride on the affected subject so long as the combined weight does not exceed the spells maximum.

Aftermath - When the spell exhausts its duration or the caster speaks the command words causing the spell to end, the object will resume its normal rate of falling (movement).

Mage/1I - Babble

Type: Illusion	Alteration: Level 1
Cast Time: 1 Second	Duration: 1 Round/Level
Range: 15' + 10'/level	Affected Area: Target creature
Mana: 1	Damage: None
Save: None	Save Affect: N/A
Components: V, S, M	Concentration: N/A
Material Comp: Piece of cotton	
Somatic Comp: Twisting the hand back and forth in the air	

Execution - This spell causes the subject's speech to become an unintelligible gibberish to all but the caster.

Affect - The spell does not actually change the words spoke, but only serves to make them incomprehensible.

Limitations - The caster may understand the subjects speech only if within hearing distance and the subject is speaking in a language know to the caster. The spell does not hinder the subject from speaking verbal components to a spell or the command words to a magical item.

Uses - A caster might use the spell on enemy so as to prevent communication with comrades. The spell could be used to allow a someone to give the spell caster a private message that cannot be understood or eavesdropped on.

Mage/1I - Cause Blindness

Type: Illusion	Alteration: Level 1
Cast Time: 1 Second	Duration: 1 Round/level (non-magical)
Range: 15' + 10'/level	Affected Area: 1 Creature
Mana: 1	Damage: None
Save: Charisma	Save Affect: Negates
Components: V, S, M	Concentration: N/A
Material Comp: Drop of black Ink	
Somatic Comp: Flicking of ink from tips of fingers in general direction of intended subject.	

Execution - This spell will cause a temporary mental block that causes the subject to be blinded.

Limitations - The affect will not any physical affect on the subject.

Erratta - Although magically induced, the affect is purely psychological and cannot be ended early by command words from the caster or remove by enchantment dispelling. There are mental restorative elements in the game, however, that might end the affect.

Mage/1I - Guise

Mage/ Illusion	Alteration: Level 1
Cast Time: 1 Second	Duration: 1 minute/level
Range: 0	Affected Area: 15' Radius
Mana: 1	Damage: None
Save: None	Save Affect: N/A
Components: V, S, M	Concentration: None
Material Comp: Bit of chalk dust	
Somatic Comp: Rubbing a small line of dust under each eye	

Execution - This spell will allow the caster to change the perception of their appeance to any other humanoid.

Limitations - To become an exact duplicate of a particular humanoid, the spell caster must touch the person being copied in order to orientate the spell. Otherwise, the copy will be poor and noticeably different. The spell will not duplicate any scents, languages, body English, etc. Over time even a perfect copy will draw attention as being unlike the original. Once the spell is cast and a guise is assumed, it cannot be changed into a different guise unless a new spell is cast.

Uses - If used to copy a person, the spell is best used from a distance so that differences in speech, scent, and body english are not noticeable.

Mage/1I - Itch

Mage/ Illusion	Alteration: Level 1
Cast Time: 1 Second	Duration: 1 minute/level
Range: 0	Affected Area: 15' Radius
Mana: 1	Damage: None
Save: None	Save Affect: N/A
Components: V, S, M	Concentration: None
Material Comp: Bit of chalk dust	
Somatic Comp: Rubbing a small line of dust under each eye	

Execution - This spell will allow the caster to change the perception of their appeance to any other humanoid.

Mage/I1 - Mesmeric Touch

Type: Illusion	Level 1
Cast Time: 1 Second	Duration: 1 Round/level (non-magical)
Range: Touch	Affected Area: 30'/level
Mana: 1	Damage: N/A
Save: Charisma	Save Affect: Negates
Components: V, S, M	Concentration: N/A
Material Component: Loco weed	
Somatic Component: Touching leaf o subject's flesh	

Execution - This spell will allow the caster to touch one natural humanoid creature in order to cause them to go into a stupor and be unable to take action.

Mage/1I - Sleep

Type: Illusion	Level 1
Cast Time: 1 Second	Duration: 1 round/level (non-magical)
Range: 15' + 10'/level	Affected Area: 15' Radius
Mana: 1	Damage: None
Save: Charisma	Affect: Negates

Sleep spell - Maximum creatures affected				
	|----------# Hit-points--------|			
Level	1-10	11-20	21-30	31-40
1	1	*	*	*
2	1D4	1	*	*
3	1D6	1-4	1-2	1
4	1D8	1D6	1D4	1-2
5	1D12	1D8	1D6	1D4

Components: V, S, M   Concentration: N/A

Material component: Pinch of sand

Somatic Comp: Tossing sand towards intended subjects

Execution - This spell will cause a comatose slumber to come upon one or more natural creatures.

Affect - The number of creatures that can be affected is dependent upon the hit-points of the intended subject/s. The caster must select a single creature on which to center the spell. The creature at the center of the spell will prioritize on the selected creature, affecting other creatures of the same species until all the creatures in a 15 foot radius are affected or the maximum number of creatures have been affected.

Limitations - Onlyu one species of creature can be affected. All the affected creatures are allowed an independent charisma saving throw. The stated maximum number of creatures for the spell includes those that make a successful save even though they are not affected. Affected creatures can be normally roused by slapping, shaking, dousing with water or any means that would wake a creature from a deep slumber.

Aftermath - Affected creatures will sleep for a minumum of the affects duration. The affected is non-magical and

Erratta - If thye spell is used on creatures that are weary or fatigued, they might well sleep normally for hours after the affect has exhausted its duration.

Mage/1I - Ventriloquism

Type: Illusion	Level 1
Cast Time: 1 Second	Duration: 1 Round/Level
Range: 15' + 10'/level	Affected Area: Hearing range
Mana: 1	Damage: None
Save: None	Affect: N/A
Components: V, S	Concentration: None

Material component - None

Somatic comp: Touching throat with one hand and pointing with other.

Execution - This spell will make the caster's voice originate from a different location.

Affect - This spell will cause the caster's voice to originate from a place other than the casters mouth. All speech, guttteral sounds, and other vocal noises area affected.

Limitations - The point of origin cannot be moved about, and the spell must be cast again to change the point of origin. The caster may cast a different spell with verbal components while under the influence of this spell, however, the spell range is based on the caster's location and not the location the verbal sounds are coming from. The enchantment may be turned on and off by command words. However, the command words for turning off must come from the point of origin and the verbal components and the command words to reinstate the enchantment must originate from the caster mouth.

Aftermath - The enchantment remains in affect until the spell exhausts its duration, the caster speaks the command words calling for the spell to end, or the enchantment is dispelled.

Mage/1N - Enlarge/Shrink Creature

Mage/Necromancy	Level: 1
Cast Time: 1 Second	Duration: 1 turn (10 minutes)/level
Range: Touch	Affected Area: Target creature
Mana: 1	Damage: None
Save: None	Save Affect: N/A
Components: V, S, M	Concentration: N/A

Material Comp: Object to be enlarged

Somatic Comp: Touching of object

Enlarge Creature Size/Weight increase			
Caster Level	Max Norm Object Size	Max Decrease	Max Increase
1	50 lbs	1/2 (-50%)	x 1½ (+50%)
2	100 pounds	1/4 (-75%)	x 2 (+100%)
3	150 pounds	1/6 (-83.5%)	x 2½ (+150%)
4	200 pounds	1/8 (-87.5%)	x 3 (+200%)
5	250 pounds	1/10 (-90%)	x 3½ (+250%)
6-	300 pounds	1/12 (-92.25%)	x 4 (+300%)

Execution -This spell will cause a touched creature to instantly growing in size and weight, up to four times its normal size.

Adjustments - After the spell is cast, the caster can touch the subject again and speak the command words altering the subject agains. The change can be repeated as long as the new size is within the stated limits and the spells duration has not expired.

Limitations - The spell can be used to affect creatures of natural size of up to 50 pounds per level of experience of the caster. Spells cannot be combined on a pariticular item to leap frog past the spells size limitations.

Mage/1N - Infravision

Mage/Necromancy	Level: 1
Cast Time: 1 Second	Duration: 1 turn/level (non-magical)
Range: Touch	Affected Area: 1 Creature
Mana: 1	Damage: N/A
Save: None	Save Affect: N/A
Components: V, S, M	Concentration: N/A

Material Comp: Owls eye

Somatic Comp: Clutching eye in fist and touching intended subject.

Execution - This spell will cause the caster's touch to endow a creature with infravision.

Aftermath - Although magically induced, the affects of this spell are physiological and cannot be ended by command words or enchantment dispelling. When the affect exhausts its duration the recipient's eye sight will begin to return to normal, and revert back completely in the course of one round.

Mage/1N - Jump

Mage/Necromancy	Level: 1
Cast Time: 1 Second	Duration: 1 turn/level (non-magical)
Range: Touch	Affected Area: 1 Creature
Mana: 1	Damage: N/A
Save: None	Save Affect: N/A
Components: V, S	Concentration: N/A

Material Comp: None

Somatic Comp: Touching of calve muscle

Execution - This spell will greatly increase the subject's calve muscles so as to allow the receipeint to jump long distance or run at accelerated speeds.

Affect - The recipients running speed and leaping distance will be increased by a factor of 4.

Uses - The spell might be used to outrun an enemy, leap to an otherwise unreachable ledge, etc.

Mage/1N - Resist Temperatures

Mage/Necromancy	Level: 1
Cast Time: 1 Second	Duration: 1 turn/level (non-magical)
Range: Touch	Affected Area: 1 Creature
Mana: 1	Damage: N/A
Save: None	Save Affect: N/A
Components: V, S	Concentration: N/A
Material components: Drop of oil	
Somatic components: Rubbing oil drop onto skin	

Execution - After casting this spell, the caster may touch a subject to endow them with an enchantment that affords tolerance to non-magical heat and cold.

Affect - The subject will be able to stand in a blazing fire or artic storm with the same comfort as if they were basking in normal room temperature. The spell will not protect clothing, carried items or other items that may have intolerance to adverse temperatures.

Limitations - This spell will not priotect against magical elemental attacks or breath weapons that employ fire, cold, etc. The spell will function only on natural creatures and has no affect on undead or magical creatures. Likwise, fires stoked by non-magical man-made means such as a kiln or a blast-furnace will be beyond the limits of the spells protection

Mage/1N - Water Breathing

Mage/Necromancy	Level: 1
Cast Time: 1 Second	Duration: 1 turn/level (non-magical)
Range: Touch	Affected Area: 1 Creature
Mana: 1	Damage: N/A
Save: None	Save Affect: N/A
Components: V, S	Concentration: N/A
Material component - Fish gill	
Somatic component - Placing of gill on neck of subject	

Execution - When this spell is cast, the fish gill that is used as the material component will grow into place and begin to function. The gill will grow to a size proportional for the subject's body, and an identical gill will grow on the other side of the subject's neck.

Affect - The gill will function as a normal fishes gill, pulling tiny air bubbles from the water and oxygenating the blood. If the subject is breathing water that is heavily polluted, the breathing will become labored and difficult, possibly forcing the subject to periodically return to the surface or move to clearer waters.

Aftermath - Once the spell is cast, the affect is non-magical in nature and cannot be magically dispelled or called to end early by use of command words. After the affect exhausts its duration, the gills will begin to lose their effectiveness and, over the course of a turn (10 minutes) will stop functioning completely and fall away from the subject's body.

Mage/1N - Water Walking

Mage	Level: 1 - Necromancy
Cast Time: 1 Second	Duration: 1 hour/level
Range: Touch	Affected Area: 1 Creature
Mana: 1	Damage: 1D8 Death
Save: Dexterity	Save Affect: Avoids for 1 Round
Components: V, S	Concentration: N/A
Material component - Drop of oil	

Somatic component - Rubbing of oil on bottoms of feet or shoes.

Execution - Even though the somatic gestures of the spell involve only the touching of the feet, the affect is spread over the entire body and will cause the subject and all carried items to be totally repulsed by water.

Affect - The subject will be able to walk, sit, or lie upon the waters surface as if it were solid terrain. Any items that are dropped will lie on the waters surface as if dropped onto the ground. Missle weapons fired down towards the water will be deflected as if fired at solid ground. Anything picked up by the subject immediately gains the same benefit, even if held for only a moment

Limitations - Turbulent waters, or waves are difficult to walk on and may require a dexterity saving throw or ability roll to retain the subjects footing.

Aftermath - The affect is immediately ended if the enchantment is dispelled or the spell caster speaks the command word for the spell to end. After the spell exhausts its duration, the subject will begin to sink and, oever the course of 1 turn (10 mintes) the affect will be lost completely.

Errata - Weight is not a factor in the spell, although the strength required to lift an object and hold it above the waters surface is requires the same strength as it if were carried above the ground.

Mage/1V - Combustion

Mage/Evocation	Level: 1
Cast Time: 1 Segment	Duration: 1 Second
Range: 15' + 10'/level	Affected Area: 2" target surface area
Mana: 1	Damage: 2D6
Save: None	Save Affect: N/A
Components: V, S, M	Concentration: N/A
Material Comp: Bit of sulphur	
Somatic Comp: Snap of fingers	

Execution - This spell will momentarily raise the temperature of a small surface area (2 inch diameter) to such a high degree that it will burst into flame.

Affect - The spell will cause a small, torch sized burst of flame that can cause 2D6 hit-points of fire damage when cast onto a creature.

Limitations - If the affected area does not have adequate fire sustaining properties (fuel, oxygen, etc), it will snuff out when the spell is over.

Uses - The spell can be used to start a fire, damage and distract an opponent, melt a 2 inch hole in armor or other metal, etc.

Mage/1V - Energy Weapon (Enchant)

Mage/Evocation	Level: 1
Cast Time: 1 Second	Duration: 1 Turn/Level
Range: Touch	Affected Area: 1 WeaponArrow/level
Mana: 1	Damage: An additional 1D4 Energy
Save: N/A	Save Affect: N/A
Components: V, S, M	Concentration: N/A
Material Comp: Small piece of flint	
Somatic Comp: Touching of arrow tip	

Execution - This spell will create will an enchanted sheath around a non-magical fighting weapon or missile weapon so that anytime it causes regular damage it will also cause an additional 1D4 hit-points of energy damage.

Mage/1V - Energy Shield

Mage/Evocation	Level: 1
Cast Time: 1 Round	Duration: 1 Turn/Level

Range: 15' + 10'/Level	Affected Area: 10' x 10' square
Mana: 1	Damage: 3D4 Energy
Save: None	Save Affect: N/A
Components: V, S, M	Concentration: None
Material Comp: Small piece of glass	
Somatic Comp: Waving motion of the hand	

Execution - This spell will create This spell creates a 10' x 10' magical wall that causes 3D4 points of energy damage to any creature that passes through it.

Description – The shield can be cast to be invisible, or apaque. It can be created be any color of the caster's chosing.

Limitations – The entire shield must be of the same color. Once the spell is cast, the color cannot be changed, and the shield cannot be moved. The shield can only be cast to be flat, vertical, and square.

Erratta – If there is not adequate space to accommodate the shield, it will be imbedded in surrounding solids.

Aftermat – The enchantment remains in affect until the spell exhausts its duration, the caster speaks the command words calling for the spell to end, or the enchantment is dispelled.

Mage/1V – Energy Touch

Mage/Evocation	Level: 1
Cast Time: 1 Second	Duration: N/A
Range: Touch	Affected Area: 1 Creature
Mana: 1	Damage: 1D4/Level Up to 10D4
Save: Dexterity	Save Affect: Avoids for 1 round
Components: V, S, M	Concentration: N/A
Material Comp: Bit of sulfur	
Somatic Comp: Crumbling sulfur in palm, then touching	

Level	Energy Damage
1	1D4 Hit-points
2	2D4 Hit-points
3	3D4 Hit-points
4	4D4 Hit-points
5	5D4 Hit-points
6	6D4 Hit-points
7	7D4 Hit-points
8	8D4 Hit-points
9	9D4 Hit-points
10-	10D4 Hit-points

Execution - This spell will allow the caster to use a touch to deliver a massive amount of energy damage.

Mage/1V - Flame Arrow

Mage/Evocation	Level: 1
Cast Time: 1 Second	Duration: 1 Round/Level
Range: Touch	Affected Area: 1 Arrow/level
Mana: 1	Damage: An additional 1D6 Fire
Save: N/A	Save Affect: N/A
Components: V, S, M	Concentration: N/A
Material Comp: Small piece of flint	
Somatic Comp: Touching of arrow tip	

Execution - This spell will create a magical flame on the tip of an arrow, a staff, or the end of any slender object. In the item as used as weapon, it will cause an additional 1D6 of fire damage.

Affect - Once the magic-user has cast this spell, he or she is able to touch one arrow or crossbow bolt (quarrel) per second the duration of the flame arrow. Each such missile so touched becomes magic, although it gains no bonuses "to hit". Each such missile must be discharged within 1 round, for after that period flame consumes it entirely, and the magic is lost. The arrow will have normal probabilities of causing combustion, and any creature subject to additional fire damage will suffer an additional 1D6 hit-point of damage from any flame arrow which hits it.

Limitations - The enchantment does not increase the to-hit. The material components for this spell are a drop of oil and a small piece of flint.

Mage/1V – Flash

Mage/Evocation	Level: 1
Cast Time: 1 Segment	Duration: N/A
Range: 0	Affected Area: Cone 60' len x 30' diam
Mana: 1	Damage: None
Save: None	Save Affect: N/A
Components: V, S	Concentration: N/A
Material comp: None	
Somatic Comp: Opening the hand in the direction of the spell	

Execution - This spell will cause a brilliant flash of light.

Affect - The flash will appear in a cone, with the point originating at the casters palm, extending outward for 60 feet, to reach a 30' diameter base.

Eratta - The flash is visible from a great distance, particularly at night, however is only affective for blinding opponents inside the area of affect. Any any seeing creatures that do not protect their eyes for will be blinded 10-40 seconds (1D4 rounds) 1D4 rounds.

Mage/1V – Nudge

Mage/Evocation	Level: 1
Cast Time: 1 Segment	Duration: N/A
Range: 15' + 10'/level	Affected Area: 2" target surface area
Mana: 1	Damage: None
Save: None	Save Affect: N/A
Components: S	Concentration: N/A
Material Comp: None	
Somatic Comp: Pushing motion with fingertips or nudging montio with elbow.	

Execution - This spell can be used to push or press an item, creature, or surface.

Affect - It will deliver approximately 10 pounds of force against the targeted surface.

Limitations - The affect will not cause any damage.

Uses - Since the casting time is very quick, a nudge spell can often be used to scrub an opponent's spell that is more po werful but has a longer cast time. The spell can also be used to poke the eye of a person in hand combat, blinding them for 1 round and giving them a -4 on roll-to-hit. The spell could be used to knock an item of a table or shelf, tap a comrade on the shoulder to get their attention, rustle a bush, or sipple the surface of water.

Mage/1V – Shatter

Mage/Enchantment	Level: 1
Cast Time: 1 Segment	Duration: N/A
Range: 15' + 10'/level	Affected Area: Target object
Mana: 1	Damage: N/A
Save: Versus drop	Save Affect: Neg
Components: V, S	Concentration: N/A
Material comp: None	
Somatic Comp: Pointing at target object with one hand and snapping fingers with other hand	

Execution - This spell will cause a breakable object to shatter as if it were dropped onto a stone floor from a height of 10 feet.

Limitations - The object will make normal breaking noises when it shatters and the pieces will scatter as if broken normally.

Mage/2A – Air Restoration

Mage/Alteration	Level: 2
Cast Time: 2 segments	Duration: 1 hour/level
Range: 15' + 10'/level	Affected Area: 30' diameter area
Mana: 2	Damage: N/A
Save: N/A	Save Affect: N/A
Components: V, S	Concentration: N/A
Material Comp: None	
Somatic Comp: Wave of the hand as if waving away smoke	

Affect - When this spell is cast, it will keep the air in the affected area fresh and oxygenated for 1 hour per level of experince of the spell caster. Any corrosive gasses, poisonous fumes or other non-breathable vapors that are introduced into the affected area will be instantly neutralized.

Limitations - The point of origin can be cast in the air or cast on an object or creature in order to be moved about.

Adjustments - While the enchantment is in affect, the caster can speak command words temporarily halting the spell and futher command words reinstating the affects of the enchantment.

Aftermath - The enchantment remains in affect until the spell exhausts its duration, the caster speaks the command words calling for the spell to end, or the enchantment is dispelled.

Mage/2A – Amplify Sound

Mage/Alteration	Level: 2
Cast Time: 2 Seconds	Duration: 1 hour/level
Range: Touch	Affected Area: 30' diameter
Mana: 2	Damage: N/A
Save: Charisma	Save Affect: Negates
Components: V	
Material component: None	
Somatic component: None	

Execution - This spell will cause all sounds inside the affected area to be amplified by a factor of 10.

Affect - The "moving silently" thieving function will be inpossible inside the affected area. Whispers will be loud and audible. A shout will defen people in the affected area for 1d6 rounds. Extremely loud noises usch as the thunder crack from a lightning bolt will defen for 1D6 hours.

Mage/2A – Crystalize

Mage/Alteration	Level: 2
Cast Time: 2 Seconds	Duration: 1 Round/Level
Range: 15' + 10'/level	Affected Area: One Metal Object
Mana: 2	Damage: N/A
Save: N/A	Save Affect: N/A
Components: V, S	Concentration: N/A
Material Comp: None	
Somatic Comp: Pointing at metal object	

Execution - This spell will cause any sort of non-magical metal to become very brittle and easy to shatter.

Uses - The spell can be used on an opponent's sword to make it shatter after the first blow, or on the irons bars of a cell in order to break them away and escape

Aftermath - After the spell is cast, and the metal is crystallized, it retains no magical nature. The affect cannot be reversed by enchantment dispelling or command words.

Eratta - The affect will not change the basic strength of the metal. A crystallized stand will support the same weight as it did before. The alteration of metal magical objects or metal creatuis will not remove or change their magical nature (unless broken). A magical wand made of metal will be fragile, but still. The affect will not remove the lifeforce of a metal magical creature, but it can easily be shattered with a single blow.

Mage/2A – Freeze

Mage/Alteration	Level: 2
Cast Time: 2 Seconds	Duration: 1 hour/level
Range: Touch	Affected Area: 1000 cubic foot
Mana: 2	Damage: N/A
Save: N/A	Save Affect: N/A
Components: V	Concentration: N/A
Material Component: Water	
Somatic Component: Placing finger to waters surface	

Execution - This spell will freeze massive amounts of water into ice.

Affect - The spell will affect up to 1,000 cubic foot (10ft x 10ft x 10ft) for each level of experience of the spell caster.

Limitations - If the spell is used to enclose a warm blood creature or a heat producing object, the ice will shatter, peltering all creatures in a 15' radius with chunks of ice, causing 3-18 (3D6) hit-points damage to each (1/2 for successful dexterity save)

Aftermath - Once frozen, the ice is, for all pratical purposes, ordinary ice and is subject ot normal adversaiuos conditions such as melting, shattering, etc.

Mage/2A - Heat Metal

Mage/Evocation	Level: 2
Cast Time: 2 Seconds	Duration: 1 round/level
Range: Touch	Affected Area: 30'/level
Mana: 2	Damage: N/A

Level	#Rounds	Affect	Damage
0-1	1	Hot to touch	1D6
2-3	2	Will cause water to sizzle	2D6
4-5	3	Glows red	3D6
6-7	4	Glows bright red	4D6
8-9	5	Glows orange, softens	5D6
10-11	6	Glows yellow, bends easily	6D6
12-	7	Glows white, liquid, can be poured	7D6

Save: Charisma	Save Affect: Negates
Components: V, S, M	Concentration: High
Material Component: Bit of Sulphur	
Somatic Component: Rubbing of sulphur on metal	

Execution - This spell will heat metal to the point that it becomes soft and pliable (or even liquid)

Damage - If a creature vulnerable to heat damage is wearing armor affected by the spell, or pressed against metal affected by the spell, they will suffer damage based on the round of the spell. At the first round, they will suffer 1D6. On the second round, they will suffer 2D6, etc.

Metal	Additional Rounds
Steel	1 Additional round
Titanium	2 Additional rounds
Mithirl	3 Additional rounds
Adamanite	4 Additional rounds

Erratta - Some very hard metals are less affected by the spell and take longer to heat up.

Mage/2A - Slippery Surface

Mage/Alteration	Level: 2
Cast Time: 2 Seconds	Duration: 1 hour/level
Range: Touch	Affected Area: 30'/level
Mana: 2	Damage: N/A
Save: N/A	Save Affect: N/A
Components: V, S, M	Conntration: N/A

Material Comp: Drop of oil
Somatic Comp: Rubbing oil drop between fingertips

Execution - This spell will ereduce the friction inside the affected area by 90%, making the surfaces slippery and difficult to manage.

Affect - It is impossible stand on a surface that is affected by a frictionless area with less then three contact points to the floor. Climbing a rope is impossible because it will slip through the fingers. Climbing a wall can only be done if there are places for hand holds. Objects that are sitting on unlevel surfaces will start to drift across the floor.

Mage/2C - Enchanted Flame

Mage/Conjuration	Level: 2
Cast Time: 2 Seconds	Duration: 1 hour/level
Range: Touch	Affected Area: 30'/level
Mana: 2	Damage: N/A
Save: N/A	Save Affect: N/A
Components: V	Concentration: N/A

Material Component: Bit of sulphur
Somatic Component: Pressing sulphur between fingers and pointing

Execution - This spell will create a small magical flame that is about the size of a typical torch.

Affect - The flame will create the the same amount of heat and light as if it were natural flame. The flame will consume no fuel or oxygen. Moving air will cause the flame to flutter, but will not blow it out. Emmersing in water will not extinguish the flame. It cannot be snuffed out moving ariby dousing in wat

Erratta - An enchanted flame can be sued to light combustibles and create natural fires.

Adjustments - If the caster speaks the command words calling for the spell to end, the fire is extinguished and must be recast in order to restore the flame.

Aftermath - The flame will burn until the spell exhausts its duration, the spell caster speaks the command word calling for the spell to end, or the enchantment is dispelled.

Mage/2C - Hold Portal

Mage/Evocation	Level: 2
Cast Time: 2 Seconds	Duration: 1 hour/level
Range: Touch	Affected Area: 30' x 30' sqft
Mana: 2	Damage: N/A
Save: N/A	Save Affect: N/A
Components: V	Concentration: None

Material Comp: Drop of glue
Somatic Comp: Rubbing glue drop between fingertips

Execution - This spell will cause an invisible wall of force to be created, effectively sealing a portal or doorwat up to 30 foot x 30 foot square.

Affect - The affect will prevent any creatures, objects, spells, sounds, or vapors from passing through. The only thing that will pass is non-magical light.

Adjustments - The spell will automatically adjust its shape and size to the opening it is cast upon, so long as the limit of 900 square feet is not exceeded. While in range, the caster may speak the command words to temporarily open the seal, or reinstate the seal.

Uses - The spell can be used to block a doorway or cave entrance, plug a bottle.

Erratta -

Aftermath - The spell is ended when the duration is exhausted, the caster speaks the command words causing the spell to end, or the enchantment is dispelled.

Mage/2C - Shield

Mage/Conjuration	Level: 2
Cast Time: 1 Segment	Duration: 1 turn/level
Range: 15'	Affected Area: Up to 10' x 10' square
Mana: 2	Damage: N/A
Save: None	Save Affect: N/A
Components: V, S	

Material Comp: Silver coin
Somatic Comp: Holding the hand flat and vertical with the palm facing away.

Execution - This spell create a vertical wall of force that can be used to hide behind to avoid being hit by missle attacks.

Description - The shield is a flat opaque white in color and is always square or rectangular in shape. It is strictly 2-dimensional and does not have a thickness. It is solid to the touch, and is impervious to all normal missle regardless of the size or weight. Even massive boulders will be easily deflected without the shield having budged. Likewise, non-magical creatures will be unable to pass through the shield. All non-magical gasses, vapors, and fluids will be deflected as well.

Limitaions - The shield is non-movable and cannot be moved about or cast on an object or creature to be moved. The shield can only be cast vertically and cannot be made to lay over a creature or item, nor can it even be cast at a slant to provide better protection from an arial attack. Any sort of magical affect, magical item, enchanted object, magical creature, or creature under the influence of an enchanntment will pass easily through the shield, disrupting the enchantment of the shield and causing it to dispel.

Aftermath - The shiled will not be dispelled if the caster is away, however, it cannot be controlled by the spell caster's command words unless the caster is withing range. The spell will remain in affect until the caster speaks the command words for the spell to end, the enchantment is dispelled, or the spell exhausts its duration.

Mage/2D - Decipher Code

Mage/Divination	Level: 2
Cast Time: 1 Second	Duration: N/A
Range: 15' + 10'/level	Affected Area: 15' radius

Mana: 2	Damage: N/A
Save: N/A	Save Affect: N/A
Components: V, S	Concentration: N/A

Material component: None
Somatic component: Horizontal sweeping motion with the hand

Execute - When this spells is cast, all entrances and exits to any enclosure will be outline with brilliantly glowing luminescent lines.

Affect - Doors, doorways. Portals, secret doors, concealed doors, corks in bottles, plugs on scroll tubes, all portals will have a glowing line around the edges.

The spell will not reveal and hidden latching mechanisms or traps on the doors

Mage/2D - Find Doors

Mage/Divination	Level: 2
Cast Time: 1 Second	Duration: N/A
Range: 15' + 10'/level	Affected Area: 15' radius
Mana: 2	Damage: N/A
Save: N/A	Save Affect: N/A
Components: V, S	Concentration: N/A

Material component: None
Somatic component: Horizontal sweeping motion with the hand

Execute - When this spells is cast, all entrances and exits to any enclosure will be outline with brilliantly glowing luminescent lines.

Affect - Doors, doorways. Portals, secret doors, concealed doors, corks in bottles, plugs on scroll tubes, all portals will have a glowing line around the edges.

The spell will not reveal and hidden latching mechanisms or traps on the doors

Aftermath - The glowing lines will remain until the spell exhaust its duration, it is magically dispelled, or the caster speaks the command words calling for the spell to end.

Mage/2D - Find Traps

Mage/Divination	Level: 2
Cast Time: 1 Second	Duration: N/A
Range: 15' + 10'/level	Affected Area: 15' radius
Mana: 2	Damage: N/A
Save: N/A	Save Affect: N/A
Components: V, S	Concentration: N/A

Material component: None
Somatic component: Touching of subject.

Execution - When this spell is cast, all mechanical type traps within the affected area will begin to glow brightly and illuminate light.

Affect - Traps illuminated by the spell are easy to see and avoid, but not always easy to disarm. Some can be as easy as closing a safety or throwing a lever. Others may require thieving abilities to neutralize.

Aftermath - Affected traps will glow until the enchantment is dispelled, the spell exhausts its duration, or the spell caster speaks the command word calling for the spell to end.

Mage/2D - Trace

Mage/Divination	Level: 2
Cast Time: 1 Second	Duration: 1 Turn + 1 Turn/Level
Range: Unlimited	Affected Area: 1 creature/item
Mana: 2	Damage: N/A
Save: N/A	Save Affect: N/A
Components: V, S	Concentration: N/A

Material component: None
Somatic component: Touching tip of finger to subject.

Execution - This spell will place a small visible mark on a creature or item that is tracable byt the caster.

Affect - At any time, the caster will be able to speak a command word and instantly know the exact direction and distance the subject is from them self.

Limitations – Magical dispelling will remove the mark. If the

Aftermath – The mark will remain on the subject until the spell exhausts its duration or the caster speaks the command word calling for the spell to end.

Mage/2E - Invisibility

Mage/Enchantment	Level: 2
Cast Time: 2 Seconds	Duration: 1 hour/level
Range: Touch	Affected Area: 1 Creature/Object
Mana: 2	Damage: N/A
Save: N/A	Save Affect: N/A
Components: V	Concentration: None

Material Comp: None
Somatic Comp: None

Execution - This spell will cover the subject with a magical shroud that will cause invisibility. *See Magical Game Standards/Invisibility*

Aftermath - The enchantment will be in force until the spell exhausts its duration, the caster speaks the command word calling for the spell to end, the enchamntment is dispelled, or the magical shroud is peirced.

Mage/2E - Levitate

Mage/Enchantment	Level: 2
Cast Time: 2 Segments	Duration: 2 minutes/level
Range: 15' + 10'/level	Affected Area: 100 pounds/level
Mana: 2	Damage: N/A
Save: None	Save Affect: N/A
Components: V, S	Concentration: None

Material Comp: None
Somatic Comp: Lifting of the horizontal open palm (raising) or lower of the horizontal open palm (lowering)

Execution - This spell will allow the caster to raise and lower one creature or object of up to 100 pounds per level of the caster.

Limitations - The spell only affect vertical movement and does not create or stop horizontal movement. A person or object raised by this spell can be blown about by heavy winds, or pushed by a comrade in order to corss a crevasse.

Aftermath - When the spell exhausts its duration the subject will start to lower to the ground at a slow rate of 10 feet/round. The spell has a tolerance which gives a residual enchantment will last, lowering the subject for up to an extra 1 round/level beyond the spells active duration. During the tolerance period, the rate of fall cannot be adjusted. If the enchantment is dispelled or the caster speaks the command words for the spell to end, the subject will plummet at normal falling rate.

Mage/2E - Enchanted Rope

Mage/Enchantment	Level: 2
Cast Time: 2 Seconds	Duration: 1 turn/level
Range: 15' + 10' /level	Affected Area: 60' length of rope
Mana: 2	Damage: N/A
Save: N/A	Save Affect: N/A
Components: V, M	

Material Component: Rope
Somatic Component: Cupping hands around rope and letting it slide through as it becomes animated

Execution - This spell will animate a rope fo upt to 60' in length. It will move about in any manner the caster desires, much the same as snake.

Affect - The rope can be made to slither across the ground, raise itself and attach, coil up, etc.

Adjustments - The rope is controlled by the use of command words that must be spoken verbally.

Limitations - The spell will not cause a rope to levitate unsupported in the air. If the rope is raised into the iar, it must leave enough of on the ground to provide an adequate base.

Aftermath - The enchantment will be in force until the spell exhausts its duration, the caster speaks the command word calling for the spell to end, of the enchamntment is dispelled.

Mage/2E - Enchanted Shelter

Mage/Enchantment	Level: 2
Cast Time: 2 rounds	Duration: 1 hour/level
Range: Touch	Affected Area: 30'/level
Mana: 2	Damage: N/A
Save: N/A	Save Affect: N/A
Components: V	Concentration: None
Material Component: None	
Somatic Component: None	

Execution - This spell creates an magical shelter that will protect the occupants from adverse temperatures, gasses, and fluids.

Adjustments - The caster is able to control the appearnce of the shelters perimeter after the spell is cast. By speaking command words, the caster can make the shelter invisible, transparent, white, black, or any shade of gray in between.

Limitations - The shelters shade must be set to be a single color. It offers no protection from missles, weapons or magics. Once the spell is cast, the shelter cannot be moved about, nor can it be cast on an object in order to be moved about.

Uses - The shelter can be used as a shelter from inclement weather, the sun

Erratta - The shelter is not affected by creatures, objects, or spells passing through it.

Aftermath - The enchantment will be in force until the spell exhausts its duration, the caster speaks the command word calling for the spell to end, of the enchamntment is dispelled.

Mage/2E - Knock

Mage/Enchantment	Level: 2
Cast Time: 2 Seconds	Duration: 1 round/level
Range: 0	Affected Area: 1 lock/obstructed hole
Mana: 2	Damage: N/A
Save: N/A	Save Affect: N/A
Components: V	Concentration: N/A
Material Component: None	
Somatic Component: None	

Execution - This spell will open any sealed, locked or plugged portal or door.

Affect - The spell will affect both magical and non-magical locking means and mechanisms. The spell will open locks as well as dislodge plugs in holes. It will break welds, lift beams barring doors, loosen chains or ropes. etc.

Limitaions - The spell will not open magical locks or seals that were placed by a mage of a higher level. It will not not perform more abstract actions to allow passage such as lowering a drawbridge, raising a portcullis, pulling a log across a crevasse, etc.

Mage/2I - Charm

Mage/Illusion	Level: 2
Cast Time: 2 Seconds	Duration: 1 turn/level
Range: Touch	Affected Area: 1 Creature
Mana: 1	Damage: None
Save: Charisma	Save Affect: Negates
Components: V, S	Concentration: N/A
Material component: Drop of wine	
Somatic component: Rubbing drop between fingertips then touching subject.	

Execution - This spell will cause the recipient to take a more favorable view of the caster and cause anything said by the caster to be taken in a more favorable way.

Limitations - The spell does not enable control of the charmed person/creature as if it were an automaton. A charmed creature would not obey a suicide command, and cannot be persuaded to do something out of character or against alignment. After a person has been charmed, they are immune to being charmed by the same mage again for a period of 24 hours.

Aftermath - Although magically induced, the affect is psychological and there is no magical duration. The affect cannot be controlled by command words or dispelled. When the spell is invoked, the caster should specify a duration. If the caster does not specify, the referee will assume that the spell is to run for maximum duraton. When the spell has exhausted its duration, the affected creature will not necessarily know that they have been influenced by a spell.

Mage/2I - Fear

Mage/Illusion	Level: 2
Cast Time: 2 Seconds	Duration: 1 second/level (non-magical)
Range: 15' + 10'/level	Affected Area: 1 Creature
Mana: 2	Damage: N/A
Save: Charisma	Save Affect: Negates
Components: V	Concentration: N/A
Material Component: None	
Somatic Component: None	

Execution - When this spell is invoked, the subject is consumed by an uncontrollable fear of the caster and will immediately run the other direction with no thought of attack, defense, hiding, or spell casting.

Affect - Affected creatures are likely to drop whatever they are holding when struck by the spell is 100% - modified charisma score. Creatures affected by fear flee at their fastest rate for the duration fo the affect.

Limitations - The spell is only affective on natural creatures.

Aftermath - Wounding, extreme fear, slapping, dousing with water, and other rousing affects will prematurely end the spells affect. Although magically induced, the affect is psychological and there is no magical duration. The affect cannot be controlled by command words or dispelled. When the spell is invoked, the caster should speciify a duration. If the caster does not specify, the referee will assume that the spell is to run for maximum duraton.

Mage/2I - Mirror Image

Mage/Illusion	Level: 2
Cast Time: 2 Seconds	Duration: 1 Round/Level
Range: 0	Affected Area: 1-6 Duplicates in 15'
Mana: 2	Damage: N/A
Save: Charisma	Save Affect: Negates
Components: V, S	Concentration: N/A
Material Component: None	

Somatic Component: None

Execution - When a mirror image spell is invoked, the spell caster causes from 1 to 6 exact duplicates of himself or herself to come into being around his or her person.

Affect - The number of image created will be 1 plus an additional 1 for every 2 levels of experiaence of the caster. The images do exactly what the magic-user does, and as the spell causes a blurring and slight distortion when it is effected, it is impossible for opponents to be certain which are the phantasms and which is the actual magic-user.

Limitations - When an image is struck by a weapon, magical or otherwise, it disappears, but any other existing images remain intact until struck. The images seem to shift from round to round, so that if the actual magic-user is struck during one round, he or she cannot be picked out from amongst his or her images the next.

Mage/3I – Sneeze

Mage/Illusion	Level: 3
Cast Time: 2 Seconds	Duration: 1 Round/level (non-mag)
Range: 15' + 10'/level	Affected Area: 1 Creature
Mana: 2	Damage: N/A
Save: Charisma	Save Affect: Negates
Components: V	Concentration: N/A
Material Component: None	
Somatic Component: None	

Execution - This spell causes the subject to become entranced and immobilized.

Mage/3I – Suggestion

Mage/Illusion	Level: 3
Cast Time: 2 Seconds	Duration: 1 Round/level (non-mag)
Range: 15' + 10'/level	Affected Area: 1 Creature
Mana: 2	Damage: N/A
Save: Charisma	Save Affect: Negates
Components: V	Concentration: N/A
Material Component: None	
Somatic Component: None	

Execution - This spell causes the subject to become entranced and immobilized.

Mage/2N – Dragon Skin

Mage/Necromancy	Level: 2
Cast Time: 2 Seconds	Duration: 1 round/level
Range: Touch	Affected Area: 1 Creature
Mana: 2	Damage: N/A
Save: N/A	Save Affect: N/A
Components: V, S, M	Concentration: N/A
Material Component: Bit of Dragon leather	
Somatic Component: Rubbing leather onto subject's skin	

Level	Dragon Leather	Armor Class Bonus
0-1	Yellow, Violet, Orange	+1
2-3	Red, Green, Blue	+2
4-5	White	+3
6-	Black	+4

Execution - The spell is used to make the subject's skin more string and less vulnerable to damage, thereby improving the character's armor class 1 point fore every 2 levels of experience of the caster.

Affect - The amount of protection available depends on the experience level of the caster. The color and texture of the subject's skin will not change, nor will the feel or sensitivity.

Aftermath - After the spell is cast, the affect is physiological and cannot be magically dispelled or ended early by command words.

Mage/2N – Fly

Mage/Necromancy	
Level: 2	
Cast Time: 2 Seconds	
Duration: 1 hour/level	
Range: Touch	
Affected Area: 1 Creature	
Mana: 2	
Damage: None	
Save: N/A	
Save Affect: N/A	
Components: V	
Concentration: None	
Material component: Feather	
Somatic Component: Sticking quill into back of subject	

Execution - When this spell is cast, when the quill of a feather is stuck into the bare skin of a subject it will divide and grow into a proportional pair wings.

Affect - The wings will be capable of lifting the subject off the ground and flying them about.

Limitations - Unless a specific duration is stated at the start of the spell, the referee will assume that the spell is cast to run for maximum duration. Cutting away the wings prematurely will cause 2-40 (2D20) hit-points of damage to the subject. Flying is difficult to learn and can cause damage if done badly. Consult the section of flying for more information.

Aftermath - Although magically induced, the spells affect is physiological and cannot be magically dispelled and cannot be ended by a command word from the caster. When the spell exhausts its duration the wings will start to shrink and lose strength, forcing the subject to land. After one round (10 seconds) the wings will wither and fall away from the subject's body. When the spell is invokled the caster should announce how long the duration of the affect is intended to last. If no such announcement is made, the referee will assume the affect is to last for maximum duration.

Mage/2N – Slow Poison

Mage/Necromancy	Level: 2
Cast Time: 1 Segment	Duration: 1 hour/level
Range: Touch	Affected Area: 1 Creature
Mana: 2	Damage: N/A
Save: N/A	Save Affect: N/A
Components: V, S	Concentration: None
Material Component - None	
Somatic Component - Touching of subject	

Execution - By casting this spell, the caster is able to slow the onset of a poisons affect on a subject's body.

Affect - The spell will not detoxify the poison or reverse any ill affects that have already taken place. The onset time and duration of the poison will be slowed by a factor of 60. The poisons affects that would normally occur in a 1 round (10 second) time frame will instead occur in a 1 turn (10 minute) time frame. This generally allows ample time for administering of healing magics or anti-venoms/anidotes (if available).

Aftermath - If the enchantment is ended or dispelled, or the spells duration is exhausted, the affects will immediately resume their normal rate of pregression.

Mage/2N - **Spider Climb**

Mage/Necromancy	Level: 2
Cast Time: 2 Seconds	Duration: 1 hour/level
Range: Touch	Affected Area: 1 Creature
Mana: 2	Damage: N/A
Save: N/A	Save Affect: N/A
Components: V, S, M	Concentration: None

Material Component - Drop of glue
Somatic Component - Rubbing on fingertips and/or feet

Execution - This spell causes the recipients touch to cling to surfaces enabling the climbing of walls and ceilings.

Limitations - Oily, powdred, or crumbling surfaces cannot be climbed in this way. The affected creature must have bare hands and feet in order to climb in this manner. During the course of the spell the recipient cannot handle or touch objects or creatures because they will cling to the hands. A spell caster will be unable to cast spells with material components because of the inability to handle them properly.

Adjustments - The spell can be cast on the hands, feet, both, or any other surface of the skin. A caster could conceivably use the spell on the naked back of an opponent, then sticking them to a ceiling to immobilize them.

Aftermath - Although magically induced, the spells affect is physiological and cannot be magically dispelled and cannot be ended by a command word from the caster. When the spell exhausts its duration the wings will start to shrink and lose strength, forcing the subject to land. After one round (10 seconds) the wings will wither and fall away from the subject's body. When the spell is invokled the caster should announce how long the duration of the affect is intended to last. If no such announcement is made, the referee will assume the affect is to last for maximum duration.

Mage/2N - **Strength**

Mage/Necromancy	Level: 2
Cast Time: 2 Seconds	Duration: 1 hour/level
Range: Touch	Affected Area: 1 Creature
Mana: 2	Damage: N/A
Save: N/A	Save Affect: N/A
Components: V, S	Concentration: None

Material Component - None
Somatic Component - Touching of subject

Natural Strength	Strength Gain
1-19	No affect
20-39	+10
40-59	+20
60-79	+40
80-	+80

Execution - This spell will increase the subject's strength.

Limitations - The spell can only be cast on natural creatures, and only while they are in natural form. The strength will only be increased based on the recipient's natural strength and the bonuses are not added to strngth altered magically.

Aftermath - Although magically induced, the spells affect is physiological and cannot be magically dispelled and cannot be ended by a command word from the caster. When the spell exhausts its duration the strength will start to ebb. After one round (10 seconds) the benefit will be gone completely. When the spell is invoked the caster should announce how long the duration of the affect is intended to last. If no such announcement is made, the referee will assume the affect is to last for maximum duration.

Mage/2V – Energy Blast

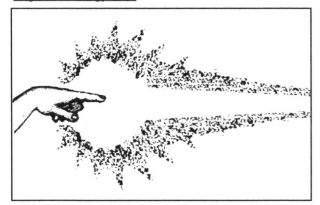

Mage/Evocation	Level: 1
Cast Time: 1 Second	Duration: 1 hour/level
Range: Touch	Affected Area: Target creature
Mana: 1	Damage: 1D4 to 7D4 Energy
Save: N/A	Save Affect: N/A
Components: V, S	Concentration: N/A

Material Component: None
Somatic Component: Pointing of finger

Level	Energy Damage
0-1	1D4 Hit-points
2-3	2D4 Hit-points
4-5	3D4 Hit-points
6-7	4D4 Hit-points
8-9	5D4 Hit-points
10-11	6D4 Hit-points
12-13	7D4 Hit-points
14-	8D4 Hit-points

Execution - By using this spell that caster causes a beam of glowing energy to shoot forth from an outstretched finger and strike a target creature.

Affect - e energy bolt will cause 1D4 points of energy damage for each level of experience of the caster, up to a mximum of 7D4.

Limitations - To target the spell, the caster must have visual contact with the intended subject. If the caster is firing blindly, the referee will determine the odds of a hit based on what is appropriate for the situation.

Erratta - See *Game Standards - Magical - Energy damage*

Mage/2V – Fire Enchant

Mage/Evocation	Evocation: Level 2
Cast Time: 2 Seconds	Duration: N/A
Range: 15' + 10'/level	Affected Area: Touch
Mana: 1	Damage: 1D6 to 10D6
Save: Dexterity	Save Affect: N/A
Components: V, S, M	Concentration: N/A

Material Comp: Bit of sulfur
Somatic Comp: Crumbling sulfur in palm, then touching target

Execution - After casting this spell, the touch of the spell caster will cause an area of the subject's body to burst into flames. The flames will cause 1D6 points of energy damage for each level of experience of the caster, up to a mximum of 10D6.

Mage/2V – Fire Shield

Mage/Evocation	Evocation: Level 2
Cast Time: 2 Seconds	Duration: N/A
Range: 15' + 10'/level	Affected Area: Touch
Mana: 1	Damage: 3D6 Fire
Save: Dexterity	Save Affect: N/A
Components: V, S, M	Concentration: N/A

Material Comp: Bit of sulfur
Somatic Comp: Crumbling sulfur in palm, then touching target

Execution - This spell will create This spell creates a 10' x 10' magical wall that causes 3D6 points of fire damage to any creature that passes through it.

Description – The shield appears at an apaque flickering orange and red square.

Limitations –Once the spell is cast, the color cannot be changed, and the shield cannot be moved, nor can it be cast onto an object or creature in order to be moved about. The shield can only be cast to be flat, vertical, and square.

Erratta – If there is not adequate space to accommodate the shield, it will be imbedded in surrounding solids. Any objects passing through the shield must make a saving throw or be consumed by fire

Aftermat – The enchantment remains in affect until the spell exhausts its duration, the caster speaks the command words calling for the spell to end, or the enchantment is dispelled.

Mage/2V – Fire Touch

Mage/Evocation	Evocation: Level 2
Cast Time: 2 Seconds	Duration: N/A
Range: 15' + 10'/level	Affected Area: Touch
Mana: 1	Damage: 1D6 to 10D6
Save: Dexterity	Save Affect: N/A
Components: V, S, M	Concentration: N/A

Material Comp: Bit of sulfur

Somatic Comp: Crumbling sulfur in palm, then touching target

Execution - After casting this spell, the touch of the spell caster will cause an area of the subject's body to burst into flames. The flames will cause 1D6 points of energy damage for each level of experience of the caster, up to a mximum of 10D6.

Level	Fire Damage
0-1	1D6 Hit-points
2-3	2D6 Hit-points
4-5	3D6 Hit-points
6-7	4D6 Hit-points
8-9	5D6 Hit-points
10-11	6D6 Hit-points
12-13	7D6 Hit-points
14-15	8D6 Hit-points
16-17	9D6 Hit-points
18-	10D6 Hit-points

Mage/2V – Freeze

Mage/Evocation	Level: 2
Cast Time: 2 Seconds	Duration: 1 hour/level
Range: Touch	Affected Area: 30'/level
Mana: 2	Damage: N/A
Save: Charisma	Save Affect: Negates
Components: V	Concentration: N/A
Material Component: Bit of Sulphur	
Somatic Component: Flicking sulphur into air	

Execution - This spell will produce a massive sphere of arial fireworks.

Affect - Any creature inside the sphere will be blinded for 1D4 rounds and defeaned for 1D6 rounds. Creatures inside the affected area will be unable to summon the concentration to cast spells or activate magical items. Creatures blinded by the affect, will suffer -4 on all to-hit rolls. Likewise, rolls-to-hit on creatures obscured by the affect will be at a -4 penalty.

Limitations - The affect will not cause any sort of damage to creatures not will it ignite combustible materials. It serves only to confure, distract, or frighten an enemy.

Erratta - Creatures are not hampered from leaving the area, however, the affect will cause most horses to rear, and frighten most creatures of low intelligence.

Mage/2V – Pyrotechnics

Mage/Evocation	Level: 2
Cast Time: 2 Seconds	Duration: 1 hour/level
Range: Touch	Affected Area: 30'/level
Mana: 2	Damage: N/A
Save: Charisma	Save Affect: Negates
Components: V	Concentration: N/A
Material Component: Bit of Sulphur	
Somatic Component: Flicking sulphur into air	

Execution - This spell will produce a massive sphere of arial fireworks.

Affect - Any creature inside the sphere will be blinded for 1D4 rounds and defeaned for 1D6 rounds. Creatures inside the affected area will be unable to summon the concentration to cast spells or activate magical items. Creatures blinded by the affect, will suffer -4 on all to-hit rolls. Likewise, rolls-to-hit on creatures obscured by the affect will be at a -4 penalty.

Limitations - The affect will not cause any sort of damage to creatures not will it ignite combustible materials. It serves only to confure, distract, or frighten an enemy.

Erratta - Creatures are not hampered from leaving the area, however, the affect will cause most horses to rear, and frighten most creatures of low intelligence.

Mage/3A - Change Mass

Mage/Alteration	Level: 2
Cast Time: 2 Seconds	Duration: 1 Round/level
Range: 15' + 10'/level	Affected Area: One solid object
Mana: 2	Damage: N/A
Save: None	Save Affect: N/A
Components: V, S	Concentration: None
Material Comp: None	

Somatic Comp: Clasping the fingers and drawing the hand down as if pulling a string (to increase), or opening the hand and raising the palm as if lifting to (decrease).

Execution - This spell is used to drastically change the weight of a non-magical item .

Affect - With this spell, the caster is able to make the weight of any single non-magical object very heavy (up to 100 * it's normal weight) or lighter than air (as much as 1/100 its normal weight lighter than air)

When the spell is invoked the caster must announce the direction and the amount of the weight change. Thereafter, the spell caster must speak a command word anytime the weight is to be changed again. When the spell exhausts it's duration, the object will begin to regain its regular mass. Within the course of an additional round, the object will be returned to normal. The object will immediately change weight if; the caster commands it to, the enchantment is dispelled.

The spell will not affect gasses of liquids. The intended subject must be solid. Clothing with interwoven fibers cannot be affected. In the case of an iron chain, only one link would be affected. The boot section of a shoe.

If the spell is used to make an object lighter than air, it will lift gently off the ground and rise into the air until it comes up against an obstruction, or reaches the maximum range of the spell. If the object rises to maximum range, it will hoover about, bobbing in the air until the

Mage/3A – Harden Metal

Mage/Alteration	Level: 3
Cast Time: 3 rounds	Duration: Hour)/Level
Range: Touch	Affected Area: 10gold piece/level
Mana: 3	Damage: N/A
Save: N/A	Save Affect: N/A
Components: V, S, M	Concentration: None
Material Component: Piece of adamanite	
Somatic Component: Dragging corner of adaminite across metal.	

Execution - Casting this spell cause metal to harden to the stiffness of adamnite.

Affect – Only a single item can be affected. The spell will have no affect if it is attempted on an item larger then the allowed affected area.

Limiations - The hardness cannot be adjusted after the spell is cast.

Mage/3A – Passwall

Mage/Alteration	Level: 3
Cast Time: 3 rounds	Duration: 1 Round (10 seconds)/Level
Range: Touch	Affected Area: Shroud
Mana: 3	Damage: N/A
Save: N/A	Save Affect: N/A
Components: V, S, M	Concentration: High
Material Component: Drop of oil	

Somatic Component: Rubbing oil between fingers.

Execution - Casting this spell will allow the subject and all carried creatures and items, to become non-corpreal and pass through walls and solid objects.

Affect - The spell will affect all items carried, regardless if they are magical or non-magical, living or inanimate. The subject cannot be struck by non-magical weapons.

Limitations - Although the spell can cause creatures or magic items to become non-corpreal, the spell cannot be used to pass through other magical objects or living tissue. Likewise, the non-corpreal subject can be struck by magical weapons or the limbs of creatures. While immersed in solid matter, the subject will be unable to see, and hearing will be reduced to ½. While passing through solid matter, the caster cannot cast spells or activate magical items.

passing through solids, the

Aftermath - When the spell exhausts its duration, the subject will start to feel drag from pasing through objects as they begin to solidify. In the course of 1 round (10 seconds) the subject will becom completely solid once again.

Mage/3A – Transparency

Mage/Alteration	Level: 3
Cast Time: 3 rounds	Duration: 1 Round (10 seconds)/Level
Range: Touch	Affected Area: Shroud
Mana: 3	Damage: N/A
Save: N/A	Save Affect: N/A
Components: V, S, M	Concentration: High

Material Component: Drop of oil

Somatic Component: Rubbing oil between fingers.

Execution - This spell will cause stone, wood, or other non-living matter to become transparent like glass. The transparency can be 1-way or 2-way in that, the spell may be cast to only allow viewing through from one side of a wall or object

Erratta – The spell wil not make an item invisible, but will make it very unnoticeable, particularly from a distance.

Mage/3A – Water to Oil

Mage/Alteration	Level: 3
Cast Time: 3 rounds	Duration: N/A
Range: 15' + 10'/level	Affected Area: 1 pint/level
Mana: 3	Damage: N/A
Save: N/A	Save Affect: N/A
Components: V, S, M	Concentration: None

Material Component: Water

Somatic Component: A swirling motion with a downward pointed finger.

Execution - Casting this spell will transform water into oil.

Limitations - If the water is in a container, it must be unsealed. If the spell is used to transform part of a larger body of water, the oil will rise to the surface and spread out.

Aftermath - Once the spell is complete, the oil is non-magical and can be used for burning, lubrication, etc.

Mage/3C – Continual Light

Mage/Conjuration	Level: 3
Cast Time: 3 Seconds	Duration: Permanent
Range: Touch	Affected Area: 30'/level
Mana: 3	Damage: N/A
Save: None	Save Affect: N/A
Components: V, S	

Material Component: None

Somatic Component: Snap of fingers

Execution - When this spell is cast, it creates a small, brilliantly glowing 2" sphere. The spell can be cast into the air (where it will remain motionless) or on an object (in order to be moved about).

Affect - The magical orb that will effectively light a surrounding 15' radius. Although different in appearance, a light sphere gives off roughly the same amount of light as a bright torch.

Adjustments - As the spell is cast, the caster selects the command words to contro it. Once the spell is cast, a continual light sphere has no direct connection to the caster. Anyone who knows the proper command words can control it and cause it to be brightened, dimmed, or turned off

Aftermath - The orb is a continual magic and, will last until is dispelled by magics that destroy continual magics. If the spell is cast onto an object, it becomes a magical item. Once cast bears no connection to the spell caster. Anyone who knows the

Limiations - A light spell cannot be cast onto living tissue nor objects or creatures already affected by continual magics. The spell might, however, be cast onto the clothing or something carried by a living or magical creature. Likewise, the spell may be cast on a container for a magical item, or an a non-magical object attached to the magical item.

Errata - A light sphere give off no heat and consumes no oxygen. It cannot be blown out, doused, or extinguished by normal means. A light sphere has no physical mass of its own. It cannot be touched.

Mage/3C - Create Food and Drink

Mage/Conjuration	Level: 2
Cast Time: 3 seconds	Duration: N/A
Range: Touch	Affected Area: 1 Creature
Mana: 3	Damage: N/A
Save: N/A	Save Affect: N/A
Components: V, S	Concentration: N/A

Material Component: None

Somatic Component: Waving off hands over food in sweeping motion

Execution - By use of this spell the caster is able to create enough food and drink to feed 1 humanoic creature for wach level of experience of the spell caster.

Affect - The spell can be used to to create any sort of common food known to the caster. The food can be created inside unsealed containers and will be at whatever temperature as would be normal for eating.

Aftermath - Once the food is created it is for all practical purposes regular food and retains no magical nature. Magically created food is subject to all normal adversarious conditions such as spoilage, contamination, etc.

Limitations - The spell cannot be used to create foods with magical, healing, or special chemical qualities.

Mage/3C - Create Oil

Mage/Conjuration	Level: 3
Cast Time: 3 Seconds	Duration: Permanent
Range: Touch	Affected Area: 30'/level
Mana: 3	Damage: N/A
Save: None	Save Affect: N/A
Components: V, S	

Material Component: None

Somatic Component: Snap of fingers

Execution - When this spell is cast, it creates a small, brilliantly glowing 2" sphere. The spell can be cast into the air (where it will remain motionless) or on an object (in order to be moved about).

Mage/3C – Reflective Shield

Mage/Conjuration	Level: 3
Cast Time: 1 Segment	Duration: 1 hour/level
Range: 0	Affected Area: 10' x 10'
Mana: 3	Damage: N/A
Save: N/A	Save Affect: N/A
Components: V	Concentration: N/A
Material Comp: None	
Somatic Comp: None	

Execution This spell create a vertical wall of force that can be used to hide behind to avoid being hit by missle attacks.

Affect - The shield can be create or adjusted to be of any color, flat or opaque, translucent or invisible, or completely reflective. It is always square or rectangular in shape. It is strictly 2-dimensional and does not have a thickness. It is solid to the touch, and is impervious to all normal missle regardless of the size or weight. Even massive boulders will be easily deflected without the shield having budged. Likewise, non-magical creatures will be unable to pass through the shield. All non-magical gasses, vapors, and fluids will be deflected as well.

Limitations - The shield is non-movable and cannot be moved about or cast on an object or creature to be moved. The shield can only be cast vertically and cannot be made to lay over a creature or item, nor can it even be cast at a slant to provide better protection from an arial attack. Any sort of magical affect, magical item, enchanted object, magical creature, or creature under the influence of an enchanntment will pass easily through the shield, disrupting the enchantment of the shield and causing it to dispel.

Aftermath - The shiled will not be dispelled if the caster is away, however, it cannot be controlled by the spell caster's command words unless the caster is withing range. The spell will remain in affect until the caster speaks the command words for the spell to end, the enchantment is dispelled, or the spell exhausts its duration.

Mage/3C – Stinking Cloud

Mage/Creation	Level: 3
Cast Time: 1 segment	Duration: 1 round/level
Range: 15' + 10'/level	Affected Area: 30'/level
Mana: 3	Damage: N/A
Save: Charisma	Save Affect: Negates
Components: V, S, M	Concentration: Medium
Material Component: Stink gland of skunk	
Somatic Component: Clutching gland to palm with thumb and pointing with remaining fingers.	

Execution - This spell creates a billowing cloud of nauseous vapors 30 foot in diameter.

Affect - All creatures caught within the cloud must make a constitution saving throw or be overcome with nauseous. Creatures failing a saving throw will be incapacitated from the fumes will be unable to take action. Affected creatures will become sick and unable to leave the cloud without assistance for one round. Creatures who manage to leave the cloud are incapacited for one additional round after emerging.

Adjustments - So long as the caster remains in range of the cloud, the caster can control the movement of the cloud up to 25 yards per round (5mph).

Limitations - The cloud causes no real damage. The cloud will always remain roughly spherical and cannot be formed into eccentric shapes. The cloud cannot be subdivided into separate smaller clouds. Winds in excess of 5 mph will blow the cloud beyond the caster's control and eventuall cause it to move out of range, which will cause it to disperse. The spell caster and members of the party are not immune to the spell should they somehow wind up inside

Concentration - After the spell is cast, the enchantment requires medium concentration to maintain. If the caster is wounded, distracted, or cast a different spell, the anchantment will instantly be dispelled.

Aftermath - When the spell exhausts its duration, the enchantment is dispelled, the cloud moves out of range of the caster, the caster's concentration is broken, or the caster speaks the command words calling for the spell to end, the cloud will begin to dissipate. In the course of one round, it will be totally dissolved and gone.

Mage/3C - Water Spray

Mage/Conjuration	Level: 3
Cast Time: 1 Second	Duration: 1 Round/Level
Range: Touch	Affected Area: 2" x 60' stream
Mana: 3	Damage: None
Save: Dexterity	Save Affect: Maintain footing
Components: S, V, M	Concentration: N/A
Material Component: Drop of water on palm	
Somatic Component: Closing fist around drop, then opening palm towards intended target.	

Execution - This spell will create a forceful stream of water that is 2 inches in diameters and will spray forth 60 feet.

Affect - This spell will immediately silence all emanations of sound from a creature or object.

Uses - The spell might be used to silence an alarm, cause a missle to strike without noise, stop a spell-caster from using spells with somatic components.

Mage/3C – Web

Mage/Conjuration	Level: 3
Cast Time: 3 Seconds	Duration: 1 turn/level
Range: Touch	Affected Area: 30' diameter web
Mana: 2	Damage: N/A
Save: Strength	Save Affect: Breaks free
Components: V, S, M	Concentration: N/A
Material Component: Cob web	
Somatic Component: Rolling web into ball and tossing at opponent	

Execution - This spell will create a large net of stick strands that will ensnage creatures in a 30' diamater area.

Limitations - Creatures trapped in the netting are allowed a strnght saving throw each round in an attempt to break free

Erratta - The netting is flammable, and if set afire, will burn anyone trapped in its strands for 3D6 hit-points of fire damage.

Aftermath - When the affect exhausts its duration the strands will start to shrink and dissolve away. In the course of a round, the webbing will become completely inert and creatures traped inside will escape. Although magically created, the webbing retains no magical nature and connot be magically dispelled or dissolved by command words.

Mage/3D – Detect Influence

Mage/Divination	Level: 3
Cast Time: 3 Seconds	Duration: N/A
Range: 0	Affected Area: Self
Mana: 3	Damage: None
Save: Dexterity	Save Affect: Avoids for 1 Round
Components: S	Concentration: N/A

Material Component: None
Somatic Component: Dragging a finger across the lower lip
Affect - This spell will cause the caster to be totally articulate in all froms of non-magical conversing. The caster will be able to comprehend, speak, read and write any form of verbal or written communication. The spell will also endow the caster with the dialects and accents as may be appropriate.

Mage/3D - Find Gold

Mage/Divination	Level: 3
Cast Time: 3 Seconds	Duration: N/A
Range: 0	Affected Area: Self
Mana: 3	Damage: None
Save: Dexterity	Save Affect: Avoids for 1 Round
Components: S	Concentration: N/A

Material Component: None
Somatic Component: Dragging a finger across the lower lip
Affect - This spell will cause the caster to be totally articulate in all froms of non-magical conversing. The caster will be able to comprehend, speak, read and write any form of verbal or written communication. The spell will also endow the caster with the dialects and accents as may be appropriate.

Mage/3D - Locate

Mage/Divination	Level: 3
Cast Time: 3 Minutes	Duration: 1 round/level
Range: Touch	Affected Area: 10' Cubic/level
Mana: 40	Damage: N/A
Save: N/A	Save Affect: N/A
Components: V, S	

Material Component: Needle, pin or other tiny metal rod
Somatic Component: Placing needle on palm of hand
Execution - This spell will reveal the direction of a creature, a type of creature, an item, or a type of item. When the spell is cast, whenever the sought after creature or item is within range, the meedle will hover a an inch or so above the caster's palm and point the direction .
Affect - As the spell is invoked, the caster will need to designate the scope of the spell. For example, the spell, might be used to locate a certain human, or the nearest human, the nearest humanoid, the nearest natural creature, the nearest creature, etc.
Limitations - The spell will needle will point directly at the subject, even if the shortest open path to the subject is a different direction. Once the spell is cast, the subject, or scope of the spell cannot be changed. To locate a individual creature or item (as opposed to a type) the caster must have had physical contact with creature or item at seom point. If the spell is used to locate a type, the needle will point to the nearest creature or object of the sought type, regardless of whether or not it is the particular individual item or creature being sought. Creatures or items in a hermetically sealed area cannot be located. . Various magics in the game can obscure an item, making it impossible to locate with a magical spell. Artifacts and relics are typically immune to location magics
Adjustments - Althought the spell cannot be adjusted, when the caster has found the subnect the needle is poiting towards, the needle can be touched to the creature or object. Thence forth, the magic will ignore the touched creature or item and point to the second nearest. As more are touched, they also become ignored. It is possible to find many individuals of a type with a single spell.

Aftermath - The spell will end when it exhausts its duration, the enchantment is dispelled, or the caster speaks the command words calling for the spell to end.

Mage/3D - Scan Item

Mage/Divination	Level: 3
Cast Time: 3 Minutes	Duration: 1 round/level
Range: 15'	Affected Area: One item
Mana: 3	Damage: N/A
Save: N/A	Save Affect: N/A
Components: V, S	

Material Component: None
Somatic Component: None
Execution - This spell reveals the basic rudimentary purpose of an object, and the simplest methods of its use.
Affect - The spell will reveal the common name of the item. If the item is magical, it will reveal the command words necessary to operate it. If the spell is used on a scroll, the name of the spell will be revealed
Limitations - The spell will not reveal if the item is an evil or cursed nature. The spell will not reveal if detailed information about the number of charges of an item, the damage it might cause, the range of its affects, etc.

Mage/3D - Tounges

Mage/Divination	Level: 3
Cast Time: 3 Seconds	Duration: N/A
Range: 0	Affected Area: Self
Mana: 3	Damage: None
Save: Dexterity	Save Affect: Avoids for 1 Round
Components: S	Concentration: N/A

Material Component: None
Somatic Component: Dragging a finger across the lower lip
Affect - This spell will cause the caster to be totally articulate in all froms of non-magical conversing. The caster will be able to comprehend, speak, read and write any form of verbal or written communication. The spell will also endow the caster with the dialects and accents as may be appropriate.
Limitations - The spell will not change the tonal qualities of the spell casters voice. The caster might sound like a ntaive of a particular area, but the affect will not be aid in the impersonatation of an idividual. The enchantment will not enable the caster to cimmunicate in the grunts and body languages of animals or any creature that communicates by means other than a spoken language.
Uses - The caster might use the spell to communicate with a stranger or interrogate a prisoner.
Aftermath - The spell will end when it exhausts its duration or the enchantment is dispelled.

Mage/3E - Dimension Walk

Mage/Enchantment	Level: 3
Cast Time: 3 Seconds	Duration: N/A
Range: 15' + 10'/Level	Affected Area: Self
Mana: 3	Damage: N/A
Save: N/A	Save Affect: N/A
Components: V	Concentration: N/A

Material component: None
Somatic component: None
Execution - This spell will teleport the caster and all carried items in any direction, including up or down, up 15 feet + 10 feet per level of experience of the caster.

Affect -

Limitations - The spell caster can only teleport to a location that can be seen visually, or to a place where the caster has already been.

Adjustments - If the intended destination is already occupied by another creature or object, the caster will instead be teleported to the closes available space to the target destination.

Uses - The spell might be used to bypass a trap or obstacle, or to return to a known location after becoming lost.

Mage/3E - Dispel Enchantment

Mage/Enchantment	Level: 3
Cast Time: 3 Seconds	Duration: N/A
Range: 15' + 10'/Level	Affected Area: Single/!5' radius
Mana: 3	Damage: None
Save: N/A	Save Affect: N/A
Components: V, S	Concentration: N/A
Material Component: None	
Somatic component: Snapping of fingers	

Execution - This spell can be cast in one of two forms. It may be used to dispel a single enchantment or all enchantments in a 15' radius.

Singular affect - When this spell is used in singular form it will remove all magics from the the creature or item it is cast upon. Any enchantments that were affecting the subject will be destroyed. If the spell is used singularly on a continual magic, (magical creature, magical item, etc) the continual magic will be neutralized for of round for every level of experince of the spell caster.

Area casting - If this spell is used in area form it has absolutely no affect on continual magics. It will, however destroy all enchantments in the affected area, When used in this form, the spell has no duration and its affect and will not prevent further magics from being introduced.

Limiations - This spell will not affect artifacts or relics. It will not prevent a creature from casting a spell, reading a scroll, or employing a magical item. When the spell is invoked in singular form, the caster can specify any duration up to the maximum of 1 round/level, but the the duration cannot be ended early by used of command words. Unless otherwise pre-stated, the referee will assume the spell was cast for maximum duration. The spell will not reverse any magically induced damage or reverse any affects that do not have a magical duration.

Mage/3E - Protective Aura

Mage/Enchantment	Level: 3
Cast Time: 3 Seconds	Duration: N/A
Range: 15' + 10'/Level	Affected Area: Single/!5' radius
Mana: 3	Damage: None
Save: N/A	Save Affect: N/A
Components: V, S	Concentration: N/A
Material Component: None	
Somatic component: Snapping of fingers	

Execution - This spell can be cast in one of two forms. It may be used to dispel a single enchantment or all enchantments in a 15' radius.

Mage/3I - Hold Person

Mage/Illusion	Level: 3
Cast Time: 2 Seconds	Duration: 1 Round/level (non-mag)
Range: 15' + 10'/level	Affected Area: 1 Creature
Mana: 2	Damage: N/A
Save: Charisma	Save Affect: Negates
Components: V	Concentration: N/A
Material Component: None	
Somatic Component: None	

Execution - This spell causes the subject to become entranced and immobilized.

Affect - The affected creature will be semi-entranced. They will not be able to gather the concentration necessary to cast spells or use command words to activate magical items. Affected creatures will be daxed, and will think, walk, and move at ½ normal speed.

Limitations - The spell is only affective on natural creatures. The affect will not force the subject to speak or act in any certain way.

Aftermath - Wounding, extreme fear, slapping, dousing with water, and other rousing affects will prematurely end the spells affect. Although magically induced, the affect is psychological and there is no magical duration. The affect cannot be controlled by command words or dispelled. When the spell is invoked, the caster should speciify a duration. If the caster does not specify, the referee will assume that the spell is to run for maximum duraton.

Mage/3I - Interrogate

Mage/Illusion	Level: 3
Cast Time: 2 Seconds	Duration: 1 Round/level (non-mag)
Range: 15' + 10'/level	Affected Area: 1 Creature
Mana: 2	Damage: N/A
Save: Charisma	Save Affect: Negates
Components: V	Concentration: N/A
Material Component: None	
Somatic Component: None	

Execution - This spell causes the subject to become entranced and immobilized.

Mage/3N - Feign Death

Mage/Necromancy	Level: 3
Cast Time: 3 turns	Duration: N/A
Range: Touch	Affected Area: 1 Creature
Mana: 3	Damage: None
Save: N/A	Save Affect: N/A
Components: V, S	Concentration: N/A
Material component: None	
Somatic component: Horizontal sweeping motion with the hand	

Execution - Casting this spell will casue a subject to appear dead. Once cast, the affect is physiological and cannot be magically dispelled.

Affect - The subject will seem completely lifeless. All bodily functions will cease and the flesh will take on a pale appearance and cool to room temperature. The subject will not require any food or air to be sustained.

Limitations - The spell has no affect upon unwilling subjects, and willing subject will be able to rouse themselves at any time. To maintain the the affect, the subject must make no voluntary movements. If the subject is moved about by external means, the affect is not dissapaited.

While under the spells affect, none of the subject's senses will function except hearing. The subject will not be aware of being moved or wounded unless they pick up on some audible clues as to what is occurring.

Erratta - While under the affect of the spell, the subject will experience no damage or discomfort from adverse temperature, so long as the temperature is warm enough to prevent freezing, and cool enough to not sear flesh.

Mage/3N - Infravision

Mage/Necromancy	Level: 3
Cast Time: 3 Seconds	Duration: N/A
Range: Touch	Affected Area: 1 Creature
Mana: 3	Damage: None
Save: N/A	Save Affect: N/A
Components: V, S	Concentration: N/A
Material component: None	
Somatic component: Laying plam across recipient's eyes	

Execution - By means of this spell the magic-user enables the recipient of infravision to see light in the infrared spectrum.

Affect - The differences in heat wave radiations can be seen up to 60'. Note that strong sources of infrared radiation (fire, lanterns, torches, etc.) tend to blind or cast "shadows" just as such light does with respect to normal vision, so the infravision is affected and does not function efficiently in the presence of such heat sources. (Invisible creatures are not usually detectable by infravision, as the infrared light waves are affected by invisibility, just as those of the ultraviolet and normal spectrums are.) The material component of this spell is either a pinch of dried corrot or an agate.

Mage/3N - Neutralize Poison

Mage/Evocation	Level: 3
Cast Time: 1 segment	Duration: 1 round/level
Range: Touch	Affected Area: N/A
Mana:3	Damaage: None
Save: N/A	Save Affect: N/A
Components: V, S	
Material Component: None	
Somatic Component: None	

Execution - This spell causes all poisons inside a single creature to become inert and harmless.

Affect - If the spell is used on person suffering the effects of poison, it will cease immediately and no further damage will be sustained (Damage already incurred will not be healed). If the spell is used on a venmous creature, it will neutralize the venoms.

All poisons and venoms will be affected regardless if they deal damage, or only cause paralyzation.

The spell will not cause venoms or poisons to change color or consitency. After being neutralized, the poison retains no magical nature from this spell, and magical dispelling will not restore the poison. If the spell is used to neutralize a venomous creature, the effects are temporary, since the magic will not alter a creatures poison producing capabilities.

Mage/3N - Wizard Eye

Mage/Evocation	Level: 3
Cast Time: 1 segment	Duration: 1 hour/level
Range: 15' + 10'/level	Affected Area: 30'/level
Mana: 2	Damage: N/A
Save: Charisma	Save Affect: Negates
Components: V, S	Concentration: Medium
Material Component: Eye	
Somatic Component: Laying palm over eye and pointing with other hand.	

Execution - This spell will allow the caster to close one eye, and send a forth magically created facsimile to see what lies ahead.

Affect – The disembodied eye, for all intents and purposes will appear and function as the natural eye it has duplicated. It will magically be kept warm, moist, and free of irritation. The eye can be moved about at a rate of 50 yards per round (10 mph)

Limitations - The eye is not protected from damage by weapons, or magic. If the eye is physically destroyed it will cause 1D8 damage to the spell caster. If it is bumped or battered, but there is no damage, the pain is transmitted back to the spell caster. The spell requires low concentration to maintain.

Concentration - Maintiaining the spell requires concentration on the part of the spell caster. If the caster is becomes unconscious, is wounded or attempts a new spell, the concentration will be broken and the eye will fall to the ground.

Erratta - If the caster is becomes unconscious, is wounded or attempts a new spell, the concentration will be broken and the eye will fall to the ground. If the enchantment is still in force, the caster can regain control of the eye when concentratin is restored.

Aftermath - The enchantment is ended when the spell exhausts its duration, the caster speaks the command word calling for the spell to end, the enchantment is dispelled, or the eye is physically destroyed.

Mage/3V - Energy Bomb

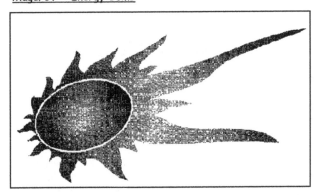

Mage/Evocation	Level: 3
Cast Time: 3 Seconds	Duration: N/A
Range: 15' + 10'/level	Affected Area: 15' radius
Mana: 2	Damage: Up to 6D4
Save: Dexterity	Save Affect: ½ damage
Components: V, S	Concentration: N/A
Material Component: None	
Somatic Component: Pointing of finger	

Execution - This spell will cause a small, one inch ball of light to shoot forth from the caster's outstretched finger, fly through the air, and burst into a ball of magical energy.

Affect - Energy damage harms only creatures and does not damage items and objects. The affect creates a flashes of light (not intense enough to temporarily blind). All creatures caught in the blast will suffer energy damage.

Mage/3V - Explosive Runes

Mage/Evocation	Level: 3
Cast Time: 3 Seconds	Duration: N/A
Range: 0	Affected Area: 15' radius
Mana: 3	Damage: 3D6
Save: None	Save Affect: None
Components: V, S, M	Concentration: N/A

Material Component: Sulphur powder
Somatic Component: drawing of symbol using powder

Execution - By tracing the mystic runes upon a book, map, scroll, reading the text will create a firey blast that will cause 3D6 hit-points of fire damage to all within a 15' radius

Affect - The spell is used to prevent unauthorized reading of written materials.

The explosive runes are difficult to detect, 5% per level of magic use experience of the reader, thieves having only a 5% chance in any event. When read, the explosive runes detonate, delivering a full 12 to 30 (6d4 + 6) hit points of damage upon the reader, who gets no saving throw, and either a like amount, or half that if saving throws are made, on creatures within the blast radius.

Adjustments - The spell caster can temporarily deactivate the spell by speaking the command words to suspend the spell, then later speaking the command words to reinstate it.

Erratta - The caster who cast this spell, and any mage that the caster gives warning to, is not affected by the rune, and can merely skim past it as the other text is read.

destroyed when the explosion takes place unless it is not normally subject to destruction by magical fire.

Mage/3V - Flame Blast

Mage/Evocation	Level: 3
Cast Time: 2 Seconds	Duration: N/A
Range: 15' + 10'/level	Affected Area: 1 Creature or Object
Mana: 3	Damage: 1D4/2 Levels up to 7D4
Save: N/A	Save Affect: N/A
Components: V	Concentration: N/

Material Component: Bit of Sulphur
Somatic Component: Pointing at target

Level	Fire Damage
0-2	1D6 Hit-points
3-6	2D6 Hit-points
6-9	3D6 Hit-points
9-12	4D6 Hit-points
12211	5D6 Hit-points
15-14	6D6 Hit-points

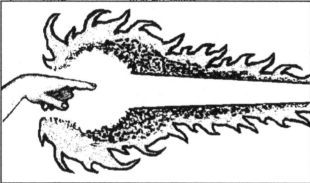

Execution - Invoking this spell will cause a bolt of fire to erupt from the caster's extended finger tip to strike a target creature or object.

Affect - The affect will cause 1-6 (1D6) Hit-points of fire damage for everly level of experience of the caster, up to a limit of 10-60 (10D6) hit-points.

Mage/3V - Frost Enchant

Mage/Evocation	Level: 3
Cast Time: 3 Seconds	Duration: N/A
Range: 0	Affected Area: 15' radius
Mana: 3	Damage: 3D6
Save: None	Save Affect: None
Components: V, S, M	Concentration: N/A

Material Component: Sulphur powder
Somatic Component: drawing of symbol using powder

Execution - By tracing the mystic runes upon a book, map, scroll, reading the text will create a firey blast that will cause 3D6 hit-points of fire damage to all within a 15' radius

Affect - The spell is used

Mage/3V - Frost Shield

Mage/Evocation	Level: 3
Cast Time: 3 Seconds	Duration: N/A
Range: 0	Affected Area: 15' radius
Mana: 3	Damage: 3D8 Frost
Save: None	Save Affect: None
Components: V, S, M	Concentration: N/A

Material Component: Sulphur powder
Somatic Component: drawing of symbol using powder

Execution - This spell will create This spell creates a 10' x 10' magical wall that causes 3D8 points of frost damage to any creature that passes through it.

Description - The will appear as a shimmering white square.

Limitations -Once the spell is cast, the color cannot be changed, and the shield cannot be moved, nor can it be cast onto an object or creature in order to be moved about. The shield can only be cast to be flat, vertical, and square.

Erratta - If there is not adequate space to accommodate the shield, it will be imbedded in surrounding solids.

Aftermath - The enchantment remains in affect until the spell exhausts its duration, the caster speaks the command words calling for the spell to end, or the enchantment is dispelled.

Mage/3V - Frost Touch

Mage/Evocation	Level: 3
Cast Time: 2 Seconds	Duration: N/A
Range: Touch	Affected Area: 30'/level
Mana: 3	Damage: N/A
Save: Dexterity	Save Affect: Avoids
Components: V, S, M	Concentration: N/A

Level	Freeze Damage
0-2	1D8
3-5	2D8
6-8	3D8
9-11	4D8
12-14	5D8
15-17	6D8
18-20	7D8
21-23	8D8
24-26	9D8
27-	10D8

Material Component: Small piece of glass
Somatic Component: None

Execution - This spell will cause the caster's touch will drain a massive amount of heat from creature touched.

Affect - The affect will cause 1-8 (1D8) Hit-points of cold

Level	Energy Damage
0-2	1D4 Hit-points
3-5	2D4 Hit-points
6-8	3D4 Hit-points
9-11	4D4 Hit-points
12-14	5D4 Hit-points
15-17	6D4 Hit-points
18-	7D4 Hit-points

damage for everly level of experience of the caster, up to a limit of 10-80 (10D8) hit-points.

Depending upon the type of creature, the amount of damage, and the are being touched, the referee may declare that the subject has been frost-bitten and, upon thawing, the frost-bitten area will turn black and will need to be amputated.

Mage/3V - Water Blast

Mage/Alteration	Level: 1
Cast Time: 1 Second	Duration: 1 Round/Level
Range: Touch	Affected Area: 1 Creature or object
Mana: 1	Damage: None
Save: Dexterity	Save Affect: Avoids
Components: S	Concentration: N/A

Material Component: None
Somatic Component: Placing a finger upright against the lips, then touching the intended subject
Affect - This spell will immediately silence all emanations of sound from a creature or object.
Uses - The spell might be used to silence an alarm, cause a missle to strike without noise, stop a spell-caster from using spells with somatic components.

Mage/3V – Wind Gust

Mage/Evocation	Level: 3
Cast Time: 3 Seconds	Duration: N/A
Range: 0	Area: 30' diamter x 15'/Level
Mana: 3	Damage: None
Save: Dexterity	Save Affect: Maintain position
Components: V, S	Concentration: N/A

Material Component: None
Somatic Component: Blowing air across palm at target
Execution - When this spell is cast, a strong puff of air originates from the mage and moves in the direction he or she is facing.
Affect - The force of this gust of wind is sufficient to extinguish candles, torches, and similar unprotected flames, It will cause protected flames -such as those of lanterns- to wildly dance. It will also fan large fires outwards in the direction of the wind's movement. It will force back small flying creatures and cause man-sized ones to be held motioniess if attempting to move into its force, and similarly slow large flying creatures by 50% for I round. It will blow over light objects.

Mage/4A – Adhesive Surface

Mage/Alteration	Level: 4
Cast Time: 4 Seconds	Duration: 1 Round/level
Range: Touch	Affected Area: 30' diameter surface
Mana: 4	Damage: None
Save: Strength	Save Affect: Able to step
Components: V, S	Concentration: None

Material Component: Bit of glue
Somatic Component: Rubbing glue between fingers, the pointing
Execution - When this spell is cast upon a wall, floor, section of ground, or other flat surface, it will become sticky to the touch.
Affect - Any creature stuck to the surface will have to make a strength saving throw to break free. A creature who is close to the edge of an adhesive area will be free after only one successful strength save. Persons closer to the middle of the area will have to make a successful roll for each step, up to a maximum of 7 steps to leave the middle (7 steps required for a human size bi-pedal to walk the 15' radius of the area. The referee will adjust this quantity lower for creatures with longer strides, and up for creatures with shorter strides). Creature attempting to leave the affect area are allowed to make one save (1 step if successful) per round.

Creatures who are attached in multiple areas from sitting or lying on the affected area will make the first saving throw at a penalty from having less leverage.

Mage/4A – Gaseous Form

Mage/Alteration	Level: 4
Cast Time: 1 segment	Duration: 1 round/level
Range: Touch	Affected Area: 1 Creature
Mana: 4	Damage: None
Save: Dexterity	Save Affect: Avoids for 1 round
Components: V, S	Concentration: None

Material Component: None
Somatic Component: Touching of subject
Execution - This spell will cause one creature and all carried items to be transformed into a billowing green cloud.
Affect - Consult *Magical Game Standards/Gaseous form*

Mage/4A – Hermetic Seal

Mage/Alteration	Level: 4
Cast Time: 1 segment	Duration: 1 round/level
Range: Touch	Affected Area: 1 Creature
Mana: 4	Damage: None
Save: Dexterity	Save Affect: Avoids for 1 round
Components: V, S	Concentration: None

Material Component: None
Somatic Component: Touching of subject
Execution - This spell will cause one creature and all carried items to be transformed into a billowing green cloud.

Mage/4A – Silence 15' Radius

Mage/Alteration	Level: 4
Cast Time: 4 Seconds	Duration: N/A
Range: Touch	Affected Area: 1 Creature
Mana: 4	Damage: None
Save: None	Save Affect: N/A
Components: V, S, M	Concentration: N/A

Material Component: None
Somatic Components: Finger to the lips as if to silence
Execution - Casting this spell will stop all sound causing vibrations in a 15 foot radius of the spell point of origin.
Affect - Creatures and objects inside the affected area will be incapable of speaking alound, communicating verbally, or casting spells with verbal components, os using magic items that require command words. Missle weapons fired into the affected area will alnd silently. Creatures struck by missles inside an affected area will be unable to cry out or sound an alarm.

Limitations - The point of origin cannot be moved after the spell has been cast, nor can the spell be cast onto a creature or item in order to be moved about. If the spell caster is inside the affected area, they will be unable to speak the command words to end the spell.

Uses - A party passing through a silenced area cannot be heard by an enemy, but also cannot communicate with each other verbally.

Aftermath - The spell will run until it exhausts its duration, the enchantment is dispelled, or the spell caster speaks the command words for the spell to end (from outside the circle).

Mage/4A - Stone to Mud

Mage/Alteration	Level: 4
Cast Time: 4 Seconds	Duration: N/A
Range: Touch	Affected Area: 1 Creature
Mana: 4	Damage: None
Save: None	Save Affect: N/A
Components: V, S, M	Concentration: N/A
Material Component: None	
Somatic Components: Finger to the lips as if to silence	

Execution - Casting this spell will stop all sound causing vibrations in a 15 foot radius of the spell point of origin.

Mage/4C - Insect Paque

Mage/Evocation	Level: 4
Cast Time: 1 segment	Duration: 1 round/level
Range: Touch	Affected Area: 1000' Cubic/level
Mana: 4	Damage: N/A
Save: Charisma	Save Affect: Negates
Components: V, S	Concentration: N/A
Material Component: Drop of water	
Somatic Component: Clutching hand around drop and blwing air through fist	

Execution - This spell will create a block of normal ice up to 1000 cubic feet (10' x 10' x 10') per level of experience of the spell caster.

Mage/4C - Wall of Ice

Mage/Evocation	Level: 4
Cast Time: 1 segment	Duration: 1 round/level
Range: Touch	Affected Area: 1000' Cubic/level
Mana: 4	Damage: N/A
Save: Charisma	Save Affect: Negates
Components: V, S	Concentration: N/A
Material Component: Drop of water	
Somatic Component: Clutching hand around drop and blwing air through fist	

Execution - This spell will create a block of normal ice up to 1000 cubic feet (10' x 10' x 10') per level of experience of the spell caster.

Affect - The ice can be created as any shape desired, smooth or rough, clear or with white splotches. Any creature attempting to walk upon smooth ice must make a dexterity saving throw or fall.

Limitations - Only a single ice block can be created and cannot be created into separate pieces. The ice cannot be made into elaborate aritistic shapes unless the caster has artistics talents

Aftermath - once the spell is cast, the ice created is for all practical purposes, ordinary ice and subject to all normal adversaious conditions such as metlting, shattering, etc.

Erratta - If the spell is cast to in case a warm-blooded creature of other warm object, the ice block will shatter, perltering all creatures in a 15' radius with ice and dealing 3D12 hit-points of pelter damage.

Mage/4C - Wall of Fire

Mage/Conjuration	
Level: 4	
Cast Time: 4 seconds	
Duration: 1 turn/level	
Range: 15' + 10'/Level	
Affected Area: 100sq'/level	
Mana: 4	
Damage: 3D6	
Save: None	
Save Affect: N/A	
Components: V, S, M	
Concentration: None	
Material Component: Piece of sulphur	
Somatic Component: Downward vertical motion with psread fingers	

Execution - This spell creates a magical curtain of flame 1 foot thick.

Mage/4D - Detect Lie

Mage/Evocation	Level: 4
Cast Time: 1 segment	Duration: 1 round/level
Range: Touch	Affected Area: 30'/level
Mana: 2	Damage: N/A
Save: Charisma	Save Affect: Negates
Components: V, S	Concentration: N/A
Material Component: None	
Somatic Component: Placing a hand to the ear as if to hear better	

Execution - This spell will allow the caster to determine if a subject is lying, telling the truh, or speaking in exaggeration.

Affect - By means of this spell the caster is able to pick up on minute, normally inaudible fluctuations in the subjects voice in order to tell if the subject is lying. A successful save indicates that the subject is able to mask these fluctuations so as to not reveal lies.

Limitations - The spell only reveals if the speaker *believes* the information is correct and not whether it is truly accurdate. The spell requires low concentration to maintain and can be held in affect throughout its duration as long as the caster is not wounded or does not attempt to cast a new spell or activate a magic item. The spell will not increase the caster's hearing range. To determine if the subject is speaking the truth, the caster must be able to hear the subject naturally.

Mage/4D - Enchant Footsteps

Mage/Divination	Level: 4
Cast Time: 4 Seconds	Duration: 1 Minute/level
Range: Touch	Affected Area: 15' Radius
Mana: 4	Damage: N/A
Save: Charisma	Save Affect: Negates
Components: V, S	Concentration: None
Material Component: None	
Somatic Component: Pointing	

Execution - This spell will allow the caster to make visible to all the trail of footprints (or tracks) made by an creature who has past. The affect wil be centered around the caster and will move as the caster moves

Affect - The tracks will be brightly illuminated and obvious. The affect wil be centered around the caster and will move as the caster moves

Adjustments - The spell caster can use command words to adjust the age of tracks that are shown. For example, in a busy city, a caster might limit the spells affect to the last five minutes to find someone who has recently past. The caster may selected a pariticular set of footprints, and use command words to turn off the illumination to any others. The affected area moves about with the caster, and is always centered on the caster's person. By this method, the caster can walk along the trail of footprints in order to find follow.

Limitations - The spell will always detect the steps from the current moment to any previous time up ot 1 hour per level of the caster. The caster cannot adjust the spell time to include a range excluding the present up to 1 hour per level of experience. For example, the caster cannot specify a range of 2 hours to 4 hours previous, and omit the last 2 hours.

Aftermath - The spell will run until it exhausts its duration, the enchantment is dispelled, or the spell caster speaks the command words for the spell to end.

Mage/4D – Find Gole

Mage/Divination	Level: 4
Cast Time: 4 rounds	Duration: 1 turn/level
Range: Touch	Affected Area: 30'/level
Mana: 4	Damage: N/A
Save: None	Save Affect: N/A
Components: V, S, M	Concentration: High
Material Component: Puddle or pool of water	
Somatic Component: Waving of hands over surface of water	

Execution - This spell will cause the visuals of the reflective surface of water to shimmer and reform into images of

Mage/4D – Scrye

Mage/Divination	Level: 4
Cast Time: 4 rounds	Duration: 1 turn/level
Range: Touch	Affected Area: 30'/level
Mana: 4	Damage: N/A
Save: None	Save Affect: N/A
Components: V, S, M	Concentration: High
Material Component: Puddle or pool of water	
Somatic Component: Waving of hands over surface of water	

Execution - This spell will cause the visuals of the reflective surface of water to shimmer and reform into images of creatures or objects being scryed. See "scrying" under . *See Game-Standards/Magical/Scroll creation*

Mage/4E – Create Potion of Invisibility

Mage/Enchantment	Level: 4
Cast Time: 4 hours	Duration: N/A
Range: Touch	Affected Area: 2 fluid ounces ink
Mana: 40	Damage: N/A
Save: N/A	Save Affect: N/A
Components: V, M	Concentration: N/A
Material Component: Pure water	
Somatic Component: None	

Execution - This spell will enchant one vial (2 fluid ounces) of Invisibility potion.

Affect - The potion is poured over the intended creature or tiem in order to create an ivisible shroud.

Mage/4E – Dimension Door

Mage/Enchantmentem	Level: 4
Cast Time: 1 segment	Duration: N/A
Range: 15' + 10'/level	Affected Area: N/A
Mana: 2	Damage: N/A
Save: N/A	Save Affect: N/A
Components: V	Concentration: N/A
Material Component: None	
Somatic Component: None	

Execution - By means of the spell, a mage can very quickly transport themselves a short distance

Effect - The spell instantaneously teleports the caster in any directio, including up or down, to any distance up to the maximum range available.

Limitations - If the targeted space is occupied, the spell will adjust itself to select the nearest space in range that will accommodate. If there is no suitable space available within the spell caster's range, the mana will be used but the teleportation will not take place.

Adjustments - The caster can invoke the spell in such a way so as to reappear facing in any chosen direction. The basic body position, however will be unchanged.

Erratta - As the casting time is only 1 segment (1/10th second), the spell can be cast while in combat between exchanges.

Mage/4E – Dimensional Chamber

Mage/Enchantment	Level: 3
Cast Time: 1 Segment	Duration: 1 hour/level
Range: 0	Affected Area: 10' x 10' x 10' cubic
Mana: 3	Damage: N/A
Save: N/A	Save Affect: N/A
Components: V	Concentration: None
Material component: None	
Somatic component: None	

Execution - This spell creates a a 10' x 10' x 10' cubic extra dimensional space that is centered around the caster. When the spell is completed, everything inside the affected area will vanish and be placed inside the extra-dimensional space.

Affect - Everthing inside the affected area will be inside the chamber when the spell is completed. Objects and creatures that were only partially in the affected area will not be in the chamber. The walls inside the chamber will be a pale gray. The ceiling of the chamber will emit an even lighting.

Limitations - When the chamber dissolves, the occupants will be returned to the same 10' x 10' x 10' are in which the spell was originally cast. Any objects or creatures that have come to occupy the same space in the meantime will be pressed aside. The spell can only be cast to be centered on the spell caster. The chamber cannot be used to trap creatures separately from the spell caster. The chamber can only be dissolved once per spell. To recreate the chamber, a new spell must be cast.

Uses - The spell is best used when the party is suffering heavy damage and needs time to regoup and heal wounds.

Erratta - The chamber will be completely sealed off from the outside world. Creatures and objects inside the chamger cannot be seen, heard, attacked, or otherwise influenced by the outside world. Likewise, anyone insde the cube cannot see, hear, scry or influence the ouside world. The chamber cannot be destroyed externally since it is no longer in the real world.

Aftermath - The chamber will dissolve when the spell exhausts the duration, caster speaks the command word calling for the enchantment to end, or someone *inside* the cube dispels the enchantment.

Mage/4E – Enchant Ink

Mage/Evocation	Level: 4
Cast Time: 4 hours	Duration: N/A
Range: Touch	Affected Area: 2 fluid ounces ink
Mana: 40	Damage: N/A
Save: N/A	Save Affect: N/A
Components: V, M	Concentration: N/A
Material Component: 2 fluid ounces ink	
Somatic Component: None	

Execution - This spell will enchant one vial (2 fluid ounces) or regular ink into magical scroll ink.

Affect - The spell will create a continual magic, in that, the dweomer will not fade due to the passage of time. Likewise, the ink is not affected enchantment dispelling.

Limitations - Enchanted ink dissolves very rapidly in the open air. Immediately after a scroll is inscribed, it must be sealed in an air tight tube to prevent fading. *See Game-Standards/Magical/Scroll creation*

Mage/4E - Invisibility, 15' Radius

Mage/Enchantment	Level: 4
Cast Time: 4 seconds	Duration: 1 Min/Level
Range: 0	Affected Area: 15' Radius
Mana: 4	Damage: N/A
Save: Charisma	Save Affect: Negates
Components: V, S	Concentration: None
Material Component: None	
Somatic Component: Circular motion over head with hand	

Execution – This spell will cause all creatures within a 15' radius to be covered with a magical shroud of invisibility as if an individual spell was cast on each.

Affect – All creatures

Limitations – The spell radius in only applicable at the ompletion of the casting. Thereafter, creatures entering the affected area will not become invisible. Likewise, creatures leaving the affected will retain the invisibility.

Aftermath – The enchantment will remain in affect until the spell exhuasts its duration, the caster speaks the command words to end the affect for on or all affected creatures, the affect is dilpelled, or the shroud is pierced by standard means that would end invisibility see *Game Standards/Magical/Invisibilitiy*

Mage/4I – Circle of Sleep

Mage/Evocation	Level: 4
Cast Time: 4 Turns	Duration: Special
Range: 15' + 10'/Level	Affected Area: One vial
Mana: 50	Damage: 3D12
Save: Dexterity	Save Affect: Avoids
Components: V, S, M	Concentration: N/A
Material Component: Hand full of sand	
Somatic Component: Sprinkling grains of sand along perimter of inteded area of affect	

Execution - This spell will create an area in which all creatures entering must make a charisma saving throw or become weary and fall into a slumber.

Affect - All natural and super-natural creatures will feel the affects of the spell when they enter the affected area and begin to feel very tired

Limitations - Creatures trying to ward off the affect are entitled to a charisma saving throw in order to be able to leave the circle. Plants, Undead creatures, and extra-dimensional creatures are not affected by this spell. Super-natural creatures can be affected, but receive a +4 bonus on their saving throw.

Erratta - Once a person leaves the circle, if they re-enter to save a comrade (or for other reason) they must make a new saving throw. Subsequent saving throw rolls are made at a +4 bonus, due to having already fought off the affects once before.

Aftermath - For potion shelf lifes and durations consult *Games-standards/Magical/Potions*

Mage/4I – Create Potion of Mana Restoration

Mage/Illusion	Level: 4
Cast Time: 4 Turns	Duration: Special
Range: 15' + 10'/Level	Affected Area: One vial
Mana: 40	Damage: N/A
Save: N/A	Save Affect: N/A
Components: V, S, M	Concentration: N/A
Material Component: Water	
Somatic Component: Gesturing over container	

Execution - This spell will convert a vial of ordinary water into a mana potion that will restore 1D8 Mana-points.

Limitations - The water must be clean and free of colors and impurities. The container must be constructed of glass. If any of these restrictions are not met, the spell and mana will be used, but the potion will not be created.

Erratta - The potion will have a light blue tint, and will have a very thin viscosity.

Aftermath - For potion shelf lifes and durations consult *Games-standards/Magical/Potions*

Mage/4I - Forget

Mage/Illusion	Level: 2
Cast Time: 2 Seconds	Duration: N/A
Range: Touch	Affected Area: 1 Creature
Mana: 2	Damage: N/A
Save: Charisma	Save Affect: Negates
Components: V	Concentration: N/A
Material Component: None	
Somatic Component: None	

Execution – This spell can be used to cause a natural creature to forget ver recent events. The spell will erase all memories from the present moment backwards to up to 1 round (10 secoonds) per level of experience of the spellc caster.

Affect - The memories affected by this spell will become buried deep within the subject's subconciuos and will not be recoverable without external assitance. The subject will experience a "blip" in time as moving creature and objects suddenl shift, due to the forgotten time fram being removed from memory.

Limitations - This spell will not interfere with any other sort of minda altering affects. Some restorative game affects can recover memories.

Aftermath - The affect is psychological and cannot be removed my enchantment dispelling. Some mind probing magics or affects, or hypnosis techniques, however, might restore the lost memories.

Mage/4I - Fumble

Mage/Illusion	Level: 4
Cast Time: 4 Turns	Duration: 1 Round
Range: 15' + 10'/Level	Affected Area: One creature
Mana: 4	Damage: N/A
Save: Charisma	Save Affect: Negates
Components: V, S, M	Concentration: Yes

Material Component: Drop of oil
Somatic Component: Swirling oil on palm with fingertip then pointing at intended subject
Execution - This spell will cause the subject to have a mishp in anthing they attempt to do.
Affect - Creatures attacking with weapons will automatically miss and have a mishap as if natural 1 were scored on the roll-to-hit. Spell casters under this affect will have the casting times of spells with somatic components doubled. Running creatures will trip and fall, those reaching for an item will fumble and drop it.
Concentration - If the caster attempts a new spell or is wounded, this spell will be ended.

Mage/4N - Reverse petrification

Mage/Evocation	Level: 4
Cast Time: 4 Turns	Duration: N/A
Range: Touch	Affected Area: One creature
Mana: 4	Damage: N/A
Save: None	Save Affect: N/A
Components: V, S, M	

Material Component: Drop of blood
Somatic Component: Rubbing of blood on surface of stone
Execution - This spell will turn one petrified item or a creature and all carried items back to their prior state.
Limitations - The spell will not affect normal stone or statues or other carvings, due to the lack of cellular structure. It will, howver, restore petrified wood to natural wood.

.

Mage/4N - Shape Change

Mage/Necromancy	Level: 4
Cast Time: 1 segment	Duration: 1 turn/level
Range: Touch	Affected Area: 30'/level
Mana: 2	Damage: None
Save: None	Save Affect: N/A
Components: V, S, M	Concentration: None

Material Component: Chameleon foot
Somatic Component: Rubbing of foot on skin
Execution - This spell will physically transform one humanoid creature into any other humanoid form.
Affect -
Limitations - To make a passable facsimile of a creature, the spell caster will have to, at one time or another that will have to have had physical contact. This spell can not be used on, or used to duplicate, plants, magical creatures or undead creatures. The spell can be used with with regard to super-natural creatures, although innate abilities will not be added, changed, or removed. Specialize skill are not duplicated. A thief might be duplicated, but the thieving skills will not be.
Uses - The caster might user the spell to disguise the subject os as tp not be recognized, or to impersonate someone else. The spell night be used to duplicate a winged creature to allow the creature to fly (flying skill required - see *Game Standards/Non-Magical/Flying*)
Erratta - The subject's mental stat and abilities will remain unchanged. While in a the new form, the subject will be able to cast spells as before, provided the new form has the vocal and gesturing abilities necessary for verbal and somatic components.
Aftermath - Although magically initiated, the affect is physiological and can not be magically dispelled or called to end with command words. When the duration has been exhausted, the subject will begin to revert to their true self. In the course of

one round, all affects of the spell will be gone and the subject will be back to normal.

Mage/4N - Telescopic Vision

Mage/Necromancy
Cast Time: 1 segment
Range: Touch
Mana: 4
Save: None
Components: V, S
Material Component: Small cincular piece of glass
Somatic Component: Holding glass over eye and peering through

Execution - This spell will endow one natural creature with telescopic vision.
Limitations - The spell will not affect normal stone

Mage/4N - Wizard Hand

Mage/Necromancy	Level: 4
Cast Time: 1 segment	Duration: 1 round/level
Range: Touch	Affected Area: One creature
Mana: 4	Damage: N/A
Save: None	Save Affect: N/A
Components: V, S	Concentration: None

Material Component: Small cincular piece of glass
Somatic Component: Holding glass over eye and peering through
Execution - This spell will endow one natural creature with telescopic vision.
Limitations - The spell will not affect normal stone

Mage/4V - Disentigrate

Mage/Evocation	Level: 4
Cast Time: 4 Seconds	Duration: N/A
Range: 15' + 10'/level	Affected Area: 1000' Cubic/level
Mana: 4	Damage: None
Save: None	Save Affect: N/A
Components: V, S	Concentration: N/A

Material Component: None
Somatic Component: Clapping of hands
Execution - This spell will obliterate massive amounts of non-living, non-magical matter.
Affect - The spell will utterly destroy all non-living, non-magical matter inside an affect area of up to 1000 Cubic foot (10' x 10' x 10') for each level of experience of the spell caster.
Limitations - The spell will not affect creatures or magical objects. The spell will not affect liquids or gasses, but only solid matter.
Uses - The spell might be used to clear rubble, make a passage, disarm (and disrobe) an enemy.

Mage/4V - Energy Orb

Mage/Evocation	Level: 4
Cast Time: 4 Seconds	Duration: N/A
Range: 15' + 10'/level	Affected Area: 1000' Cubic/level
Mana: 4	Damage: None

Save: None   Save Affect: N/A
Components: V, S   Concentration: N/A
Material Component: None
Somatic Component: Clapping of hands

Execution - This spell will create will a enchanted orb that will fire a 3D4 energy blast at any creature, that approaches within a 15' radius without first speaking the command words to deactivate the orb

Mage/4V - Electric Touch

Mage/Evocation	Level: 4
Cast Time: 4 Seconds	Duration: N/A
Range: Touch	Affected Area: 1 Creature
Mana: 4	Damage: 1D10/4 Levels up to 10D10
Save: Dexterity	Save Affect: Avoids 1 Round
Components: V, S, M	Concentration: None

Material Component: Piece of silver
Somatic Component: Touching silver to subject

Execution - After this spell is cast, the caster's touch send a massive amount electric votage into the next creature the caster touches.

Level	Electric Damage
0-3	1D10 Hit-points
4-7	2D10 Hit-points
8-11	3D10 Hit-points
12-15	4D10 Hit-points
16-19	5D10 Hit-points
20-23	6D10 Hit-points
24-27	7D10 Hit-points
28-31	8D10 Hit-points
32-35	9D10 Hit-points
36-	10D10 Hit-points

Affect - The affect will cause 1-10 (1D10) Hit-points of electrical damage for everly level of experience of the caster, up to a limit of 10-10 (10D10) hit-points.

Erratta - If the caster touches a subject in water or dips their hand into a pool, all creatures in the water within a 15 foot radius will receive full damage from the spell..

Mage/4V - Fireball

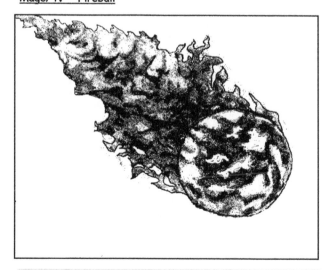

Mage/Evocation	Level: 4

Cast Time: 4 Seconds	Duration: N/A
Range: Touch	Affected Area: 30' diameter
Mana: 4	Damage: 1D6/4 Levels up to 7D6
Save: Dexterity	Save Affect: ½ Damage
Components: V, S, M	

Level	Fire Damage
0-3	1D6 Hit-points
4-7	2D6 Hit-points
12-15	3D6 Hit-points
16-19	4D6 Hit-points
20-23	5D6 Hit-points
24-27	6D6 Hit-points
28-	7D6 Hit-points

Material Component: Bit of Sulphur
Somatic Component: Tossing sulphur

Execution - This spell will cause glowing, fiery, pea-size sphere to shoot forth from the caster's extended finger to a predetermined range or spot, then explode into a 30 foot diameter ball of fire.

Affect - The fireball will engulf all objects and creatures in a 15' radius. Creatures will receive damage, and object must make a saving throw versus magical fire or be consumed.

Limitations - Those creatures who attamept to dodge the fireball are allowed to make a dexterity saving throw. A successful saving throw indicates that the subject was only partially burned and will suffer only ½ damage.

Eratta - If the spell is cast in an enclosed area, the affected area will conform itself to fit the shape of the area, up to a maximum of 30 feet from the point of origin. Creatures inside a confined area that is consumed in the blaze are not permitted a saving throw as there is not space to dodge to. If the fireball is used in a completely sealed area, the referee may call for a saving throw to determine if the sealed area has been bursted open.

Mage/4V - Icy Blast

Mage/Evocation	Level: 4

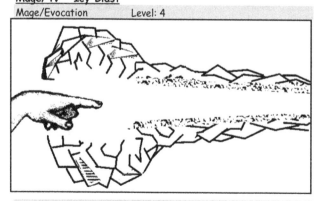

Cast Time: 4 Seconds	Duration: N/A
Range: 15 + 10/level	Affected Area: One target
Mana: 4	Damage: 1D84 Levels up to 8D8
Save: None	Save Affect: N/A
Components: V, S, M	Concentration: N/A

Material Component: Piece of Glass
Somatic Component: Clutching glass and pointing

Execution - By invoking this spell, the aster causes a whitish-bkue beak of light to emit from the caster's extended finger and

Level	Cold Damage
0-3	1D8 Hit-points
4-7	2D8 Hit-points
12-15	3D8 Hit-points
16-19	4D8 Hit-points
20-23	5D8 Hit-points
24-27	6D8 Hit-points
28-31	7D8 Hit-points
32-	8D8 Hit-points

strike a target creature or character. The affect will cause 1-8 (1D8) Hit-points of cold damage for everly level of experience of the caster, up to a limit of 7-56 (7D8) hit-points of cold damage.

Depending upon the type of creature, the amount of damage, and the are being touched, the referee may declare that the subject has been frost-bitten and, upon thawing, the frost-bitten area will turn black and will need to be amputated.

Mage/4V- Lightning Enchant

Mage/Evocation	Level: 4
Cast Time: 1 segment	Duration: 1 round/level
Range: Touch	Affected Area: 30'/level
Mana: 2	Damage: N/A
Save: Charisma	Save Affect: Negates
Components: V, S	Concentration: None
Material Component: Small piece of glass	
Somatic Component: None	

Execution - After invoking this spell, the caster can touch or punch a creature and do a massive amount of bludgeon damage (if the caster uses a punch, the standard punch damage of 1D4 is also added)

Mage/4V- Lightning Shield

Mage/Evocation	Level: 4
Cast Time: 1 segment	Duration: 1 round/level
Range: Touch	Affected Area: 30'/level
Mana: 2	Damage: 3D10 Lightning
Save: Charisma	Save Affect: Negates
Components: V, S	Concentration: None
Material Component: Small piece of glass	
Somatic Component: None	

Execution - This spell will create This spell creates a 10' x 10' magical wall that causes 3D10 points of lightning damage to any creature that passes through it.

Description – The will appear as a shimmering bluish-white square.

Limitations –Once the spell is cast, the color cannot be changed, and the shield cannot be moved, nor can it be cast onto an object or creature in order to be moved about. The shield can only be cast to be flat, vertical, and square.

Erratta – If there is not adequate space to accommodate the shield, it will be imbedded in surrounding solids.

Aftermath – The enchantment remains in affect until the spell exhausts its duration, the caster speaks the command words calling for the spell to end, or the enchantment is dispelled.

Mage/4V- Power Fist

Mage/Evocation	Level: 4
Cast Time: 1 segment	Duration: 1 round/level
Range: Touch	Affected Area: 30'/level

Mana: 2	Damage: N/A
Save: Charisma	Save Affect: Negates
Components: V, S	Concentration: None
Material Component: Small piece of glass	
Somatic Component: None	

Execution - After invoking this spell, the caster can touch or punch a creature and do a massive amount of bludgeon damage (if the caster uses a punch, the standard punch damage of 1D4 is also added)

Affect - Creatures caught in the initial blaze or passing throught the flames will suffer 3D6 hit-points of burn damage. All items caught in the blaze must make a saving throw against magical fire or be consumed.

Adjustments - The spell caster can speak command words to temporarily extinguish the wall of fire, adjust the flames, or make an opening to pass through.

Limitations - The wall will always be 1 foot thick, flat, vertical and rectangular. A wall of fire cannot be moved about by the caster or by moving air. Large amounts of water will momentarily extinguish areas of the blaze allowing passage. Missles fired through a wall of fire will be at a -4 to-hit penalty due to lack of visual contact with the target.

Aftermath - The flames will remain until they are extinguished, the enchantment is dispelled, the spell exhausts its duration, or the spell caster calls for the spell to end.

Mage/5A – Soften Shape

Mage/Alteration	Level: 5
Cast Time: 5 seconds	Duration: 1 minute/level
Range: Touch	Affected Area: 10lbs/level
Mana: 5	Damage: N/A
Save: None	Save Affect: N/A
Components: V, S. M	Concentration: High
Material Component: Object	
Somatic Component: Molding of object	

Execution - This spell will soften any non-magical solid object so as to make pliable with the consistency of clay. The spell may be used to mold stone, iron, glass, non-living wood, ceramics, etc.

Concentration - After the spell is cast, the enchantment requires medium concentration to maintain. If the caster is wounded, distracted, or cast a different spell, the anchantment will instantly be dispelled.

Limitations - Statues, jewelry pieces, or weapons created fashioned by this spell will be crude and sloppy unless the caster already possesses artistic talents, as the spell does not imbue the caster with such. Only one object per casting of the spell can be affected. For example, if the spell is used on a chain, only one link would be affected, however, multiple spells could be used to combine the links into a single ball of matter. The spell can affect up to 10 pounds of matter per level. If the spell is used on an object larger than the maximum, only part of the object will be affected.

Aftermath - When the spell exhaust it's duration, the object will begin to stiffen and lose its pliability. Within the course of 1 round (10 seconds) it will totally solidify. If the enchantment is dispelled, the caster's concentration is broken, or the caster speaks the command word calling for the spell to end, it will solidify instantaneously.

Mage/5A – Temperature point

Mage/Alteration	Level: 5
Cast Time: 5 seconds	Duration: 1 Turn/Level

Range: Touch	Affected Area: 10' Cubic/level
Mana: 5	Damage: N/A
Save: Nonw	Save Affect: N/A
Components: V, S	Concentration: None
Material Component: None	
Somatic Component: Rubbing the tip of finger on palm	

Execution - This spell will cause a 2 inch area to emit or draw heat from the surrounding area.

Affect -

Concentration - After the spell is cast, the enchantment requires medium concentration to maintain. If the caster is wounded, distracted, or cast a different spell, the anchantment will instantly be dispelled.

Mage/5A - Wild Wood

Mage/Alteration	Level: 5
Cast Time: 5 seconds	Duration: 1 Turn/Level
Range: Touch	Affected Area: 10' Cubic/level
Mana: 5	Damage: N/A
Save: Nonw	Save Affect: N/A
Components: V, S	Concentration: None
Material Component: None	
Somatic Component: Rubbing the tip of finger on palm	

Execution - This spell will cause a 2 inch area to emit or draw heat from the surrounding area.

Affect -

Concentration - After the spell is cast, the enchantment requires medium concentration to maintain. If the caster is wounded, distracted, or cast a different spell, the anchantment will instantly be dispelled.

Mage/5C - Continual Stream

Mage/Conjuration	Level: 5
Cast Time: 1 segment	Duration: Minute/Level
Range: 15' + 10'/level	Affected Area: 30' Diam Cloud
Mana: 5	Damage: N/A
Save: Constitution	Save Affect: May leave cloud
Components: V, S, M	Concentration: Medium
Material Component: Bit of sulfur	
Somatic Component: None	

Execution - This spell will create billowing cloud of poisonous green vapors that will cause damage to natural creatures who breathe its fumes.

Mage/5C - Poison Cloud

Mage/Conjuration	Level: 5
Cast Time: 1 segment	Duration: Minute/Level
Range: 15' + 10'/level	Affected Area: 30' Diam Cloud
Mana: 5	Damage: N/A
Save: Constitution	Save Affect: May leave cloud
Components: V, S, M	Concentration: Medium
Material Component: Bit of sulfur	
Somatic Component: None	

Execution - This spell will create billowing cloud of poisonous green vapors that will cause damage to natural creatures who breathe its fumes.

Affect - The cloud will cause 1 hit-point of damage for each round (10 seconds) that is spent breathing the vapors. Those inside may make a constution saving throw in an attempt to exit the cloud. Those failing a saving throw will be incapacitated an unable to take action for the remainder of the round.

Adjustments - The movement of the cloud is directed by the spell caster. The cloud can be moved at 25 yards per round (5 mph) relative to the surrounding air.

Limitations - The spell caster and any comrades are not immune to the affects of the cloud, should they somehow wind up inside Creatures iside the cloud are permitted a constitution saving throw per round in an attempt to leave. Missle attacks that pass through the cloud will be at -4 to-hit penalty due to a lack of visual contact with the target.

Concentration - After the spell is cast, the enchantment requires medium concentration to maintain. If the caster is wounded, distracted, or cast a different spell, the anchantment will instantly be dispelled.

Aftermath - When the spell exhausts its duration, the enchantment is dispelled, the cloud moves out of range of the caster, the caster's concentration is broken, or the caster speaks the command words calling for the spell to end, the cloud will begin to dissipate. In the course of one round, it will be totally dissolved and gone.

Mage/5C - Wall of Stone

Mage/Conjuration	Level: 5
Cast Time: 1 segment	Duration: N/A
Range: Touch	Affected Area: 100' Sqft/level
Mana: 5	Damage: N/A
Save: None	Save Affect: N/A
Components: V, S, M	Concentration: N/A
Material Component: Small piece of iron	
Somatic Component: Closing piece of iron in one fist and pointing with hand of other	

Execution - This spell will create a massive rectangular wall of stone up to 1/2 foot thick. Up to 100 square feet (10 x 10) per level can be created.

Affect - The wall can be created any thickiness up to ½ foot, and any square footage up to the maximum. The wall can be created vertically, horizontally, or tilted/turned to any angle. If there is not adequate space for the wall to be formed, the wall be seated into the surrounding non-magical, non-living matter. Such matter is replaced by the iron as the wall is created

If the wall should be cast so as to fall on creatures, those creature who attempt to dodge will be permitted a dexterity saving throw. A successful saving throw indicates that the wall was avoided and no damage is take. Otherwise, the creatures will suffer 3D12 apeice. Creatures trapped underneath may make one strength saving throw per round in an attempt to get free. Those not making a successful throw remain pinned beneath the weight of the wall

Limitations - The wall will always flat, rectangular (or square) and 6 inches thick. If the spell is cast in such a way as to create the wall in space already occupied by living tissue or magics, the mana and the spell will be used but the wall will not be created.

Mage/5D - Continual Locate

Mage/Divination	Level: 4
Cast Time: 1 segment	Duration: Permanent
Range: Touch	Affected Area: 10' Cubic/level
Mana: 40	Damage: N/A
Save: Charisma	Save Affect: Negates
Components: V, S	Concentration: N/A
Material Component: Needle, pin or other tiny metal rod	
Somatic Component: Placing needle on palm of hand	

Execution - This spell will create a magical item that will reveal the direction of a creature, a type of creature, an item, or a type of item.

Affect - When the spell is cast, whenever the sought after creature or item is within range, the meedle will hover a an inch or so above the caster's palm and point the direction .

Adjustments - As the spell is invoked, the caster will need to designate the scope of the spell. For example, the spell, might be used to locate a certain human, or the nearest human, the nearest humanoid, the nearest natural creature, the nearest creature, etc. Once the parameters have been set for what is being located, they cannot be changed without casting a new spell.

Limitations - The spell will needle will point directly at the subject, even if the shortest open path to the subject is a different direction. Once the spell is cast, the subject, or scope of the spell cannot be changed. To locate a individual creature or item (as opposed to a type) the caster must have had physical contact with creature or item at seom point. If the spell is used to locate a type, the needle will point to the nearest creature or object of the sought type, regardless of whether or not it is the particular individual item or creature being sought. Creatures or items in a hermetically sealed area cannot be located. . Various magics in the game can obscure an item, making it impossible to locate with a magical spell. Artifacts and relics are typically immune to location magics

Adjustments - Althought the spell cannot be adjusted, when the caster has found the subnect the needle is poiting towards, the needle can be touched to the creature or object. Thence forth, the magic will ignore the touched creature or item and point to the second nearest. As more are touched, they also become ignored. It is possible to find many individuals of a type with a single spell.

Aftermath - The spell will end when it exhausts its duration, the enchantment is dispelled, or the caster speaks the command words calling for the spell to end.

Mage/5D – Probe Item

Mage/Evocation	Level: 5
Cast Time: 1 segment	Duration: 4 hours
Range: 15' + 10'/Level	Affected Area: 10' Cubic/level
Mana: 5	Damage: N/A
Save: N/A	Save Affect: N/A
Components: V, S, M	

Material Component: Item
Somatic Component: Rubbing of finger along item while

Execution – This spell will released detailed information about the magical nature of an item.

Affect - The spell will reveal the basic steps necessary to activate the item, the affects it will cause, the amount of damage it deals, range, number of charges, etc.

Limitations - The spell has no or limited affect on items that are magically obscured. The spell will not detect a cursed or evil nature to the item. It will not reveal any sort of glyphs, magical traps, or other protective magics. The spell will not reveal any non-magical information about the item such as who last owned it, how it was created, if it is trapped mechanincally, etc.

Mage/5D – Seek

Mage/Evocation	Level: 6
Cast Time: 1 segment	Duration: 6 hours
Range: 15' + 10'/level	Affected Area: 10' Cubic/level
Mana: 60	Damage: N/A

Save: Charisma	Save Affect: Negates
Components: V, S	

Material Component: Needle, pin or other tiny metal rod
Somatic Component: Placing needle on palm of hand

Execution - This spell will divine the shortest unobstructed path way to an item or creatures.

Affect - The spell will seek the shortest path. As the caster approached an intersection or fork, the needle will point

Uses - The spell is useful most useful when used to find a way through underground passages or very large structures with internal walls

Limitations - The enchantment will not distinguish whether or not there is adequate space for the caser to pass. If a tiny ventilation tube is the shortest route that has an unobstructed passage, that is the direction the needle will point. In the outdoors, the spell functions mostly like a locate, in that it will usually point directly at the target, only changing direction when the caster nears an obstruction.

Aftermath - The spell will end when it exhausts its duration, the enchantment is dispelled, or the caster speaks the command words calling for the spell to end.

Mage/5D - True Seeing

Mage/Divination	Level: 5
Cast Time: 5 Rounds	Duration: N/A
Range: 0	Affected Area: 15' Radius
Mana: 5	Damage: None
Save: N/A	Save Affect: N/A
Components: V, S, M	Concentration: N/A

Material Component: Water droplets
Somatic Components: Tilting back the head and placing a drop of water on each eye, then looking in the direction of the intended point of origin.

Execution - This spell will allow the caster to gain a heightened awareness of items and creatures in the affected area.

Affect - The caster will be aware of all doors, traps, invisible or magically disguised, or magically altered creature and items within the affected area. Creatures that have been physically altered, even if no residual magic remains, will be obvious

Limitations - The spell will not be affected onm objects outside the affected area, even if they are in the spell caster's line of sight.

Mage/5E - Cube of Force

Mage/Evocation	Level: 5
Cast Time: 1 segment	Duration: 4 hours
Range: Touch	Affected Area: 1000 Cubic/level
Mana: 5	Damage: N/A
Save: Charisma	Save Affect: Negates
Components: V, S	

Material Component: Small piece of glass
Somatic Component: None

Execution - This spell will create a 10 foot x 10 foot x 10' foot cube that will have impenetrable walls. The only thing that pass through is non-magical light.

Affect - All 6 sides of the cube will be impenetrable by spells, weapons, or magic. No sound, nor any form of magical cimmunication can enter or escape the cube. The cube cannot be teleported into or out of by any means. The air inside the cube is kept magically refreshed and oxygenated. The temperature is kept automatically to 70 degrees farenheit. IF the spell is

Limitations - Although magics cannot penetrate the cube, there is nothing in the cubes nature to prevent spells from being cast inside the cube. The cube moved after it is cast, nor can it be be cast on an boject in order to be moved about. Any creature or item partially in the affected area will be able to enter or exit. Once they are move in or out from the edge of the perimeter, the cube walls will seal behind them.

Uses - The spell can be used to trap an enemy, or provide safe harbor for a character or party to regroup and institue healing.

Aftermath - The spell will end when it exhausts its duration, the enchantment is dispelled, or the caster speaks the command words calling for the spell to end.

Mage/5E - Destroy Magic

Mage/Enchantment	Level: 5
Cast Time: 5 Seconds	Duration: N/A
Range: Touch	Affected Area: One Magical Item
Mana: 40	Damage: N/A
Save: N/A	Save Affect: Negates
Components: V, S	
Material Component: Pinch of dust	
Somatic Component: None	

Execution - This spell will allow the caster to touch a magical item, a magical creature, or other continual magic and destroy the magical nature.

Affect - The spell will completely and permanently remove all magics

Limitations - If the spell is used on a magical creature, the creature is allowed a charisma saving throw. A successful throw indicates that the spell was ineffective in destroying the continual magics that the creature retains it's life force. This spell has no affect on non-magical creatures or items.

Mage/5E - Magic Bottle

Mage/Enchantment	Level: 5
Cast Time: 5 seconds	Duration: Special
Range: Touch	Affected Area: 60' x 30' cone
Mana: 5	Damage: Special
Save: N/A	Save Affect: N/A
Components: V, S, M	Concentration: None
Material Component: Bottle	
Somatic Component: Pointing mouth of bottle side towards area to be affected.	

Execution - This spell will cause an ordinary bottle to vacuum in a vast amount of gasses, liquids, or matter small enough to be sucked into the opening.

Affect - The vacuum created is of magical nature and not bound by the same laws of physics as a normal vacuum caused by atmospheric pressure. All gasses, and liquids in a cone shaped area that begins with the point at the neck of the bottle, spreads for a length of 60 feet, and ends at a circular base 30 feet in diameter. The amount of matter that the bottle can consume is dependent upon the length of the spell. While the affect is working, the spell will clear 1000 cubic feet of space per round.

As new pressure equalizes and more gasses or liquids come into the affected area, they will be conusmed also. Likewise, if the position of the bottle is changed, the affected area will be shifted, changing the areas that are vacuumed inside. Very ligh objects that are too large to be drawn into the bottle will be to

be drawn into the opening will be swept around by the moving ari, but not drawn to the whole.

If the bottle is plugged before the spell reaches its duration, the contents will remain "in flux" and will reform until the bottle is opened, even after the magic has faded and is gone. Gasous creatures that are inside the bottle will be conscious but will not age, be able to speak, cast spells, or take other action.

Limitations - The spell cannot be used on a container with multiple openings, or a single opening more than 2 inches in diameter.

Aftermath - The affect is ended when the anchantment is dispelled or the spell caster speaks the command words calling for the spell to end. If the bottle is not plugged when the enchantment ends, the contents will immediately begin to gush, and trying to cap the bottle while the contents are exiting will be impossible. If the bottle is capped while the enchantment is in affect, the contents will remain inside until the bottle is unplugged or broken, even after the enchantment is gone.

Mage/5E - Teleport

Mage/Enchantment	Level: 5
Cast Time: 5 seconds	Duration: N/A
Range: 1 mile/level	Affected Area: One creature
Mana: 5	Damage: N/A
Save: Dexterity	Save Affect: Avoids
Components: V, S	Concentration: N/A
Material Component: Drop of olive oil	
Somatic Component: Visualizing the destination and rubbing a streak of oil down the subjects face.	

Execution - By means of this spell, the caster is able to transport their person and all carried items to a destination

Limitations - The spell cannot be used to teleport into or out of a hermetically sealed area. To orient the spell, the caster must have personally been in the exact destination, or be able to see the location visually. Invoking the spell requires contact with subject while casting takes place, therefore, the spell is not a 'touch' type of spell. An unwilling party cannot be teleported unless they are restrained or unconcious

Adjustments - If the space is occupied by other matter, the destination of the spell will be shifted to the nearest an occupied space capable of accommodating the spell caster along with carried items.

Mage/5E - Wall of Force

Mage/Evocation	Level: 5
Cast Time: 1 segment	Duration: 1 hour + 1 hour/level
Range: Touch	Affected Area: 10' Cubic/level
Mana: 5	Damage: N/A
Save: N/A	Save Affect: N/A
Components: V, S	Concentration: None
Material Component: None	
Somatic Component: Making a closed fist with one hand and cupping the other hand around it	

Execution - This spell will create an invisible barrier that will have impenetrable walls. The only thing that will pass through is non-magical light.

Affect - The wall will be impenetrable by spells, weapons, or magic. No sound, nor any form of magical cimmunication can enter or escape the cube.

Limitations - The wall cannot be moved after it is cast, nor can it be be cast on an object in order to be moved about. Any creature or item partially in the affected area will be able to enter or exit. Once they are move in or out from the edge of the perimeter, the cube walls will seal behind them.

Uses - The spell can be used to trap an enemy, or provide safe harbor for a character or party to regroup and institue healing.

Adjustments - The caster can, if desired, shape the wall to a hemispherical or spherical shape.

with an area equal to his or her ability, maximum of 20 square feet per level of experience. The material component for this spell is a pinch of powdered diamond

Erratta - A wall of forece is strictly 2-dimensional and has no thickness.

Aftermath - The spell will end when it exhausts its duration, the enchantment is dispelled, or the caster speaks the command words calling for the spell to end.

Mage/5I - Berserk

Mage/Evocation	Level: 5
Cast Time: 5 Turns	Duration: Special
Range: Touch	Affected Area: One vial
Mana: 50	Damage: N/A
Save: Dexterity	Save Affect: Avoids
Components: V, S, M	Concentration: N/A

Material Component: Small piece of iron
Somatic Component: Closing piece of iron in one fist and pointing with hand of other

Execution - When this spell is invoked, the subject will physically attack the any creature within a 15' radius, selecting the nearest creature first, until it is dead, then moving onto other within the 15' radius.

Mage/5I - Create Potion of Extra Mana Restoration

Mage/Evocation	Level: 5
Cast Time: 5 Turns	Duration: Special
Range: Touch	Affected Area: One vial
Mana: 50	Damage: N/A
Save: Dexterity	Save Affect: Avoids
Components: V, S, M	Concentration: N/A

Material Component: Small piece of iron
Somatic Component: Closing piece of iron in one fist and pointing with hand of other

Execution - This spell will convert a vial of ordinary water into a mana potion that will restore 2D10 Mana-points.

Affect - massive rectangular wall of iron up to 1/2 foot thick. Up to 100 square feet (10 x 10) per level can be created.

Limitations - The water must be clean and free of colors and impurities. The container must be constructed of glass. If any of these restrictions are not met, the spell and mana will be used, but the potion will not be created.

Erratta - The potion will have a light blue tint, and will have a very thin viscosity.

Aftermath - For potion shelf lifes and durations consult *Games-standards/Magical/Potions*

Mage/5I - Telekinesis

Mage/Evocation	Level: 5
Cast Time: 1 segment	Duration: 1 Round/level
Range: 15' + 10'/level	Affected Area: 30'/level
Mana: 5	Damage: N/A
Save: Charisma	Save Affect: Negates
Components: V, S	Concentration: None

Material Component: Small piece of glass

Somatic Component: None

Execution - This spell will endow the caster with telekinetic abilities alowing the use of the mind to lift, move, and hold objects and creatures up to 250 lbs (2500 gold piece weight)

Limitations - The caster will only be able to affect objects that are in visual contact. If visual contact is lost, the item can be held in place, or dropped, but cannot be moved further until the contact is restored. Multiple items cannont be moved of held at the same time. Liquids or gasses cannot be handled in this way.

Mage/5N - Continual Wizard Eye

Mage/Evocation	Level: 3
Cast Time: 5 Turns	Duration: Permanent
Range: 15' + 10'/level	Affected Area: Eye
Mana: 5	Damage: N/A
Save: : N/A	Save Affect: N/A
Components: V, S, M	Concentration: None

Material Component: Eye
Somatic Component: Laying palm over eye and pointing with other hand.

Execution - This spell will create a magical creature, or sorts, under the spell caster's control. The caster will close one eye, and send a forth magically created facsimile to see what lies ahead.

Affect - The disembodied eye, for all intents and purposes will appear and function as the natural eye it has duplicated. It will magically be kept warm, moist, and free of irritation. The eye can be moved about at a rate of 50 yards per round (10 mph). The eye requires no sleep, and will watch over the spell caster while the nost is sleeping. When the eye is not being commanded, ti will float in close proximity to the spell caster.

Limitations - The eye is not protected from damage by weapons, or magic. If the eye is physically destroyed it will cause 1D8 damage to the spell caster. If it is bumped or battered, but there is no damage, the pain is transmitted back to the spell caster. The spell requires low concentration to maintain.

Erratta - The eye will have 20 hit-points (separate from the spell cast's hit-poinst) and an effective armor class of 0 (due to its smallness and maneuverability)

Aftermath - The eye will die if the magic is destroyed, or if the eye takes 10 or more hit-points of damage.

Mage/5N - Regenerate

Mage/Necromancy	Level: 5
Cast Time: 1 segment	Duration: Special (non-magical)
Range: Touch	Affected Area: 1 Amputation
Mana: 5	Damage: None
Save: N/A	Save Affect: N/A
Components: V, S, M	Concentration: N/A

Material Component: Bit of bone
Somatic Component: Pressing bone bit or severed limb to stump.

Execution - This spell will regrow lost limbs and body parts that have been severed, removed, or damaged.

Affect - The replacement will be an exact duplicate of the original. There will be no scars (other then burn), no loss of strength, or other lingering detrimental affects.

Limitations - The subject must be alive, conscious, and have one more hit-points and one or more mana-points. The spell will only affect in area of the body. If the victim has suffered additional losses, additional spells will be required. The regrowth of the limb will not restore lost hit-points. Limbs lost due to burns can be regrown, but they will have scarring.

Duration - The duration is non magical. Once the spell is cast, the affect is physiological and cannot be halted by command words or enchantment dispelling. The amount of time required to regrow the limb depends on the type and size of the limb. A hobbit's finger will take about a turn (10 minutes), whereas a giants, might take 2 or 3 turns. A hand of foot will take about an hour. Major limbs will require anywhere from 6 to 12 hours.

Mage/5N – X-Ray Vision

Mage/Necromancy	Level: 5
Cast Time: 5 Seconds	Duration: 1 Turn/Level
Range: Touch	Affected Area: Eyes
Mana: 5	Damage: N/A
Save: None	Save Affect: N/A
Components: V, S	Concentration: None
Material Component: Jelly from the eye of an eagle	
Somatic Component: Touching jelly to eye	

Execution - When this spell is cast the caster gains the ability to look through up to 10' of solid matter.

Affect - The spell-caster will be able to see through any sort of non-metallic, non-magical material. Secret doors, mechanical traps, hidden or lost creatures or items will become obvious to the spell caster. The caster will be able to look behind doors, through walls, and into sealed containers.

Limitations - The caster will not be able to see through metal, or magical items. When peering through walls, the caster will not be able to see colors. The affect will ot give the viewr the ability to determin if a creature or object has been magically altered (other then not being able to see through it). It will not give the viewer the ablility to invisible objects or creatures.

Aftermath - Although magically induced the affect is physiological and cannot be magically dispelled or ended early by command words.

Mage/5V – Cone of Cold

Mage/Evocation	Level: 5
Cast Time: 5 Seconds	Duration: N/A
Range: 0	Affected Area: 60' x 30' cone
Mana: 5	Damage: N/A
Save: Dexterity	Save Affect: ½ Damage
Components: V, S, M	Concentration: N/A
Material Component: Piece of crytal	
Somatic Component: Pointing crystal toward target with one hand and spreading other fingers of other hand just above crystal.	

Execution - This spell will draw a massive amount of heat from a cone shaped area.

Affect – The cone shaped affected area will begin with the point at the spell caster's outstretched finger and extend outward 60' to a 30' diameter base. If the cone is directed toward the surface of water, it will freeze a slab of ice one foot thick. The size and ovalness of the slab will depend on the closeness and the angle.

Limitations – Any creature attempting to dodge the affect is permitted to make a dexterity saving throw. Creatures making a successful saving throw were able to dodge and roll away, thereby, being only partly affected and receiving only half damage.

Erratta - Inside the affected area, any containers that hold liquid freeze, requiring a saving throw to determin if the containers have burst. Glass, ceramics, and other breakables will require a saving throw to determine if they have broken due to the sudden change in temperature.

Aftermath - Any ice created by this spell is, for all practical purposes, ordinary ice and subject to normal adversarious conditions such as melting, shattering, etc.

Level	Cold Damage
0-4	1D8 Hit-points
5-9	2D8 Hit-points
10-14	3D8 Hit-points
15-19	4D8 Hit-points
20-24	5D8 Hit-points
25-29	6D8 Hit-points
30-	7D8 Hit-points

Mage/5V – Dentonate

Mage/Evocation	Level: 5
Cast Time: 5 Seconds	Duration: N/A
Range: 0	Affected Area: 60' x 30' cone
Mana: 5	Damage: N/A
Save: Dexterity	Save Affect: ½ Damage
Components: V, S, M	Concentration: N/A
Material Component: Piece of crytal	
Somatic Component: Pointing crystal toward target with one hand and spreading other fingers of other hand just above crystal.	

Execution - This spell will draw a massive amount of heat from a cone shaped area.

Mage/5V – Energy Barrier (Continual)

Mage/Evocation	Level: 5
Cast Time: 5 Seconds	Duration: N/A
Range: 0	Affected Area: 60' x 30' cone
Mana: 5	Damage: N/A
Save: Dexterity	Save Affect: ½ Damage
Components: V, S, M	Concentration: N/A
Material Component: Piece of crytal	
Somatic Component: Pointing crystal toward target with one hand and spreading other fingers of other hand just above crystal.	

Execution - This spell will draw a massive amount of heat from a cone shaped area.

Mage/5V – Energy Weapon (Continual)

Mage/Evocation	Level: 5
Cast Time: 5 Seconds	Duration: N/A
Range: 0	Affected Area: 60' x 30' cone
Mana: 5	Damage: N/A

Save: Dexterity   Save Affect: ½ Damage
Components: V, S, M   Concentration: N/A
Material Component: Piece of crytal
Somatic Component: Pointing crystal toward target with one hand and spreading other fingers of other hand just above crystal.
Execution - This spell will draw a massive amount of heat from a cone shaped area.

Mage/5V - Lightning Bolt

Mage/Evocation	Level: 5
Cast Time: 5 Seconds	Duration: N/A
Range: 0	Affected Area: 10' /Level
Mana: 5	Damage: 1D10/5 Levels up ot 8D10

Level	Electical Damage
0-4	1D10
5-9	2D10
10-14	3D10
15-19	4D10
20-24	5D10
25-29	6D10
30-34	7D10
35-	8D10

Save: None	Save Affect: N/A
Components: V, S, M	Concentration: N/A

Material Component: Piece of silver
Somatic Component: Clutching rod and pointing finger
Execution - When this spell is casr a powerful bolt of lightning , 60 feet long x 6 inches wide, shoots forth from the caster's extended finger to strike a target.
Affect - The bolt will cause 1-10 (1D10) hit-points of damage for each 5 levels of experience of the spell caster.
Save
Repercusions - A lightning bolt produces a defeaning crack of thunder and a blinding flash of light. Any creatures or characters who are caught unawares will be blinded and defeaned for 1-4 (1D4) rounds. If a lightning bolt is fired inside an unstable tunnel or building, the referee may determine that the shock to the structure has caused a collapse.
Adjudication - A non-conductive surface will deflect a lightning bolt. If a lightning bolt is fired squarely at a non-conductive surface it will be deflected back towards the caster. If fired

towards a non-conductive surface at an angle, it will be deflected at an equal opposing angle.

Mage/5V - Power Shield

Mage/Alteration	Level: 6
Cast Time: 6 Rounds	Duration: N/A
Range: 15' + 10'/Level	Affected Area: 100' Sqft/level
Mana: 6	Damage: 3D12 blunt
Save: None	Save Affect: N/A
Components: V, S	Concentration: N/A

Material Component: None
Somatic Component: Pointing toward target
Execution - This spell will create This spell creates a 10' x 10' magical wall that causes 3D12 points of blunt damage to any creature that passes through it.
Description - The will appear as a shimmering purple square.
Limitations –Once the spell is cast, the color cannot be changed, and the shield cannot be moved, nor can it be cast onto an object or creature in order to be moved about. The shield can only be cast to be flat, vertical, and square.
Erratta - If there is not adequate space to accommodate the shield, it will be imbedded in surrounding solids.
Aftermath – The enchantment remains in affect until the spell exhausts its duration, the caster speaks the command words calling for the spell to end, or the enchantment is dispelled.

Mage/6A - Gravity field

Mage/Alteration	Level: 6
Cast Time: 6 Seconds	Duration: 1 Minute/Level
Range: 15' + 10'/Level	Affected Area: 15' Radius
Mana: 6	Damage: N/A
Save: None	Save Affect: N/A
Components: V, S, M	Concentration: Hign

Material Component: Lead pellet
Somatic Component: Tossing pelled toward area to be affected
Execution - This spell will create an area in which the spell caster can alter the affects of gravity, effectively increasing or decreasing the weight of all objects and creatures inside
Concentration - After the spell is cast, the enchantment requires medium concentration to maintain. If the caster is wounded, distracted, or cast a different spell, the anchantment will instantly be dispelled.

Mage/6A - Metal Control

Mage/Alteration	Level: 6
Cast Time: 6 Seconds	Duration: 1 Minute/Level
Range: 15' + 10'/Level	Affected Area: 15' Radius
Mana: 6	Damage: N/A
Save: None	Save Affect: N/A
Components: V, S, M	Concentration: Hign

Material Component: Lead pellet
Somatic Component: Tossing pelled toward area to be affected
Execution - This spell will create an area in which the spell caster can alter the affects of gravity, effectively increasing or decreasing the weight of all objects and creatures inside
Concentration - After the spell is cast, the enchantment requires medium concentration to maintain. If the caster is wounded, distracted, or cast a different spell, the anchantment will instantly be dispelled.

Mage/6A - Transmutation

Mage/Alteration	Level: 6

Cast Time: 6 Rounds	Duration: N/A
Range: 15' + 10'/Level	Affected Area: 100' Sqft/level
Mana: 6	Damage: None
Save: None	Save Affect: N/A
Components: V, S	Concentration: N/A
Material Component: None	
Somatic Component: Pointing toward target	

Execution - This spell will reform non-magical, non-living gas, solid or liquid into another of the same class.

Limitations - The spell will not affect, or used to create, creatures, magical items, precious metals, or extremely hard meatals usch as steel titanium, mithril, or adamanite. Complex substances or crafted objects can be transmuted from, but not created via this spell, such as posoins, armor, sword, etc.
The transmutation must be of the same basic types. Gasses can only be transmuted into gasses, liquids into liquids, solids into solids.

Uses - The spell can be used to create oil from water, turn stone to mud, steel to wood, and vice-versa.

Aftermath - The affect is permanent. It has no magical duration nor any continued magical nature.

Mage/6C – Field of Swords

Mage/Evocation	Level: 6
Cast Time: 6 Seconds	Duration: N/A
Range: 15' + 10'/Level	Affected Area: 15' Radius
Mana: 6	Damage: 3D12
Save: Dexterity	Save Affect: ½ Damage
Components: V, S, M	Concentration: N/A
Material Component: Dagger (any)	
Somatic Component: Jabbing the point into the air	

Execution - This spell will cause a many sword-like iron spires to rise up out of the ground (or floor) causing 3D8 damage to any one standing on the affected area when it is cast, or later passing hurriedly through it.

Affect -

Mage/6C – Wall of Iron

Mage/Evocation	Level: 6
Cast Time: 6 Seconds	Duration: N/A
Range: 15' + 10'/Level	Affected Area: 100' Sqft/level
Mana: 6	Damage: 3D12
Save: Dexterity	Save Affect: Avoids
Components: V, S, M	Concentration: N/A
Material Component: Small piece of iron	
Somatic Component: Closing piece of iron in one fist and pointing with hand of other	

Execution - This spell will create a massive rectangular wall of iron up to 1/2 foot thick. Up to 100 square feet (10 x 10) per level can be created.

Affect - The wall can be created any thickness up to ½ foot, and any square footage up to the maximum. The wall can be created vertically, horizontally, or tilted/turned to any angle. If there is not adequate space for the wall to be formed, the wall be seated into the surrounding non-magical, non-living matter. Such matter is replaced by the iron as the wall is created

If the wall should be cast so as to fall on creatures, those creature who attempt to dodge will be permitted a dexterity saving throw. A successful saving throw indicates that the wall was avoided and no damage is take. Otherwise, the creatures will suffer 3D12 apeice. Creatures trapped underneath may make one strength saving throw per round in an attempt to get free. Those not making a successful throw remain pinned beneath the weight of the wall

Limitations - The wall will always flat, rectangular (or square) and 6 inches thick. If the spell is cast in such a way as to create the wall in space already occupied by living tissue or magics, the mana and the spell will be used but the wall will not be created.

Aftermath - The wall created by this spell is not magical. Other then the manner it was created for game purposes, it is ordinary iron.

Mage/6D - Legend Lore

Mage/Divination	Level: 6
Cast Time: 6 Turns	Duration: 6 hours
Range: Touch	Affected Area: 10' Cubic/level
Mana: 60	Damage: N/A
Save: None	Save Affect: N/A
Components: V, S	Concentration: None
Material Component: Incense and strips of ivory	
Somatic Component: Placing needle on palm of hand	

Execution - This spell is used to determine information available regarding a known person, place or thing. If the person or thing is at hand, or if the mage is in the place in question, the likelihood of the spell producing results is far greater.

Mage/6E – Charge Item

Mage/Enchantment	Level: 6
Cast Time: 6 hours	Duration: Special
Range: Touch	Affected Area: One magical item
Mana: 60	Damage: N/A
Save: Charisma	Save Affect: Negates
Components: V, M	Concentration: N/A
Material Component: Chargeable magical item	
Somatic Component: None	

Execution - When this spell will is invoked, the caster will have a percentile change, equal to their intelligence, or raising the number of charges for any chargeable magical item by one charge.

Affect - The spell can be used on any magical item that has a rechargeable nature

Limitations - This spell requires a lengthy cast time and a massive amount of mana to accomplish. If the casters concentrations is broken at any time during casting, the full mana will be used, and the spell will have no affect. Casting this spell is of such a diffculty that each use requires a percentile roll aganst the caster's intelligence in order to complete it successfully. If the roll is missed, the full mana will be used, and the spell will have no affect. If the spell is used in an attempt to charge the item beyond its maximum, the item will explode, and everyone within a 15' radius will suffer 3D6 hit-points of pelter damage

Erratta - The item being recharged need not be of a type normally useable by the spell caster.

Mage/6E – Create Invisibility Item

Mage/Enchantment	Level: 6
Cast Time: 6 Seconds	Duration: Permanent
Range: Touch	Affected Area: 1 Item
Mana: 60	Damage: N/A
Save: N/A	Save Affect: N/A
Components: V, M	Concentration: N/A
Material Component: Ring, cloak, cap, or other jewelry or clothing	
Somatic Component: None	

Execution - This spell will create continual magics that will create a magical item that will cause its user to become invisible.

Adjustments - The item can be made to be triggered by command words or by placing the item on, touching it or wielding it.
Uses - The spell can be used on hats, garments, rings, other jewelry, stones, etc.
Limitations - The magic can only be placed on fine quality items that are finely crafted from upper grade materials. The invisibility will be under all the same limitations and game restrictions as other types of invisibility. Consult *Game Standards/Magical/Invisibility.*
Aftermath - The item retains no connection to the person who created it. Anyone gains possession of it, and can operate it, may use it.

Mage/6E - Dimensional Portal

Mage/Enchantment	Level: 6
Cast Time: 6 Turns (1 hour)	Duration: 1 Day/level
Range: N/A	Affected Area: 30' Diameter circle
Mana: 8	Damage: None
Save: None	Save Affect: N/A
Components: V, S	Concentration: None

Material Component: None
Somatic Component: Drawing a square in the air with fingertips

Execution - This spell will create a 10' x 10' portals which cam be liknked to a seconds portal created the same way by the same mage. Creatures and objects can walk through in order to be teleported.
Affect - The spell caster must cast the spel lonce, at one location, then cast the same spell again at a second time. The spell caster will visualize the portal to be linked to as the second spell is cast.
Limitations - The spell caster must be at the physical location to create the portal. A portal cannot be linked up to a portal cast by a different mage. Once two portals are linked, they cannot be switched to a different portal unless one of the two is destroyed. A portal can not be linked with more then one other portal.
Erratta - The portals are independent magically. The durations of oneRemoval of one portal leaves the other unlinked, but not dispelled. A spell caster may have/create any number or unlinked portals to have on hand in order to later be linked. The portal is only visible from one side. Persons and objects passing through the backside of a portal will not be teleported. If the portal is cast over a doorway, persons passing through might be unaware that they have been teleported.

Mage/6E - Enchant Armor

Mage/Evocation	Level: 6
Cast Time: 6 Seconds	Duration: 4 hours
Range: 15' + 10'/Level	Affected Area: 100' Sqft/level
Mana: 50	Damage: 3D12
Save: Dexterity	Save Affect: Avoids
Components: V, S, M	Concentration: N/A

Material Component: Small piece of iron
Somatic Component: Closing piece of iron in one fist and pointing with hand of other

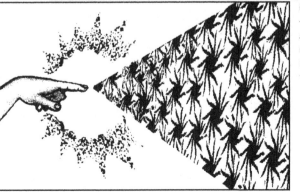 **Execution** - The spell will magically increase the

protectiveness of armor.
Limitations – The type of armor determines the
Erratta – Materials that support magical bonuses to armor class also have non-magical bonuses due to their greater tensile strength as opposed to more common materials. Consult Gamebook/Aarmor

Mage/6E - Magic Sink

Mage/Evocation	Level: 8
Cast Time: 8 Turns (80 min)	Duration: Permanent
Range: N/A	Affected Area: 30' Diameter circle
Mana: 8	Damage: None
Save: None	Save Affect: N/A
Components: V, S	

Material Component: Mana poition
Somatic Component: Touching fingertip into potion them drawing a circular area on ground or floor.

Execution - This spell can be used to create an area in which magics will not function. The affect will not dispel or destroy the magic, but only render it inert while in the affected area.
Affect - Magical items entering the affected area will not function while inside. Magical creatures are unable to enter the magical area, for as soon as they begin to place a limb inside it will lose mobility. Enchantments will be automatically dispelled.
Uses - In a society where magics are frequently used, this necessary spell to be
Erratta - This spell is usually permanent and non-revocable. Essentially, it creates a permanent "dead spot" for magics of any sort. The affect cannot be removed by other magics, since they also rendered inert.

Mage/6E – Invisibility Item

Mage/Evocation	Level: 8
Cast Time: 8 Turns (80 min)	Duration: Permanent
Range: N/A	Affected Area: 30' Diameter circle
Mana: 8	Damage: None
Save: None	Save Affect: N/A
Components: V, S	

Material Component: Mana poition
Somatic Component: Touching fingertip into potion them drawing a circular area on ground or floor.

Execution - This spell can be used to create continual magic on an a piece of clothing, jewelry or other worn garment to give the wearer a cloak of invisibilty

Mage/6I – Berserk

Mage/Illusion	Level: 6
Cast Time: 6 Turns	Duration: Special
Range: Touch	Affected Area: One vial
Mana: 60	Damage: N/A
Save: N/A	Save Affect: N/A
Components: V, S, M	Concentration: N/A

Material Component: Vial of pure water
Somatic Component: Slightly agitating containter to move fluid
Execution - This spell will cause the target creature to attack the nearest other creature within 15'.

Mage/6I – Create Potion of Intensive Mana Restoration

Mage/Illusion	Level: 6
Cast Time: 6 Turns	Duration: Special
Range: Touch	Affected Area: One vial

Mana: 60	Damage: N/A
Save: N/A	Save Affect: N/A
Components: V, S, M	Concentration: N/A

Material Component: Vial of pure water
Somatic Component: Slightly agitating containter to move fluid
Execution - This spell will convert a vial of ordinary water into a mana potion that will restore 3D12 Mana-points.
Limitations - The water must be clean and free of colors and impurities. The container must be constructed of glass. If any of these restrictions are not met, the spell and mana will be used, but the potion will not be created.
Erratta - The potion will have a light blue tint, and will have a very thin viscosity.
Aftermath - For potion shelf lifes and durations consult *Games-standards/Magical/Potions*

Mage/6I – Mana Feed

Mage/Evocation	Level: 6
Cast Time: 1 Segment	Duration: N/A
Range: Touch	Affected Area: 10' Cubic/level
Mana: 60	Damage: None
Save: N/A	Save Affect: N/A
Components: V, S	Concentration Required: N/A

Material Component: Mana poition
Somatic Component: Touching fingertip into potion them drawing a circular area on ground or floor.
Execution - By means of this spell, the caster may create an area that drains all creatures entering its perimeter to 4 mana points (unless their mana points are already lower)

Mage/6I – Mana Sink

Mage/Evocation	Level: 6
Cast Time: 1 segment	Duration: 6 seconds
Range: Touch	Affected Area: 10' Cubic/level
Mana: 60	Damage: 1D12/ 6 Levels - Pelter
Save: Charisma	Save Affect: Negates
Components: V, S, M	Concentration Required: No

Material Component: Mana poition
Somatic Component: Touching fingertip into potion them drawing a circular area on ground or floor.
Execution - By means of this spell, the caster may create an area that drains all creatures entering its perimeter to 4 mana points (unless their mana points are already lower)
Affect - The drainage will occur at a rate of 4 points per round until the creature has less then 4 mana points remaining. If a creatures mana points are restored, the affect will be triggered again until the creature is once

Mage/6I - Mind Control

Mage/Illusion	Level: 6
Cast Time: 6 rounds	Duration: 1 Round/Level
Range: Touch	Affected Area: One creature
Mana: 60	Damage: None
Save: Charisma	Save Affect: Negates
Components: V	Concentration: High

Material Component: None
Somatic Component: None
Execution - This spell will place a magical command on a natural creature to perform a task.
Affect - The task can be to carry out some service, or refrain from some action or course of activity, as desired by the spell

caster. The subject will be immediately set out to perform the task to the best of their ability. Since the task is psychological in nature, the subject will perform the the task as they *think* the caster intended it to be performed. Therefore, the subject will be unable to twist the intent or deviation from the spell caster's task.
Limitations - Only a single, very specific task can be named in the spell. Once cast, explantations of how the task should be performed cannot be added later. The creature must be intelligent, conscious, and under its own volition. While a geos cannot compel a creature to kill itself, or to perform acts which are likely to result in certain death, it can cause almost any other course of action. The spell causes the geased creature to follow the instructions until the geos is completed.
Aftermath - The affect is psychological and cannot be removed with by enchantment dispelling. The spell caster can end the affect, not by command words, but merely telling the subject they are released from the task.

Mage/6I – Interrogate

Mage/Evocation	Level: 6
Cast Time: 1 segment	Duration: 6 seconds
Range: Touch	Affected Area: 10' Cubic/level
Mana: 60	Damage: None
Save: Charisma	Save Affect: Negates
Components: V, S, M	Concentration Required: Yes

Material Component: Subject
Somatic Component: Placing the finger points on the temples of the subject..
Execution - By means of this spell, the caster can compel the subject to answer questions.
Limitations- The drainage will occur at a rate of 4 points per round until the creature has less then 4 mana points remaining. If a creatures mana points are restored, the affect will be triggered again until the creature is once again reduced to 4 mana points.

Mage/6N – Continual Wizard Hand

Mage/Evocation	Level: 6
Cast Time: 6 Seconds	Duration: 1 hour/level
Range: 15' + 10'/level	Affected Area: 30'/level
Mana: 6	Damage: N/A
Save: N/A	Save Affect: N/A
Components: V, S. M	Concentration Required: Yes

Material Component: Hand
Somatic Component: Laying palm over hand then pointing.
Execution - This spell will allow the caster to create a disembodied hand, and send it forth magically.
Affect – The disembodied eye, for all intents and purposes will appear and function as the natural eye it has duplicated. It will magically be kept warm, moist, and free of irritation. The eye can be moved about at a rate of 50 yards per round (10 mph)
Limitations - The hand is not protected from damage by weapons, or magic. If the hand is physically destroyed it will cause 1D8 damage to the spell caster. If it is bumped or battered, but there is no damage, the pain is transmitted back to the spell caster.
Concentration - Maintiaining the spell requires concentration on the part of the spell caster. If the caster is becomes unconscious, is wounded or attempts a new spell, the concentration will be broken and the eye will fall to the ground.

Erratta - If the caster is becomes unconscious, is wounded or attempts a new spell, the concentration will be broken and the hand will fall to the ground. If the enchantment is still in force, the caster can regain control of the eye when concentratin is restored.

Aftermath - The enchantment is ended when the spell exhausts its duration, the caster speaks the command word calling for the spell to end, the enchantment is dispelled, or the eye is physically destroyed.

Mage/6N – Power Sink

Mage/Evocation	Level: 8
Cast Time: 8 Turns (80 min)	Duration: Permanent
Range: N/A	Affected Area: 30' Diameter circle
Mana: 8	Damage: None
Save: None	Save Affect: N/A
Components: V, S	
Material Component: Poison	
Somatic Component: Touching fingertip into poison them drawing a circular area on ground or floor.	

Excecution

Mage/6N – Polymorph

Mage/Necromancy	Level: 4
Cast Time: 1 segment	Duration: 1 round/level
Range: Touch	Affected Area: 30'/level
Mana: 2	Damage: N/A
Save: Charisma	Save Affect: Negates
Components: V, S	
Material Component: Chameleon foot	
Somatic Component: Rubbing of foot on skin	

Execution - This spell will physically transform a natural creature into any other sort of natural creature.

Mage/6V – Chain Lightning

Mage/Evocation	Level: 6
Cast Time: 6 Seconds	Duration: N/A
Range: 15' + 10'/Level	Affected Area: 15' Radius
Mana: 6	Damage: 1D10/6 Levels up to 7D10
Save: Dexterity	Save Affect: ½ damage
Components: V, S, M	Concentration: N/A
Material Component: Piece of silver	
Somatic Component: Clutching rod and pointing finger	

Level	Electical Damage
0-5	1D10
6-11	2D10
12-15	3D10
18-20	4D10
24-25	5D10
30-30	6D10
36-	7D10

Execution - This spell will fire a lightning bolt at a single target which will bounce from creature to creature until it strikes all creatures within a 30 foot diamater of the original target.

Limitations - A creature who attempts to dodge the lightning bollt is allowed a dexterity saving throw. A successful saving throw indicates that the creature was able to turn or dive away, thereby causing only ½ damage. If a lightning bolt is fired inside an unstable tunnel or building, the referee may determine that the shock to the structure has caused a collapse.

Erratta - A lightning bolt produces a defeaning crack of thunder and a blinding flash of light. Any creatures or characters who are caught unawares will be blinded and defeaned for 1-4 (1D4) rounds.

Mage/6V– Delayed Blast Fireball

Mage/Evocation	Level:6
Cast Time: 6 Rounds	Duration: 1 Minute/Level
Range: 0	Affected Area: 10' Cubic/level
Mana: 6	Damage: 1D6/6 Levels up to 7D6
Save: Dexterity	Save Affect: ½ Damage
Components: V, S, M	Concentration: None
Material Component: Bit of sulphur	
Somatic Component: None	

Level	Burn Damage
0-5	1D6
6-8	2D6
12-17	3D6
18-23	4D6
24-29	5D6
30-35	6D6
36-	7D6

Execution – This spell will create a fiery red pea-sized sphere the can be preprogrammed to explode into a ball of fire at a preset time or distance.

Affect - A delayed blast fireball differs from a regular fireball in that it will not explode prior to reaching its preset range. IF can be ricochted around corners and off objects or creatures. Once the pshere has traveled to its preset range, it will drop to the ground and smoulder until the preset time limit has elapsed. Once the fireball has reached the preset range, it becomes vulnerable to impact (as a normal fireball) and touching it or smashing it will cause it to explode. The fireball will engulf all objects and creatures in a 15' radius. Creatures will receive damage, and object must make a saving throw versus magical fire or be consumed.

Limitations - Those creatures who attamept to dodge the fireball are allowed to make a dexterity saving throw. A successful saving throw indicates that the subject was only partially burned and will suffer only ½ damage.

Eratta - If the spell is cast in an enclosed area, the affected area will conform itself to fit the shape of the area, up to a maximum of 30 feet from the point of origin. Creatures inside a confined area that is consumed in the blaze are not permitted a saving throw as there is not space to dodge to. If the fireball is used in a completely sealed area, the referee may call for a saving throw to determine if the sealed area has been bursted open.

Mage/6V – Energy Orb (Continual)

Mage/Necromancy	Level: 4
Cast Time: 1 segment	Duration: 1 round/level
Range: Touch	Affected Area: 30'/level
Mana: 2	Damage: N/A
Save: Charisma	Save Affect: Negates
Components: V, S	
Material Component: Chameleon foot	
Somatic Component: Rubbing of foot on skin	

Execution - This spell will physically transform a natural creature into any other sort of natural creature

Mage/6V – Fire Weapon (Continual)

Mage/Necromancy	Level: 4
Cast Time: 1 segment	Duration: 1 round/level
Range: Touch	Affected Area: 30'/level
Mana: 2	Damage: N/A
Save: Charisma	Save Affect: Negates
Components: V, S	

Material Component: Chameleon foot
Somatic Component: Rubbing of foot on skin

Execution - This spell will physically transform a natural creature into any other sort of natural creature

Mage/6V – Frost Orb (Enchantl)

Mage/Necromancy	Level: 4
Cast Time: 1 segment	Duration: 1 round/level
Range: Touch	Affected Area: 30'/level
Mana: 2	Damage: N/A
Save: Charisma	Save Affect: Negates
Components: V, S	

Material Component: Chameleon foot
Somatic Component: Rubbing of foot on skin

Execution - This spell will physically transform a natural creature into any other sort of natural creature

Mage/6V – Meteor Blast

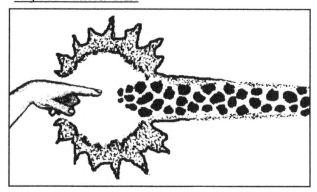

Mage/Evocation	Level: 6
Cast Time: 6 Seconds	Duration: N/A
Range: 15' + 10'/Level	Affected Area: 1 Target
Mana: 6	Damage: 1D12/ 6 Levels up to 8D12
Save: None	Save Affect: N/A
Components: V, S	Concentration: N/A

Material Component: Small stone
Somatic Component: Clutching stone and pointing

Level	Pelter Damage
0-5	1D12
6-11	2D12
12-15	3D12
18-20	4D12
24-25	5D12
30-30	6D12
36-35	7D12
40-	8D12

Execution - This spell will cause a stream of small stonre, 1-2 inches in diameter, to shoot forth from the spell caster's outstretched finger and strike a target.
Affect - The stones will move at 100 mph and will cause pelter damage to all cratures struck by the stones.
Limitations - The stones will only travel in a straight line, and only in a singular stream.
Aftermath - Although magically created, the stones of themselves are non-magical and are not stopped by any sort of barriers that prevent the entry of magic but not non-magical objects.

Mage/7A – Continual Temperature point

Mage/Alteration	Level: 7
Cast Time: 7 Rounds	Duration: Permanent
Range: Touch	Affected Area: Varies
Mana: 7	Damage: N/A
Save: None	Save Affect: N/A
Components: V, S	Concentration: None

Material Component: None
Somatic Component: None

Execution - This spell will cause a 2 inch area to emit or draw heat from the surrounding area.

Mage/7A – Solidification

Mage/Alteration	Level: 7
Cast Time: 7 Rounds	Duration: Permanent
Range: Touch	Affected Area: Varies
Mana: 7	Damage: N/A
Save: None	Save Affect: N/A
Components: V, S	Concentration: None

Material Component: None
Somatic Component: None

Execution - This spell will cause a 2 inch area to emit or draw heat from the surrounding area.

Mage/7A – Incendiary Cloud

Mage/Alteration	Level: 7
Cast Time: 7 Rounds	Duration: Permanent
Range: Touch	Affected Area: Varies
Mana: 7	Damage: N/A
Save: None	Save Affect: N/A
Components: V, S	Concentration: None

Material Component: None
Somatic Component: None

Execution - This spell will cause a 2 inch area to emit or draw heat from the surrounding area.

Mage/7D – Continual Seek

Mage/Evocation	Level: 6
Cast Time: 1 segment	Duration: 6 hours
Range: 15' + 10'/level	Affected Area: 10' Cubic/level
Mana: 60	Damage: N/A
Save: Charisma	Save Affect: Negates
Components: V, S	Concentration: N/A

Material Component: Needle, pin or other tiny metal rod

Somatic Component: Placing needle on palm of hand

Execution - This spell will create a magical item that will divine the shortest unobstructed path way to an item or creatures.

Affect - The item will be created to seek an item, creature, or type of creature or item. Once the spell is completed, the target of the item cannot be changed. The spell will seek the shortest path. As the caster approached an intersection or fork, the needle will point

Uses - The spell is useful most useful when used to find a way through underground passages or very large structures with internal walls

Limitations - The enchantment will not distinguish whether or not there is adequate space for the caser to pass. If a tiny ventilation tube is the short unobstructed passage, that is the direction the needle will point. In the outdoors, the spell functions mostly like a locate, in that it will usually

Mage/7D - Scan Intent

Mage/Evocation	Level: 6
Cast Time: 1 segment	Duration: 6 hours
Range: 15' + 10'/level	Affected Area: 10' Cubic/level
Mana: 60	Damage: N/A
Save: Charisma	Save Affect: Negates
Components: V, S	Concentration: N/A

Material Component: Needle, pin or other tiny metal rod
Somatic Component: Placing needle on palm of hand

Execution - This spell will allow the caster to read the surface thoughts and determine the basic intent of the subject

Mage/7E - Magic Sink

Mage/Enchantment	Level: 7
Cast Time: 7 Minutes	Duration: 1 Hour/Level
Range: N/A	Affected Area: 30' Diameter circle
Mana: 7	Damage: None
Save: None	Save Affect: N/A
Components: V, S	Concentration: N/A

Material Component: Mana poition
Somatic Component: Touching fingertip into potion them drawing a circular area on ground or floor.

Execution - This spell will create a magical "dead area" where no spells or magical affects will function.

Mage/7E - Mass Teleport

Mage/Enchantment	Level: 7
Cast Time: 7 Minutes	Duration: N/A
Range: 1 Mile/level	Affected Area: 1 Person/Level
Mana: 7	Damage: None
Save: None	Save Affect: N/A
Components: V, S	Concentration: N/A

Material Component: None
Somatic Component: Clasping palms

Execution - This spell will enable the caster to teleport 1 person/creature per level, plus all carried items. All creature touching the caster, or touching creatures touching the caster will be teleported.

Affect - create a magical "dead area" where no spells or magical affects will function.

Limitations - All creatures in the chain will be teleported whether the caster wants them or not, or is aware of them or nat. Only thos creatures who are in contact during the entire casting will be teleport. To orient the spell, the caster must select a location that they have personally visited before.

Mage/7E - Obscure Magic

Mage/Enchantment	Level: 4
Cast Time: 7 Mintes	Duration: 4 hours
Range: Touch	Affected Area: 10' Cubic/level
Mana: 70	Damage: N/A
Save: Charisma	Save Affect: Negates
Components: V, S	Concentration: N/A

Material Component: Magical Item
Somatic Component: Rubbing of finger tips over item

Execution - This spell will render an item immune to being identified, or any of its magical nature revealed by magical means, as well as making it immune to all scrye, location, seek, or other methods of seeing the item, or finding its location. It can also be used to disguise the item to make it appear less valuable.

Affect- The affect of this spell is a continual magic that is pemanent and becomes interlaced with all other continual magics of the item or creature. It is normally impossible to remove the continual magics of this spell (temporarily or permanaetly) without also removing all other magical properties of the item or creature. If the item is made from precious metals and gems, the spell can be cast in such a way as to make the item appear to be made of ordinary iron.

Limitations - This spell cannot be used to interlace with the magic on artifacts or relices, although ti is normally unnecessary since artifacts and relics are already magically obscure by there very nature. If the spell is also used to disguise the item, only the appearance will be changed. Encrusted jewels will feel raised to the touch although visually, they will appear flat.

Adjustments - The spell can be cast so as to release no information at all, or when its properties are magically divined, release a word or phrase.

Uses- A mage will often use this spell so that magical possessions cannot be sought magically by others, as well as to befuddle a new owner on how it is to be used. Usually, if the spell is used to allow the release of a word or phrase, the words will be cryptic and have a meaning that makes sense only to the spell caster. For example, a wand of fire might be set to release the words "red stick" to remind the rightful owner or its use/purpose.

Mage/7I - Berserk 15' radius

Mage/Illusion	Level: 7
Cast Time: 7 hours	Duration: N/A
Range: Touch	Affected Area: 1 Creature
Mana: 70	Damage: 1D12/ 6 Levels - Pelter
Save: Charisma	Save Affect: Negates
Components: V, S	

Material Component: Tissue sample
Somatic Component: Lightly rubbing of sample with fingertips

Execution - This spell will place temporarily increase a creature's mana capacity by 1 point per level of the spell caster.

Limitations - The spell only increases the subject's maximum mana capacity and does not rais the current mana level to match. Mana potions or other mana increasing techniques must be utilized for the new capacity to be fulfilled.

Mage/7I - Enhance Mana Capacity

Mage/Illusion	Level: 7
Cast Time: 7 hours	Duration: N/A
Range: Touch	Affected Area: 1 Creature
Mana: 70	Damage: 1D12/ 6 Levels - Pelter
Save: Charisma	Save Affect: Negates
Components: V, S	

Material Component: Tissue sample

Somatic Component: Lightly rubbing of sample with fingertips
Execution - This spell will place temporarily increase a creature's mana capacity by 1 point per level of the spell caster.
Limitations - The spell only increases the subject's maximum mana capacity and does not rais the current mana level to match. Mana potions or other mana increasing techniques must be utilized for the new capacity to be fulfilled.

Mage/7N - Enhance Physical Capacity

Mage/Necromancy	Level: 7
Cast Time: 7 hours	Duration: N/A
Range: Touch	Affected Area: 1 Creature
Mana: 70	Damage: 1D12/ 6 Levels - Pelter
Save: Charisma	Save Affect: Negates
Components: V, S	Concentration: N/A

Material Component: Tissue sample
Somatic Component: Lightly rubbing of sample with fingertips
Execution - This spell will temporarily raise the subject's hit-points based on the natural hit-point tally

Mage/7V - Frost Barrier (Continual)

Mage/Evocation	Level: 7
Cast Time: 7 Seconds	Duration N/A
Range: Touch	Affected Area: 60' x 30' Conel
Mana: 40	Damage: 1D12/ 7 Levels - Bludgeon
Save: Dexterity	Save Affect: ½ damage
Components: V, S, M	Concentration: N/A

Material Component: Small stone
Somatic Component: None
Execution - This spell causes a wide spary of of 1-2 inch non-magical stones to spray forth striking creatures and objects in a cone shaped affected area. When this spell is cast, a cone shaped blast of of stones 1-4 inches in diameter spurts forth from the spell caster's outstretched finger.

Mage/7V - Frost Weapon (Continual)

Mage/Evocation	Level: 7
Cast Time: 7 Seconds	Duration N/A
Range: Touch	Affected Area: 60' x 30' Conel
Mana: 40	Damage: 1D12/ 7 Levels - Bludgeon
Save: Dexterity	Save Affect: ½ damage
Components: V, S, M	Concentration: N/A

Material Component: Small stone
Somatic Component: None
Execution - This spell causes a wide spary of of 1-2 inch non-magical stones to spray forth striking creatures and objects in a cone shaped affected area. When this spell is cast, a cone shaped blast of of stones 1-4 inches in diameter spurts forth from the spell caster's outstretched finger.

Mage/7V - Fire Orb (Continual)

Mage/Evocation	Level: 7
Cast Time: 7 Seconds	Duration N/A
Range: Touch	Affected Area: 60' x 30' Conel
Mana: 40	Damage: 1D12/ 7 Levels - Bludgeon
Save: Dexterity	Save Affect: ½ damage
Components: V, S, M	Concentration: N/A

Material Component: Small stone
Somatic Component: None
Execution - This spell causes a wide spary of of 1-2 inch non-magical stones to spray forth striking creatures and objects in a cone shaped affected area. When this spell is cast, a cone

shaped blast of of stones 1-4 inches in diameter spurts forth from the spell caster's outstretched finger.

Mage/7V - Lightning Fire Orb (Enchant)

Mage/Evocation	Level: 7
Cast Time: 7 Seconds	Duration N/A
Range: Touch	Affected Area: 60' x 30' Conel
Mana: 40	Damage: 1D12/ 7 Levels - Bludgeon
Save: Dexterity	Save Affect: ½ damage
Components: V, S, M	Concentration: N/A

Material Component: Small stone
Somatic Component: None
Execution - This spell causes a wide spary of of 1-2 inch non-magical stones to spray forth striking creatures and objects in a cone shaped affected area. When this spell is cast, a cone shaped blast of of stones 1-4 inches in diameter spurts forth from the spell caster's outstretched finger.

Mage/7V - Meteor Spray

Mage/Evocation	Level: 7
Cast Time: 7 Seconds	Duration N/A
Range: Touch	Affected Area: 60' x 30' Conel
Mana: 40	Damage: 1D12/ 7 Levels - Bludgeon
Save: Dexterity	Save Affect: ½ damage
Components: V, S, M	Concentration: N/A

Material Component: Small stone
Somatic Component: None
Execution - This spell causes a wide spary of of 1-2 inch non-magical stones to spray forth striking creatures and objects in a cone shaped affected area. When this spell is cast, a cone shaped blast of of stones 1-4 inches in diameter spurts forth from the spell caster's outstretched finger.

Level	Pelter Damage
0-6	1D12
7-13	2D12
14-20	3D12
21-27	4D12
28-34	5D12
35-41	6D12
42-	7D12

Affect - The stones will move at 100 mph and will cause pelter damage to all cratures struck by the stones.
Limitations - The stones will only travel in a straight line, and only in a singular stream.
Aftermath - Although magically created, the stones of themselves are non-magical and are not stopped by any sort of barriers that

Mage/7V - Poison Barrier

Mage/Evocation	Level: 7
Cast Time: 7 Seconds	Duration N/A
Range: Touch	Affected Area: 60' x 30' Conel
Mana: 40	Damage: 1D12/ 7 Levels - Bludgeon
Save: Dexterity	Save Affect: ½ damage
Components: V, S, M	Concentration: N/A

Material Component: Small stone
Somatic Component: None
Execution - This spell causes a wide spary of 1-2 inch non-magical stones to spray forth striking creatures and objects in a cone shaped affected area. When this spell is cast, a cone shaped blast of of stones 1-4 inches in diameter spurts forth from the spell caster's outstretched finger.

Mage/7V – Poison Finger

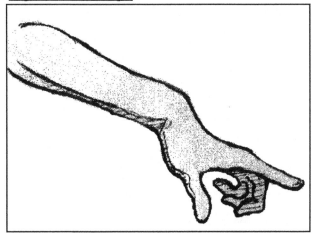

Mage/Evocation	Level: 7
Cast Time: 7 Seconds	Duration: N/A
Range: Touch	Affected Area: 1 Creature
Mana: 40	Damage: 1D20/ 7 Levels - Death Magic
Save: Dexterity	Save Affect: Avoids
Components: V, S, M	Concentration: None

Level	Death Magic Damage
0-6	1D20 Death Magic
7-13	2D20 Death Magic
14-20	3D20 Death Magic
21-27	4D20 Death Magic
28-34	5D20 Death Magic
35-41	6D20 Death Magic
42-48	7D20 Death Magic
49-55	8D20 Death Magic
56-61	9D20 Death Magic
62-	10D20 Death Magic

Material Component: Lotus leaf
Somatic Component: Touching of subject's flesh
Execution - By means of this spell the caster is able to deliver a massive amount of death magic damage onto a subject prevent the entry of magic but not non-magical objects.

Mage/8A – Transformation

Mage/Evocation	Level: 6
Cast Time: 6 Seconds	Duration: 4 hours
Range: 15' + 10'/Level	Affected Area: 100' Sqft/level
Mana: 50	Damage: 3D12
Save: Dexterity	Save Affect: Avoids
Components: V, S, M	Concentration: N/A

Material Component: Small piece of iron
Somatic Component: Closing piece of iron in one fist and pointing with hand of other
Execution - This spell will reform non-magical, non-living gas, solid or liquid into another gas, solid, or liquid.

Mage/8A – Transform Metal

Mage/Evocation	Level: 6
Cast Time: 6 Seconds	Duration: 4 hours
Range: 15' + 10'/Level	Affected Area: 100' Sqft/level
Mana: 50	Damage: 3D12

Save: Dexterity	Save Affect: Avoids
Components: V, S, M	Concentration: N/A

Material Component: Small piece of iron
Somatic Component: Closing piece of iron in one fist and pointing with hand of other
Execution - This spell causes a wide spary of of 1-2 inch non-magical stones to spray forth striking creatures and objects in a cone shaped affected area.

Mage/8A – Continual Gravity Field

Mage/Alteration	Level: 8
Cast Time: 8 Minutes	Duration: Permanent
Range: Touch	Affected Area: 15' Radius
Mana: 8	Damage: None
Save: Strength	Save Affect: Able to leave
Components: V, S, M	

Material Component: Lead pellet
Somatic Component: Tossing pelled toward area to be affected
Execution - This spell will render an item immune to being identified, or any of its magical nature revealed by magical means,

Mage/8C – Gate

Mage/Evocation	Level: 8
Cast Time: 1 segment	Duration: 6 seconds
Range: Touch	Affected Area: 10' Cubic/level
Mana: 80	Damage: 1D12/ 6 Levels - Pelter
Save: Charisma	Save Affect: Negates
Components: V, S, M	Concentration: N/A

Material Component: Mana poition
Somatic Component: Touching fingertip into potion them drawing a circular area on ground or floor.
Execution - By means of this spell the caster is able transfer 80 of their personal mana points from themselves into a recipient. If the additional mana points would place

Mage/8C – Stone Rain

Mage/Evocation	Level: 8
Cast Time: 1 segment	Duration: 6 seconds
Range: Touch	Affected Area: 10' Cubic/level
Mana: 80	Damage: 1D12/ 6 Levels - Pelter
Save: Charisma	Save Affect: Negates
Components: V, S, M	Concentration: N/A

Material Component: Mana poition
Somatic Component: Touching fingertip into potion them drawing a circular area on ground or floor.
Execution - By means of this spell the caster is able transfer 80 of their personal mana points from themselves into a recipient. If the additional mana points would place

Mage/8D – Scan Area

Mage/Evocation	Level: 8
Cast Time: 1 segment	Duration: 6 seconds
Range: Touch	Affected Area: 10' Cubic/level
Mana: 80	Damage: 1D12/ 6 Levels - Pelter
Save: Charisma	Save Affect: Negates
Components: V, S, M	Concentration: N/A

Material Component: Mana poition
Somatic Component: Touching fingertip into potion them drawing a circular area on ground or floor.

Execution - By means of this spell the caster is able transfer 80 of their personal mana points from themselves into a recipient. If the additional mana points would place

Mage/8I – Conitinnal Mana Sink

Mage/Evocation	Level: 8
Cast Time: 1 segment	Duration: 6 seconds
Range: Touch	Affected Area: 10' Cubic/level
Mana: 80	Damage: 1D12/ 6 Levels - Pelter
Save: Charisma	Save Affect: Negates
Components: V, S, M	Concentration: N/A

Material Component: Mana poition
Somatic Component: Touching fingertip into potion them drawing a circular area on ground or floor.

Level	Bludgeon Damage
1-7	1D20
8-14	2D20
15-21	3D20
22-28	4D20
29-35	5D20
36-42	6D20
43-	7D20

Execution - By means of this spell the caster is able transfer 80 of their personal mana points from themselves into a recipient. If the additional mana points would place

Mage/8I – Incapacitate

Mage/Illusion	Level: 6
Cast Time: 1 segment	Duration: 6 seconds
Range: Touch	Affected Area: 10' Cubic/level
Mana: 80	Damage: 1D12/ 6 Levels - Pelter
Save: Charisma	Save Affect: Negates
Components: V, S, M	Concentration: N/A

Material Component: Lotus leaf
Somatic Component: Touching flesh of recipient
Execution - By means of this spell the caster is able transfer 80 of their personal mana points from themselves into a recipient. If the additional mana points would place

Mage/8I – Mind Probe

Mage/Illusion	Level: 6
Cast Time: 1 segment	Duration: 6 seconds
Range: Touch	Affected Area: 10' Cubic/level
Mana: 80	Damage: 1D12/ 6 Levels - Pelter
Save: Charisma	Save Affect: Negates
Components: V, S, M	Concentration: N/A

Material Component: Lotus leaf
Somatic Component: Touching flesh of recipient
Execution - By means of this spell the caster is able transfer 80 of their personal mana points from themselves into a recipient. If the additional mana points would place

Mage/8I – Mind Link

Mage/Illusion	Level: 8
Cast Time: 1 segment	Duration: Permanent
Range: Touch	Affected Area: 10' Cubic/level
Mana: 60	Damage: N/A
Save: Charisma	Save Affect: Negates
Components: V, S	Concentration: N/A

Material Component: Needle, pin or other tiny metal rod

Somatic Component: Placing needle on palm of hand
Execution - This spell generate continual magics necessary to create a magical item. The item will divine the shortest unobstructed path way to an item or creatures.
Affect - The spell will seek the shortest path. As the caster approached an intersection or fork, the needle will point
Uses - The spell is useful most useful when used to find a way through underground passages or very large structures with internal walls
Limitations - The item will not distinguish whether or not there is adequate space for the caser to pass. If a tiny ventilation tube is the shortest route that has an unobstructed passage, that is the direction the needle will point. In the outdoors, the spell functions mostly like a locate, in that it will usually point directly at the target, only changing direction when the caster nears an obstruction.
Aftermath - The item bears no connection to the spell caster who created it. Anyone who comes to posses, knows the command words, and how it functions, can operate the item. Enchantment dispelling will temporarily neutralize this item but only if it is singularly focused. Breaking or bending the item, or destroy magic affects will remove the continual magics.

Mage/8E – Control Magic

Mage/Enchantment	Level: 6
Cast Time: 8 Turns	Duration: Permanent
Range: 0	Affected Area: 10' x 10' square
Mana: 8	Damage: None
Save: None	Save Affect: N/A
Components: V, S	Concentration: None

Material Component: None
Somatic Component: Drawing a square in the air with fingertips
Execution – This spell will allow the caster to seize control of a continual magic or enchantment.
Limitations - The spell caster must cast the spel lonce, at one location, then cast the same spell again at a second time. The spell caster will visualize the portal to be linked to as the second spell is cast.

Mage/8E - Magical Armor

Mage/Enchantment	Level: 6
Cast Time: 8 Turns	Duration: Permanent
Range: 0	Affected Area: 10' x 10' square
Mana: 8	Damage: None
Save: None	Save Affect: N/A
Components: V, S	Concentration: None

Material Component: None
Somatic Component: Drawing a square in the air with fingertips
Execution - This spell will create continual magics upon helmet, shield or body armor that will enhance the armorclass of the wearer.
Affect - The spell caster must cast the spel lonce, at one location, then cast the same spell again at a second time. The spell caster will visualize the portal to be linked to as the second spell is cast.

Mage/8E - Magical Portal

Mage/Enchantment	Level: 6
Cast Time: 8 Turns	Duration: Permanent
Range: 0	Affected Area: 10' x 10' square
Mana: 8	Damage: None

Save: None   Save Affect: N/A
Components: V, S   Concentration: None
Material Component: None
Somatic Component: Drawing a square in the air with fingertips

Execution - This spell will create a 10' x 10' continual magic portal which can be linked to a second portal created the same way by the same mage. Creatures and objects can walk through in order to be teleported.

Affect - The spell caster must cast the spel lonce, at one location, then cast the same spell again at a second time. The spell caster will visualize the portal to be linked to as the second spell is cast.

Limitations - The spell caster must be at the physical location to create the portal. A portal cannot be linked up to a portal cast by a different mage. Once two portals are linked, they cannot be switched to a different portal unless one of the two is destroyed. A portal can not be linked with more then one other portal.

Erratta - The portals are independent magically. The durations of oneRemoval of one portal leaves the other unlinked, but not dispelled. A spell caster may have/create any number or unlinked portals to have on hand in order to later be linked. The portal is only visible from one side. Persons and objects passing through the backside of a portal will not be teleported. If the portal is cast over a doorway, persons passing through might be unaware that they have been teleported.

Mage/8N – Bodily Transformmantion

Mage/Necromancy	Level: 4
Cast Time: 8 Seconds	Duration: 1 round/level
Range: Touch	Affected Area: 30'/level
Mana: 2	Damage: N/A
Save: Charisma	Save Affect: Negates
Components: V, S	

Material Component: Chameleon foot
Somatic Component: Rubbing of foot on skin

Execution - This spell will physically transform a natural creature into any other sort of natural creature.

Mage/8N – Clone

Mage/Necromancy	Level: 8
Cast Time: 8 hours	Duration: N/A
Range: Touch	Affected Area: 1 Creature
Mana: 80	Damage: 1D12/ 6 Levels - Pelter
Save: None	Save Affect: Negates
Components: V, S	Concentration: N/A

Material Component: Tissue sample
Somatic Component: Lightly rubbing of sample with fingertips

Execution - This spell will create an exact duplicate of any natural creature from a tissue sample

Affect - If the spell is used to create a duplicate of a dead player character, the clone will be a player character. If the spell is used to create a clone of a living player character, the clone will be a non-player-character under control of the referee.

Limitations - The clone will be duplicate of the original as it was when the tissue sample was taken. Any changes, acquisition or experience, since the sample twas taken will not be carried over to the clone. If the original character still exists, there will quickly become an inherent jealousy, due to having conflicting claims to friends, wealth, and possessions. Eventualy that will lead to distrust, then animosity. Sooner or later, one will kill the other. Usually, the clone (controlled by the referee) will waste no time in trying to kill off the player-character in a pre-emptive

first strike. Which ever is the survivor will fall under the control of the player.

Aftermath - The affect is permanet has no lingering magical nature. The clone is, for all intents and purposes, a natural creature.

Mage/8V – Power Sink (Continual)

Mage/Evocation	Level: 8
Cast Time: 8 Turns (80 min)	Duration: Permanent
Range: N/A	Affected Area: 30' Diameter circle
Mana: 8	Damage: None
Save: None	Save Affect: N/A
Components: V, S	Concentration: N/A

Material Component: Poison
Somatic Component: Touching fingertip into poison them drawing a circular area on ground or floor.

Mage/8V – Death Ray

Mage/Evocation	Level: 8
Cast Time: 1 segment	Duration: 8 seconds
Range: Touch	Affected Area: 10' Cubic/level
Mana: 8	Damage: 1D12/ 6 Levels - Pelter
Save: None	Save Affect: N/A
Components: V, S, M	Concentration: N/A

Material Component: Lotus leaf
Somatic Component: Clutching leaf and pointing finger

Level	Death Magic Damage
0-7	1D12 Hit-points
8-15	2D12 (2D6) Hit-points
16-23	3D12 (3D6) Hit-points
24-31	4D12 (4D6) Hit-points
32-39	5D12 (5D6) Hit-points
40-47	6D12 (6D6) Hit-points
48-55	7D12 (7D6) Hit-points
56-63	8D12 (8D6) Hit-points
64-71	9D12 (9D6) Hit-points
72-	10D12 (10D6) Hit-points

Execution - When this spell is cast a thin brilliant beam of green light will emerge from the caster's outstretched finger and strike a target creature. The ray will cause 1D20 hit-points of death magic damage to
Affect

Limitations - This spell has no affect on undead creatures. The light cannot pass through an area or magical destruction or enchantment dispelling.

Erratta - Although magical in nature, the rat of light will function as normal light. It will pass through clear objects or water and can be ricocheted off of reflective surfaces.

Mage/8V – Frost Orb (Continual)

Mage/Necromancy	Level: 8
Cast Time: 8 hours	Duration: N/A
Range: Touch	Affected Area: 1 Creature
Mana: 80	Damage: 1D12/ 6 Levels - Pelter
Save: None	Save Affect: Negates
Components: V, S	Concentration: N/A

Material Component: Tissue sample
Somatic Component: Lightly rubbing of sample with fingertips

Execution - This spell will create an exact duplicate of any natural creature from a tissue sample

Mage/8V – Lightning Barrier (Continual)

Mage/Necromancy	Level: 8
Cast Time: 8 hours	Duration: N/A
Range: Touch	Affected Area: 1 Creature
Mana: 80	Damage: 1D12/ 6 Levels - Pelter
Save: None	Save Affect: Negates
Components: V, S	Concentration: N/A
Material Component: Tissue sample	
Somatic Component: Lightly rubbing of sample with fingertips	

Mage/8V – Poison Shield

Mage/Necromancy	Level: 8
Cast Time: 8 hours	Duration: N/A
Range: Touch	Affected Area: 1 Creature
Mana: 80	Damage: 3D20
Save: None	Save Affect: Negates
Components: V, S	Concentration: N/A
Material Component: Tissue sample	
Somatic Component: Lightly rubbing of sample with fingertips	

Execution - This spell will create a 10' x 10' magical wall that causes 3D12 points of blunt damage to any creature that passes through it.

Description – The will appear as a shimmering green square.

Limitations –Once the spell is cast, the color cannot be changed, and the shield cannot be moved, nor can it be cast onto an object or creature in order to be moved about. The shield can only be cast to be flat, vertical, and square.

Erratta – If there is not adequate space to accommodate the shield, it will be imbedded in surrounding solids.

Aftermath – The enchantment remains in affect until the spell exhausts its duration, the caster speaks the command words calling for the spell to end, or the enchantment is dispelled.

Mage/9A – Phantom Substance

Mage/Conjuration	Level: 9
Cast Time: 9 Seconds	Duration: 1 Round/Level
Range: 15' + 10'/Level	Affected Area: Up to 15' Radius
Mana: 9	Damage: N/A
Save: None	Save Affect: N/A
Components: V, S, M	Concentration: High
Material Component: Drop of alcohol	
Somatic Component: Rubbing drop on palm	

Execution - This spell will allow the spell caster to control the nature of a non-magical, non-living substance so as to make it solid, completely non-solid, or any stage in between.

Affect - The magic does not make the substances soft so as to make them pliable, but rather, makes them non-solid shadows. At the highest level of intensity, the substance can be moved through as it were non-existent. The spell will hot change the appearance or shape of the affected object.

Uses - The spell can be used to desolidify the floor beneath an enemy so as to have them fall through. The spell could be used to partially remove the solidity so as to have an enemy sink to their ankles, then resolidfy so as to leave them trapped. The spell might be used to hide treasure inside a rock, a latch mechanism inside a wall, etc.

Limitations - Living and magical substances cannot be desolidified, however, those will pass through objects that have beed desolidified. Ony one sort of substance can be affected, however the scope of the affect can be adjusted. For example, the caster may specify that all non-living, non-magical matter in the affected are be affected, or they might select that only metal be affected, or they might select that only gold be affected. Likewise, the caster can control the affected area

Adjustments - At anytime during the spells duration, the caster can speak the commands words that will change the solidity, or the scope, or the size and extent of the affected area. For example, the caster may change the scope by specifying that all non-living, non-magical matter be affected, or they might select that only metal be affected, or they might select that only gold be affected. Likewise, the caster can control the extent of the affected area and declare that only a single gold piece be affected, a single pile.

Erratta - While an are is affected, it is in flux between dimensions and cannot be moved or altered. For example, the spell could not be used on gold to have the coins rain down out of a container since the gold would become immovable while affected (although the bag could be affecte to let the gold pass through). Likewise, affected objects are immune to geing torn, burned or otherwise disturbed until they return to their normal state.

Mage/9C – Black Hole

Mage/Conjuration	Level: 9
Cast Time: 1 segment	Duration: 1 Round/Level
Range: 15' + 10'/Level	Affected Area: 15' Radius
Mana: 9	Damage: Death
Save: Strength	Save Affect: Resists being pulled in
Components: V, S, M	Concentration: High
Material Component: Small black pearl	
Somatic Component: Rubbing pearl between palms then throwing in direction of point of origin	

Execution - When the spell is cast it will create a black 2 inch diameter magical sphere that will draw into itself all creatures and items that are not affixed to the ground, a tree, or other permanent structure.

Mage/9D – Exestential Vision

Mage/Divination	Level: 9
Cast Time: 1 segment	Duration: Permanent
Range: Touch	Affected Area: 10' Cubic/level
Mana: 60	Damage: N/A
Save: Charisma	Save Affect: Negates
Components: V, S	Concentration: N/A
Material Component: Needle, pin or other tiny metal rod	
Somatic Component: Placing needle on palm of hand	

Execution - This spell will wndow the caster with a special 3-dimenisional vision that will allow the caster to "look" in all directions

Mage/9D – Lond Distance Scan

Mage/Divination	Level: 9
Cast Time: 1 segment	Duration: Permanent
Range: Touch	Affected Area: 10' Cubic/level
Mana: 60	Damage: N/A
Save: Charisma	Save Affect: Negates
Components: V, S	Concentration: N/A
Material Component: Needle, pin or other tiny metal rod	
Somatic Component: Placing needle on palm of hand	

Execution - This spell will wndow the caster with a special 3-dimenisional vision that will allow the caster to "look" in all directions

Mage/9E - Continual Magic Sink

Mage/Enchantment	Level: 9
Cast Time: 9 Turns (90 min)	Duration: Permanent
Range: N/A	Affected Area: 30' Diameter circle
Mana: 9	Damage: None
Save: None	Save Affect: N/A
Components: V, S	Concentration: N/A

Material Component: Mana poition
Somatic Component: Touching fingertip into potion them drawing a circular area on ground or floor.
Execution - This spell will create a magical "dead area" where no spells or magical affects will function.

Mage/9E - Planar Portal

Mage/Enchantment	Level: 9
Cast Time: 9 days	Duration: 1 Second/Level
Range: Touch	Affected Area: Varies
Mana: 9,000	Damage: None
Save: N/A	Save Affect: N/A
Components: V, S, M	Concentration: High

Material Component: 4-leaf clover
Somatic Component: None
Execution - This spell can be used to open a portal to another dimension.

Mage/9E - Wish

Mage/Enchantment	Level: 9
Cast Time: 9 days	Duration: N/A
Range: Touch	Affected Area: Varies
Mana: 9,000	Damage: 1D12/ 6 Levels - Pelter
Save: N/A	Save Affect: N/A
Components: V, S, M	

Material Component: 4-leaf clover
Somatic Component: None
Execution - A wish is the most powerful spell in the game. It's casting is hugely difficult and once cast, the wish is usually inscribed onto a scroll or placed into an item.
Requirements - To cast a wish spell (or inscribe it) requires 9 days(216 hours) of continous spell casting to invoke, during which the spell caster must expend 90,000 mana points (approxiamately 400 mana points per hour). Since this huge amount of mana is beyond the kin of most mages, successful casting usually requires a team of mages to take turns in a roataion of replenishing their personal mana from mana storage items, then transferring their mana into the spell caster. The spell caster will need to be awake and sharply focused for 9 days without any relief. Prior to starting a wish spell, the spell caster will need to initiate some sort of magical or chemical stimulant that will carry them through the entire cast time. If the spell caster pauses, or is distracted for even a moment during the spell casting, the magi will be spoiled and the mana will be used.

Mage/9I - Incarnate

Mage/Illusion	Level: 9
Cast Time: 9 days	Duration: 1 Turn/Level
Range: Touch	Affected Area: Varies
Mana: 9,000	Damage: None
Save: N/A	Save Affect: N/A
Components: V, S, M	Concentration: High

Material Component: Gem
Somatic Component: Touching gem to subject
Execution - This spell will allow the caster's psyche to invade another living body. The psyche of the host body is either exchanged into the caster's body, or retained in the host body but pressed aside.

Mage/9I - Mind Spike

Mage/Illusion	Level: 9
Cast Time: 9 Seconds	Duration: N/A
Range: Touch	Affected Area: One creature
Mana: 9	Damage: 1D20
Save: Charisma	Save Affect: ½ Damage
Components: V	Concentration: N/A

Material Component: None
Somatic Component: None
Execution - This spell will cause the subject to have an intense spasm of pain along with 1D20 hit-points of damage on any creature that the spell caster has physically touched at on time or another. The caster need not be able to see or know the location of the subject.
Affect -

Mage/9I - Soul Trap

Mage/Illusion	Level: 9
Cast Time: 9 days	Duration: Permanent
Range: Touch	Affected Area: Varies
Mana: 9,000	Damage: None
Save: N/A	Save Affect: N/A
Components: V, S, M	Concentration: High

Material Component: Gem
Somatic Component: Touching gem to subject
Execution - This spell can be used to draw a creatures psyche out of their person and trap it inside a precious gem.

Mage/9N - Magic Morph

Mage/Necromancy	Level: 9
Cast Time: 9 Seconds	Duration: 1 Round/Level
Range: 0	Affected Area: Self
Mana: 9	Damage: N/A
Save: N/A	Save Affect: Negates
Components: V, S, M	Concentration: N/A

Material Component: Tissue sample of creature to duplicated
Somatic Component: Rubbing of foot on skin
Execution - This spell will physically transform the spell caster into any other sort of creature. All physical attributes, along with any special physical abilities, innate magical abilities, breath weapons, attack methods, etc will be duplicated. Any normal spell abilities, clothing, carried items, etc will not be duplicated.

Mage/9V - Death Prism

Mage/Evocation	Level: 9
Cast Time: 1 segment	Duration: 9 seconds
Range: 15' + 10'/level	Affected Area: 15' Radius
Mana: 9	Damage: 1D20/9 Levels - Death Magic
Save: Dextierity	Save Affect: ½ Damage
Components: V, S, M	Concentration: N/A

Material Component: Lotus leaf

Somatic Component: Rolling leaf into ball and tossing in direction
of intended point of origin

Level	Death Magic Damage
0-8	1D20 Hit-points
9-17	2D20 (2D6) Hit-points
18-26	3D20 (3D6) Hit-points
27-35	4D20 (4D6) Hit-points
25-30	5D20 (5D6) Hit-points
31-36	6D20 (6D6) Hit-points
37-	7D20 (7D6) Hit-points

Psychic Feats & Runes

Psychic/F1 - Bend Metal

Druid	Level: 6
Cast Time: 1 segment	Duration: 6 seconds
Range: Touch	Affected Area: 10' Cubic/level
Mana: 40	Damage: 1D12/ 6 Levels - Pelter
Save: Charisma	Save Affect: Negates
Components: V, S	

Material Component: Bit of sulphur
Somatic Component: None

Execution - This feat will allow a pyshic ot bend ordinary metals.

Affect - The metal can be bent,.

Limitations - BY USE FO THIS DISCPLIVE A PSYCHIC CAN CAUSE A METAL OBJECT TO BEND, RIPPLE, OR BECOME DISTORTED. THE PSYCHIC CAN NOT USE THE DISCPLINE TO MOLD METAL INTO ANY PARTICULAR SHAPE VERY STRONG METALS SUCH AS TITANIUM, MITHRIL, AND ADAMANITE WILL NOT BE AFFECTED BY THIS DISCIPLINE. MAGICED AND ENCHANTED ITEMS CAN USUALLY BE BENT WITH AFFFECTING THE MAGICAL NATURE OF THE ITEM. ENCHANTED SWORDS AND ARMOR USUALLY WILL NOT BE AFFECTED SINCE THE CREATION OF SUCH REQUIRES THE USE OF STRONG METALS

Psychic/R1 - Heat Rune

Druid	Level: 6
Cast Time: 1 segment	Duration: 6 seconds
Range: Touch	Affected Area: 10' Cubic/level
Mana: 40	Damage: 1D12/ 6 Levels - Pelter
Save: Charisma	Save Affect: Negates
Components: V, S	

Material Component: Bit of sulphur
Somatic Component: None

Psychic/R1 - Healing Rune

Druid	Level: 6
Cast Time: 1 segment	Duration: 6 seconds
Range: Touch	Affected Area: 10' Cubic/level
Mana: 40	Damage: 1D12/ 6 Levels - Pelter
Save: Charisma	Save Affect: Negates
Components: V, S	

Material Component: Bit of sulphur
Somatic Component: None

Psychic/R1 - Light Rune

Druid	Level: 6
Cast Time: 1 segment	Duration: 6 seconds
Range: Touch	Affected Area: 10' Cubic/level
Mana: 40	Damage: 1D12/ 6 Levels - Pelter
Save: Charisma	Save Affect: Negates
Components: V, S	

Material Component: Bit of sulphur
Somatic Component: None

Psychic/R2 - Sonic Rune

Druid	Level: 6
Cast Time: 1 segment	Duration: 6 seconds
Range: Touch	Affected Area: 10' Cubic/level
Mana: 40	Damage: 1D12/ 6 Levels - Pelter
Save: Charisma	Save Affect: Negates
Components: V, S	

Material Component: Bit of sulphur
Somatic Component: None

Psychic/R3 - Exploding Rune

Druid	Level: 6
Cast Time: 1 segment	Duration: 6 seconds
Range: Touch	Affected Area: 10' Cubic/level
Mana: 40	Damage: 1D12/ 6 Levels - Pelter
Save: Charisma	Save Affect: Negates
Components: V, S	

Material Component: Bit of sulphur
Somatic Component: None

Maps

Scale

0 25 50 75 100 150 200 250 300 Miles

River	
Trail	
Road	
Desert	
Swamps	
Plains	
Forrest	
Hills	
Mountains	

Beon

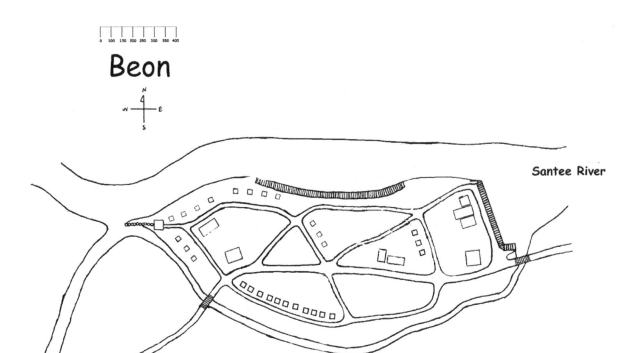

Santee River

Charone

Stancroft

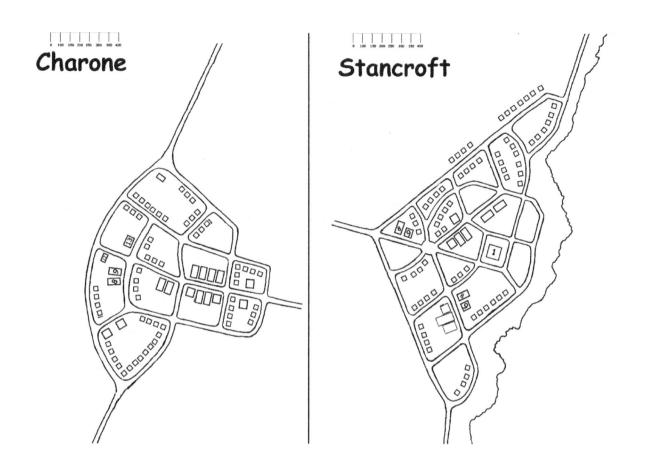

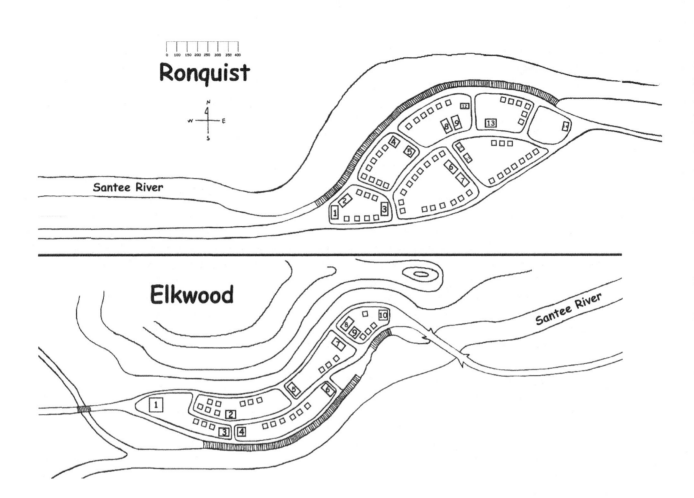

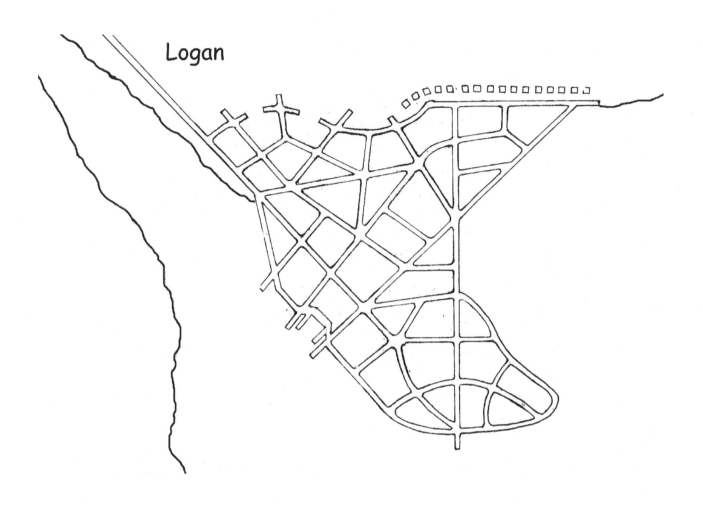

Logan

Rastin

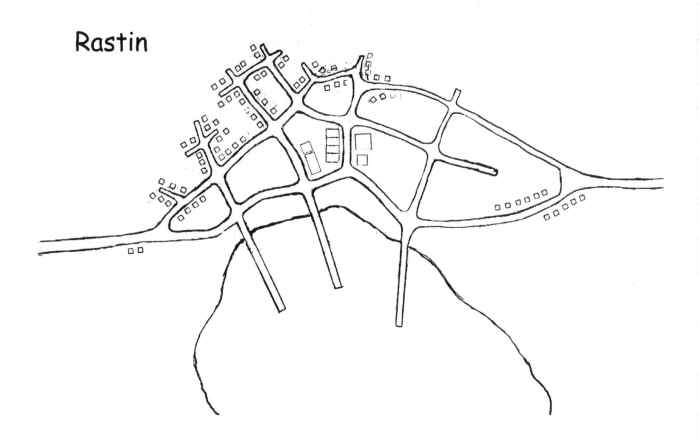

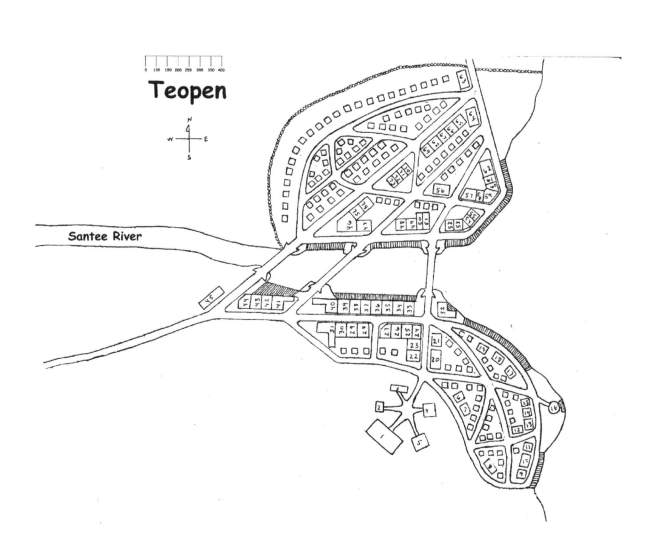

Teopen

Santee River

Glossary

Abilities – Ability scores designate what a character is capable of. The values range from 1 to 100. Each character has a score for 4 mental abilities, 4 physical abilities, and 6 senses.

Armor Class - A value running from 0 (no armor) to 20 (highest armor class in the game) that designates how difficult it is to make a successful roll-to-hit on the character.

Base-to-Hit – The unmodified score required to hit by a character to make a successful attack an armor class. A base-to-hit is arrived at by adding the characters THAC0 to the opponents armor class.

Character – Any player-character (player controlled) or non-player-character (referee controlled) character in the game.

Class – The proffesion of a character. A character's class determines the type of skills they have, the type of equipment they can have, and the nature of the powers they can acquire.

Continual Magic – Any sort of permanent magic that requires no assitance or intervention to stay in force. Continual Magics stay in affect until the spell caster calls for the spell to end or it is dispelled by someone else.

Creatue – Any character or monster in the game.

Difficulty Adjustment – A percentile bonus or penalty applied to an ability roll to make a task increase or decrease the difficulty of a task.

Enchantment - A non-permanent form of magic that deteriorates with time.

Melee - A 10 second round of battle including several exchanges, in which opponents battle each other.

Monster – Any creature controlled by the referee which is not of a humanoid race.

Level (Experience) - A number ranging from 0 to 99 that designates how far a character has advanced in their chosen class. Experience levels are gained by the awarding of experience by the referee, based on real time spent playing the character. With each 1,000 experience points awarded, the character advances a level.

Living Creatures - Any creature which has more than 0 hit-points is considered "living", regardless of the nature of the life force. Undead creatures, magical creatures, etc are all considered "living" for most game purposes

POINT OF ORIGIN - THE POINT FORM WHICH A SPELL IS TO BE INITIATED FROM OR IS TO BE CENTERED ON. THE POINT OF ORIGIN CAN BE PLACED AT ANY DISTANCE WITHIN THE RANGE ALLOWED FOR A SPELL

RACE - THE TYPE AND BREED OF A CHARACTER

Roll-to-hit – The rolling of a 20-sided die in attempt to produce a high enough number to cause a damage to an opponent.

Round – 1 melee, 10 seconmds, 1/6 of a minute

Score-to-hit - The adjusted minimum value a player must roll on a 20-sided die for their character to make n successful attack on an opponent. The score to hit is calculated by adding the THAC0 to the opponent's armor class, then adding all adjustments.

Second - 1/10 of a round, 10 Segments

Segment - 1/10 of a second

THACO – (To-hit Armor Class Zero)The minimum number a character must roll on a 20-sided die to hit a creature with no armor.

Made in the USA
Monee, IL
20 January 2020